Whate

Whatever Next!

Hazel Wood

*Illustrations by
Denise Bates*

First published in the United Kingdom 2007

Copyright © Hazel Wood 2007
Illustrations copyright © Denise Bates 2007

The moral rights of the author and illustrator have been asserted.

All rights reserved. No part of this publication may be reproduced, stored in a retrieval system, or transmitted, in any form or by any means, without the prior permission in writing of the publishers, or as expressly permitted by law, or under terms agreed with the appropriate reprographic rights organisation. Enquiries concerning reproduction outside the scope of the above should be sent to the publishers at the address below.

The Anima Centre Limited, 1 Wine Street Terrace, Bradford on Avon
Wiltshire BA15 1NP, United Kingdom
Telephone: 01225 866612   Email: team@theanimacentre.com

British Library Cataloguing in Publication Data
A CIP catalogue record for this book is available from the British Library

ISBN: 978-0-9551616-1-2

Typeset in Bookman Old Style 9/13pt

Printed and bound by
JFDi Print Services Ltd, Bradford on Avon, Wiltshire BA15 1LB

Contents

Childhood and the first taste of freedom ... 1

The war years ... 39

Back to the real world ... 103

Georgians at play ... 151

A *special* kind of travel ... 193

Reflections ... 301

Childhood and the first taste of freedom

One

The outbreak of the Second World War was for me a liberation – no use pretending otherwise – and this despite a happy childhood with two elder brothers in a close-knit family with caring parents.

Ours was a fairly conventional Scottish upbringing, disciplined to the extent that we, as children, were told once to desist from doing something which our parents considered unacceptable, and were expected to obey. Otherwise out would come the 'tawse', in our case a type of heel-less galosh, pliant and harmless, which hurt our pride much more than our anatomy. Many parents today look upon any kind of physical punishment as grotesque, but personally speaking I never harboured any resentment towards either parent, with whom I remained on close terms all their lives. We were comfortably off without being very wealthy and wanted for nothing, although my father encouraged us to be thrifty and, like most children of similar circumstances, we took our privileges for granted.

My mother, Dorothy Margaret Bertram, was the daughter of John and Jessie Bertram, the former being what was then termed a 'gentleman farmer', with a farm and land at Addinston in the Scottish Borders. Being the eldest of three girls, she was considered to be the son he never had and was treated accordingly. From the age of four she was perched, first in a wicker basket contraption and later on a saddle, upon a mount which must have seemed to her a hundred hands high. A faded sepia photograph shows my mother at a very early age, clad in voluminous skirts, clutching a riding whip in a tightly clenched fist, mutiny engraved on her face. Not surprisingly she never cared much for either horses or the countryside in later life, but I am sure that her early equestrian experiences were partly responsible for her erect carriage, which she retained all her life.

Her two younger sisters, Kathleen and Harriet, were very close as children, so when the latter died very prematurely, it was not surprising that the former resented my mother's presence and they were never particularly close in later years.

However, I always got on very well with my Aunt Kathleen, who was soft and pliable with an air of helplessness about her which appealed to men. She had one daughter, Jean, by her first husband, Paul Leared, who was killed in the First World War, and later married Donald Macaulay, a full-blooded Scot who rather awed me as a child by his overpowering masculinity, and by whom she had two sons, Donald and Jock. The latter I hardly knew as he went off to be a sheep farmer in Australia but I kept well in touch with my cousins Jean and Donald. I always felt a great respect for the latter since he opened the very first launderette in Edinburgh, at a time when such an enterprise invited some criticism from the more snobbish Edinburgh population, he being a fairly conservative lawyer.

My mother had an innate gaiety, an infectious laugh and a wonderful sense of the ridiculous, which made her popular with the young and encouraged her children to bring their friends home. Indeed, some of those, as well as some of her contemporaries, found her somewhat forbidding at first encounter, for she had a disconcerting way of scrutinising a new acquaintance with some critical regard. Once a friend, however, there was a no more entertaining or amusing companion to be with. True, at times, she covered her offspring with embarrassment by criticising someone or something rather loudly, but when faced with our cringing confusion, dismissed her action with the argument that the louder one spoke, no-one listened, but if one whispered everyone did the opposite.

She had an extravagant streak in her make-up but luckily had independent means. "Always make sure you have a separate bank account", she would counsel newly-married wives. Having one herself, she was able, so she thought, to keep many of her indulgences hidden from my father, who was distinctly thrifty. He was not fooled. My mother loved giving presents as much as my father hated receiving them. She had a flair for spotting something unusual in the unlikeliest of places that she knew instinctively would be a perfect present for a particular recipient. She began to collect early English and Scottish pottery when it was still largely regarded as merely the poor relation of porcelain, and often bought a load of junk at a local sale for next to nothing, amongst which would be one good piece.

As her collection grew, so did its value, and today part of it can be seen at the Museum of Scotland in Edinburgh. In later life, as prices inevitably rose and pottery became much sought after, she would pay quite a lot for a piece of Whieldon or agate-ware, which she would smuggle into her display case, happily unaware that my father would remark to me drily some days later, "I see that your mother has added to her collection". At least this double subterfuge act kept the peace between them.

My father, Douglas Mure Wood, always known as Dougal, came from an Edinburgh family with legal connections. He was one of five children with two brothers, Bill and George, and two sisters, Ethel and Jessie. I cannot recall either grandparent and never knew my Aunt Ethel, who married and died young together with her husband, leaving two children, Jim and Margaret. On the other hand, Uncle George and Aunt Jessie lived round the corner from us in Edinburgh. They were both unmarried and were looked after by Millie, their housekeeper. Uncle George and Uncle Bill both followed the family tradition, the latter becoming a barrister in England and the former a Writer to the Signet, or lawyer, in Edinburgh.

Uncle George was a stickler for time. On each of our visits as children, he would stand with his watch at the ready to ensure we did not outstay our welcome. To the end of his long life his hair remained glossy and almost jet black, but we never succeeded in discovering whether it was a cleverly disguised wig or an equally clever dye. His sister, my Aunt Jessie, became a well-known figure in Edinburgh's girl guide movement, as well as being very keen on country dancing which, I am ashamed to say, my brothers and I took pleasure in mimicking.

I saw more of my Uncle Bill after I went to boarding school in England. He had married Iris Lyon, of a gentle and kind disposition, and an artist of some talent. They had three daughters – Briar, Gill and Carol – the latter tragically dying at the age of six from leukaemia. As a child I was not wholly at ease with my Uncle Bill, who could sometimes be abrupt in manner. However, from my time at school in the south, both uncle and aunt could not have been kinder to me, even after my breaking two of his best wine-glasses in quick succession when helping with the drying-up after lunch on one occasion.

My father, like most hardworking men of his generation, had ambitions for his children – always a great mistake. Trained as a chartered accountant, he later became immersed in the world of investment trusts and finance, being appointed to an increasing number of company boards as the years advanced.

One of his tasks as Chairman of the then Commercial Bank of Scotland was to attend a Board lunch every Thursday, followed by the burning of old and used bank notes, a practice we children thought heretical. My father was a kind man and had many friends. He was popular with women, being a good raconteur, and had a certain racy wit. Generous in many ways, he had certain economic foibles, associated perhaps with a rather narrow Scottish upbringing. One such was a horror of wasting electricity. With east winds causing draughts to howl around our high-ceilinged Edinburgh house – reducing the interior temperature perilously near to zero unless you were standing close to a burning coal fire – he would shout to my mother, "Dorothy, your electric fire is on in the bedroom", (no thought of central heating in those days). In order to avoid a scene, his wife would say, "Yes dear" and switch it off. In later years she grew bolder, or perhaps merely colder, and would reply, "I know dear and it's staying on", after which there would be a period of reserve on my father's part. He considered receiving presents a waste of money and upset my mother considerably on one occasion by returning to the suppliers her birthday present, a much needed pair of pyjamas, as being quite unnecessary.

Dining out also posed problems as my mother, who enjoyed her food, and spotting something tempting from the *à la carte* menu, would have her attention smartly drawn to the set menu at the *prix fixe*. As a young man he had travelled widely on business, in large part to the United States, where he had just escaped being blown up in the New York subway bomb in 1927. On another occasion, while travelling by train in some remote part of Arizona, a fellow traveller, on hearing that he came from Scotland, complimented him on his good English. Travelling remained one of his great pleasures throughout his life. He and I used to pore over maps together, planning itineraries to various parts of the globe, a pastime that stood me in good stead in later life.

My mother was an excellent manager. She had the fortunate knack of being able to retain her domestic staff, several of whom remained or were in touch with my family for most of their lives. For much of my childhood, 'below stairs' consisted of Katharine the cook, May the tablemaid and her sister, Bella the housemaid. Katharine, or Katie as she allowed me to call her in later years, was small and wiry with pebble glasses, without which she could scarcely see across the room, and carried about her a rather defensive air. However, an outwardly ungracious manner concealed a fierce loyalty. Usually her stubbornness would respond to my mother's mixture of firmness and coaxing, resulting in her agreeing, albeit grudgingly, to a proposition formerly viewed with deep suspicion.

May, being without moods, got on famously with her. Buxom and rather gipsy-like in looks, she enjoyed life and was always ready to laugh at our jokes and to listen to the chatter of my two brothers and myself. Ballroom dancing was her hobby and well into her seventies she attended her local dancing club. She married after the war but her husband died at an early age, after which she returned to my mother's employment on a daily basis. Her sister, Bella, was large and placid, totally reliable and comfortable to be with. She left us to look after her mother but remained in touch with me until she died on Christmas Day, at the age of ninety, by then living with May. Her place as housemaid was taken by Penelope who came from quite different stock. Small-boned and petite with fair hair neatly tied in a bun, she was as porcelain compared with her more robust colleagues – and the more unapproachable.

My two brothers, George and John, who were four years and seventeen months respectively older than me, were as different as chalk from cheese. George, being the oldest of us, viewed life rather worriedly whilst John was the eternal showman. They were despatched to boarding school at the usual age of eight while I, from the age of six, acquired a governess – Miss Provan, or Pro as she became known, to whom I was much devoted. She had quite a strong Scottish accent and was given to admitting ingeniously from time to time that she "had never thought of that" which surprisingly, far from irritating my parents, they found rather endearing. Her marriage and my subsequent departure to boarding school at the age of twelve proved one of my first great disillusionments in life.

Puddy, the sealyham terrier, completed the household in those early pre-war days. A one-man dog, he gave his entire devotion to my mother but tolerated the rest of us. She returned his devotion despite his being an inveterate sheep-chaser and hen-destroyer. Many an irate farmer had to be paid off for the price of a mangled chicken – invariably the best layer – and even tying a feathered victim round his neck did nothing to cure Puddy of his evil ways, only giving us the added burden of cleansing him of hen fleas.

In Edinburgh, he used to accompany me and my mother on shopping jaunts, firmly tethered to a lead. Even so, the sight of him caused a number of acquaintances, leading dogs of a gentler disposition, to give us a wide berth – much to my mother's relief. One of our regular visits was to Mr Muir the butcher, who considered my mother 'elegant' and would keep his choicest cuts for her. Puddy would also be given a scrap or two, which he received as his due. On one occasion, however, when I was about six, Mr Muir was absent and his place taken by Bruce, his surly assistant, with no such altruistic leanings. Puddy had somehow escaped his lead and was creating havoc by chasing the shop's cat between an alleyway of sheep's carcasses that swung wildly from their hooks about our heads, showering us with blood and scattering the sawdust beneath our feet. "That dog of yours, Mistress Wood", darkly intoned Bruce as he viciously chopped up a scrag end of mutton for Irish stew, "will end at the knackers". I had no idea what was meant by the knackers and thought at first it had something to do with the jingle "knick-knack, paddy whack, give a dog a bone" but from Bruce's set mouth as he wrapped up our purchases, I could see that no such generous thought had entered his head. I was reading 'Strewelpeter' at the time, illustrated with pictures of an alarming orange-headed giant with six-inch long fingernails, and a caption entitled "snip-snap-snip went the scissorman". Somehow he entered my thoughts. Perhaps he was on his way to give Puddy his just rewards.

Shortly after this episode, it seemed that our cherished dog had met his Waterloo and might have to be put down. I and my two brothers, our governess Pro, and Puddy were out for a walk one Sunday afternoon in the then countrified vicinity of Ravelston Dykes, today a maze of new development.

Puddy suddenly espied a canine stranger to whom he took an instant dislike. Flying at it with bared fangs, he took Pro completely by surprise, dragging the lead from her grasp.

Unfortunately he found a trousered leg between himself and his prey and after a commendable effort on Pro's part, was finally dragged from the fray with a sizeable piece of material between his jaws.

Appalled and apprehensive, I stood transfixed on the footpath waiting to hear our friend denounced as a danger and menace to the neighbourhood. Here at last would come the knacker or scissorman to meter out dire punishment to the wretched Puddy, however hazy in my head that punishment might be. The thought was too much for me. I began to bawl. Pro looked more and more flustered; George pretended he belonged to another family across the road; John revelled in the affair as being sufficiently dramatic to enliven a humdrum family walk, while the culprit stood in his usual belligerent attitude, a triumphant leer partially obscured by the telltale evidence of the rather good quality Lovat tweed hanging from his lower jaw. The only person who appeared totally calm in the circumstances was the victim.

"Quite understandable", he murmured, graciously offering my snivelling self an immaculately laundered handkerchief into which I hiccoughed gratefully. "He was protecting his family against the invading hordes", he continued, smiling into my tear-stained face. I gazed incredulously at the insignificant pooch, the cause of Puddy's onslaught. The invading horde scarcely accorded with my image taken from the illustrated scenes from the Bible, but I let that pass and returned his benevolence with a watery smile.

Pro had the wit, at least, to ask our benefactor for his name and address, so that we could replace his damaged trousers. He informed us, however, that he would take his trousers to a first-class invisible-mending establishment with which he would be perfectly satisfied. A visiting card disclosed the fact that he was the President of the Edinburgh branch of the RSPCA. The fragment of cloth was duly removed from Puddy's reluctant jaws and we continued our walk, for my part both elated and chastened. For months to come, my hero in every fairy tale I read had silvery hair, kindly eyes and was clad in Lovat tweed. Despite his peccadilloes, Puddy survived until the venerable age of thirteen, when he was found in the local millstream, near which we garaged our car, no doubt following a heart attack while in pursuit of further prey.

Our house in Edinburgh, at 25 Douglas Crescent, was one of those Victorian crescent houses which were built on the fringes of the New Town. Of solid grey stone, the buildings had a rather dour frontage, their massive plate glass windows lacking the graceful astragals of earlier decades. A flight of stone steps led up to a very dark green painted door surmounted by a glass fanlight on which was embossed the figure 25. More stone steps led from the pavement to the basement encased by dark green iron railings, and were used solely for 'trade' and the domestic staff.

Above the basement were three storeys of generously proportioned, high-ceilinged rooms, those at the front overlooking gardens that were for the sole use of the inhabitants of Douglas Crescent and their friends. These stretched down to the Water of Leith and afforded all sorts of scope for children's games and escapades. Once within the iron railings, with the clang of the garden gate behind us and the key up an elasticated knicker leg, there was a wealth of excitements and forbidden ploys to indulge in. The creeping up on unsuspecting old ladies asleep in their deck chairs and fleeing before our exploding giggles awoke them; the ganging up with the children from No.13 against the rather prim little trio from No.21 who always had gleaming shoes and disciplined hair; the joyful terror of breaking bounds and escaping by the lower gate (strictly forbidden) and crossing a busy street to the sweetie shop on the corner for a pennyworth of toffee rolls (my choice), sherbet pouches (John's favourite) or George's weakness for Hawick Ba's, a form of peppermint gob-stopper – without being detected by 'authority' or by any officious neighbour who might report to 'authority'. Then there was always the hope of a skirmish with the boys from the Dean Village who would taunt us and occasionally throw stones from the other side of the stone wall that separated the gardens from the Water of Leith, a shallow stream that served the miller's wheel on the far bank, before making its sluggish way to the Firth of Forth.

The children's quarters were at the top of the house and consisted of the nursery, three bedrooms, a bathroom and pantry. When small, we had our meals sent up to the top floor from the kitchen, seemingly a world away, by means of a two-tiered lift that was hauled up by fierce pulls on its ropes. Its arrival was announced by a hoot on a horn, which resembled an old-fashioned ear-trumpet and by which one could shout messages to Katharine or May below if more cabbage etc. was required – unlikely in those days of boiling vegetables to death.

I will, however, give credit to Katharine for dishes at which she excelled and which stand out in my memory for all time. One was a savoury of cheese aigrettes, an exquisite concoction of cheese and choux pastry dropped into boiling fat, emerging golden crisp and meltingly satisfying. Another was an Irish stew made with scrag-end of mutton smothered with stovie potatoes and onions, and yet another was her shortbread, a buttery delight at which from time to time I was allowed to assist in its making. Her puff pastry was also outstandingly light in texture and in later life, I never returned to London from a visit home without taking with me a great wadge of Katie's pastry.

Our nursery, a spacious bow-fronted room with views on a clear day reaching to the Firth of Forth, had a dark green curtain cutting off the window recess from the rest of the room. This afforded a natural stage from which to launch amateur theatricals, to which our parents, staff, friends and their parents, and Puddy the sealyham were lured.

John was usually the star turn of these performances, having a winning charm, guile and sense of showmanship. George played the more prosaic roles, such as the family doctor, lawyer or upright citizen, while the buffoon or comic part was allotted to me, who was also in charge of the props and was general dogsbody. We cajoled some of our friends to take part in our plays, either protesting or eager to show off. However, it was not uncommon for one of the smaller players to be so overcome with shyness or the excitement of appearing in public that he or she had to be removed from the stage by a humiliated parent.

My bedroom boasted a fireplace, the fire only lit when I was ill or on my first night back from boarding school in winter. It was one of my greatest treats to lie in bed in the dark and watch the firelight flicker on the ceiling or count the 'soldiers', effervescent sparks of flame, on the fireback.

After Pro left, my brothers each had a room to themselves but during term-time I was alone on the top floor and I recall prolonging the hour of bedtime for as long as I could. This was not so much wilfulness on my part, but so that I could postpone the moment when I had to leave the warmth and security of the smoking room on the ground floor and embark on the, to me, frightening climb up the two flights of stairs to the safety of my own room. Because of my father's obsession with saving electricity, the staircase and hall were plunged into inky blackness, with one light on each landing. With pumping heart I would scuttle up to the first landing, fighting down the mounting fears of lurking bogeymen, carefully extinguish the light behind me before scrambling up the next flight and ensuing switch, the shadows almost palpably closing in on me. When I finally reached the haven of my well-lit bedroom, it took several minutes before my hammering heart returned to normal. I don't think my mother, normally a sensitive enough person, ever realised the trauma of these evening terrors. Of course, at the age of twelve or thirteen, I was far too proud and afraid of being deemed childish to admit to such cowardice.

The drawing room was directly below the nursery, a beautifully proportioned room with a huge open fireplace. It was only used for special occasions, such as my mother's bridge parties; during the Christmas holidays or for dinner parties. In the latter event, the three of us would lean over the banisters in our night clothes to watch the adults leave the drawing room and descend the staircase to the dining room – the men resplendent in tails or dinner jackets and the women in 'grande tenue'. We would loiter about in a frenzy of impatience until May was to be seen removing the remains of the first course from the dining room and put it on the lift. We would then make a headlong dash down the two flights of stairs – Pro must have been below stairs 'helping out' – and while May's back was turned, raid the leftovers before they disappeared from view. Sometimes frustrated greed would prove too much on the part of the slowest, culminating in an undignified scuffle that would speedily be brought to an end by the re-appearance of May with a forceful admonishment to "get up them stairs ye greedy wee pigs".

The dining room on the ground floor, with bow-fronted windows, was furnished with good solid mahogany and hung with deep blue damask curtains. Over the dining table was suspended one of those then fashionable lampshades of an apricot material, circular in shape enclosing five individual lamps. This contraption could be moved up or down at will according to the height of the floral centrepiece or silver trophies that sometimes graced the table. On the sideboard – again of good solid mahogany – stood an array of silver candlesticks and Georgian decanters, my father being a serious port and claret drinker. At Christmastide a vast Stilton cheese took pride of place next to an equally vast Melton Mowbray pie, annual presents to the family from my godmother, who otherwise played no important part in my life. One year just before returning to school, when the cheese was far from its first youth, my brother John and I were misguided enough to examine its crumbling edifice through a magnifying glass. We were horrified yet fascinated by the results and even went as far as scooping up a crumb or two with the idea of instigating a race meeting at which we would enter our two increasingly active contestants. My mother could never understand why both John and I suddenly went off cheese for a time.

The kitchen in the basement, with black cooking range and pulleys overhead for the drying of herbs or linen, was flanked by the laundry room. It contained two large stone tubs, which took care of all the weekly washing – always on a Monday – including at intervals the dog. Scouring board, mangle and flat irons – intrinsic items in most households of that period – are to be found in many museums or National Trust kitchens today.

Regular visits were paid each week by the knife-grinder, coalman and muffin seller – and every Saturday morning, whatever the weather, an elderly and swarthy Italian gypsy-looking lady would take up her stance by the garden railings and trundle out Neapolitan tunes on her portable hurdy-gurdy. One of us children was always at hand to run across the road to deposit our pennies in the cap proffered by the wizened monkey perched atop the organ.

Two

Every summer, the entire household would set off for the Highlands, where my parents would rent a farmhouse or such for a couple of months during the school holidays. Trunks would be packed as well as numerous suitcases, including a particularly memorable russet coloured kit bag of huge proportions that contained everyone's Wellington boots, walking shoes and my father's shooting stockings. My parents, the two boys and Puddy would then set off in our large open Renault tourer – while I (who was always car sick), Pro and the three maids would travel separately by train. I can still remember the excitement of those train journeys: the hiss of steam as the engine stoked up, the waving of the flag by the guard; and the wicker basket containing our lunch – ham sandwiches, apples, chocolate biscuits and Kate's shortbread, accompanied by ginger beer in a stone bottle for me and tea in a silver-stoppered thermos flask for my companions. All alas! replaced nowadays by diesel engine, impersonal crew and uninviting buffet car. The trunk containing the linen and kitchen equipment would travel in the guard's van and on arrival at our destination would be transferred to the local carrier, who would convey it and us to our rented abode so that all could be got in readiness before the Renault and its occupants arrived.

Our summer residences differed from year to year. Sometimes it would be a farmhouse, at others a house on an estate. One year we rented a large and decaying country manse for six weeks, where we were all bitten grievously by fleas. These were traced eventually to the adjacent stable block and kennels, where a mangy old collie dog appeared to be the sole occupant, apart from its fleas.

The first few days of each holiday were spent by me and my brothers in exploring the territory: finding suitable streams to dam and trees to climb; discovering the more unlikely nesting places for the hens that roamed unrestrictedly around the farmyard and neighbouring fields. We 'helped' with the milking – I don't know which suffered the more after my first attempt, the cow's udders or my fingers – and with the harvesting.

One of my greatest delights was to ride home on top of the hay cart, my nose peeling from the sun and my legs scratched from the stubbled stooks on which we were perched. From aloft one could survey the garnered fields and heather tufted hills, soft-shadowed in the evening light, and inhale the mingled fragrance of dung and cow parsley that rose from the rutted tracks and hedges below.

We had quite a social life during our holidays and while my father shot or fished, my mother or Pro would act as chauffeur and convey us to neighbouring friends for tennis or croquet. There would also be the inevitable garden fêtes at which we shied Aunt Sally for coconuts, staked our claim for hidden treasure and blindfoldedly stuck pins to win the pig, a prize that forever eluded us – much to my parents' relief. Quite often we went on picnics, one of our favourite sites being on Loch Garten, now the well-guarded haunt of the osprey.

We would kindle a fire on the then deserted shores and, while potatoes were roasting in its embers, we children would bathe in the ice-cold but invigorating peat-coloured water. My mother would read and smoke Turkish cigarettes, the smell of which would mingle with the scent of geranium oil with which we were all anointed as a repellent to the midges that swarmed around our heads. More deadly was the bite of a cleg, or horse-fly, which could cause an arm or leg to swell in an alarming manner.

Our larder was always well-stocked with game, thanks to my father's prowess with gun or rod – and included grouse, partridge, woodcock, snipe, pheasant and the occasional salmon or sea trout, according to the season. Hares also figured on the menu as Katharine was a dab-hand at hare soup, well laced with port – although she always complained that "the smell o' a' that bluid fair turns me stomach". My father, being a keen angler, would on occasion during term-time drag his reluctant wife on a fishing holiday. In later life she was relieved and grateful to learn that I had inherited my father's love of the sport and would gladly go off with him in her stead.

Other holidays were spent at North Berwick, some twenty-one miles east of Edinburgh, where we first rented a house each year before acquiring our own. We spent hours scrambling over the rocks along the shoreline to discover what treasures each sea pool contained – minuscule crabs, sea horses, waving fronds of ferns. Stamping on seaweed resulted in the satisfying plop as branches burst beneath our bare feet. Collecting shells occupied us for hours, especially the amassing of cowries, which were used as counters in the numerous games of cards we played. The sands also engaged our architectural skills in the art of sandcastle making.

Here also we endured the exquisite agony of bathing in the North Sea. Blue with cold we would emerge, shivering and shrieking – to be given our "chittering piece", usually a gingernut, and be exhorted to run up and down the beach till our limbs returned to normal and our faces glowed with health. Nearby was the municipal pool, where we all learned to swim properly under the watchful but stern eyes of Mr. McCracken or his assistant, Mr. Lemon. The former's method was to instruct you to jump in at the deep end, and when you emerged gasping and spluttering, to push a long handled pole under your chin to keep your head above water and to urge you to "be a frog, lassie, and swim". Somehow I did just that.

After the summer holidays it was always a wrench to go back to our respective schools. My brothers first attended a newly opened preparatory school at Dunbar called Belhaven Hill, now one of the most prestigious of its kind in Scotland. They were then packed off to Rugby, popular with many Scottish families as being well-placed on the London Midland Scottish (LMS) line, mid-way between Edinburgh and London.

I started off my academic life at the age of five as a day girl at St. Monica's, which for some years had as its headmistress a French lady called Miss Henry. It was she who instilled in us a fair knowledge of her native language by insisting that we learn six new French words every day, which is probably the reason why my French vocabulary far exceeds my grammar today. I was then despatched to an establishment called Highfield, a boarding school near Bushey, at that time in the depths of the Hertfordshire countryside, with more pretensions I suspect than a reputation for academic learning. I suspect also that it was part of my mother's plan for me to be near London so as to give her the excuse for shrugging off the somewhat restricted confines of Edinburgh society, in exchange for a brief spell in the headier precincts of Knightsbridge.

My father disliked these visits as he imagined his lifestyle to be disrupted. At the first sign of an impending departure, he would develop some hitherto unsuspected malaise destined to keep my mother at home. Brushing aside her suggestion of calling the doctor as being unnecessarily fussy and alarmist, the symptoms would mysteriously vanish once the taxi to the station had been cancelled. My mother eventually grew wise to this ruse and with the connivance of our three treasures below stairs, she would conceal her plans until the last moment, when she would announce that she was off to Hazel's half-term and that "the girls will look after you". Hazel's half-term was a fallacy as we had one weekend per term, which was usually spent with friends in the south, and an extra day during the summer term, when it was usually my father who took me out, combined with a business trip to London.

I had a happy relationship with both my parents, but preferred to have either one on their own. They had totally differing views as to what a day out in London should comprise – and my father could be jealous if my mother and I appeared to be enjoying each other's company too much.

My father loved hobnobbing with all and sundry. He would enter into conversation with anyone who took his fancy – be it some down-at-heel old tramp or one of the many prostitutes who abounded in Curzon Street in those days. I suppose having a young girl in tow was a safeguard against their advances. He preferred low life to high society, mainly because it was cheaper, and we would stroll through St James's Park licking ice-cream cornets, or sit riveted for hours at Wimbledon on 'rover' tickets with only the occasional London bun to sustain us. But he could also be generous. I recall one sizzlingly hot June day out from school when I opted to see a performance of 'French Without Tears', then playing at the Criterion Theatre on Piccadilly Circus. We lunched beforehand at the Criterion Restaurant, where in 1934 – for the princely sum of 8/6d (about 42p) – you could eat resplendently. I remember my father's expression of disbelief as I demolished a large assortment of *hors d'oeuvres*, a whole *poussin* plus accompaniments, finishing with a pyramidal concoction of ice-cream and strawberries. He was obviously unused to a healthy schoolgirl's appetite. On my return to school we had to submit an essay on "My day out", which won me the school prize, although the only words I remember writing were "back to matron and gargle".

Although Highfield was not renowned for its academic accomplishments, my mother liked the headmistress, Mrs Robley-Browne, a somewhat engulfing lady given to swooping movements and with rich red hair, which remained unchanged till the day she died, well into her eighties. She was tucked away in the top flat of the building known as 'The Nest' where she lived with her husband, a diminutive retired naval captain, inevitably known by the girls as 'wobbly-bwown', to whom she was devoted and he to her. Sab, a black labrador, invariably accompanied one or other of them at all times. Mrs RB, as she was called by her charges, was very keen on amateur theatricals. Every year, she would hire the Steiner Hall for her pupils to display their talents for dancing, singing and acting. I never became one of her star turns at any of these but was usually allotted a secondary role in the school play, more often than not with a comic flavour.

On one never-to-be-forgotten occasion I was cast as the nursemaid in a Chinese fairy tale, which spanned a lapse of thirty years between scenes. This necessitated me having to be made up to age accordingly. Inadvertently I confused the moment and appeared as an old woman a scene too soon. As the curtain went up, the enormity of my faux-pas engulfed me. I became paralysed with shame. The villain of the piece (one of my classmates), who had abducted my charge in the previous scene, regarded me with bewilderment, which gradually gave way to dawning comprehension. As he intoned the words "Tell me, lovely young maiden, can you direct me to the Emperor's palace?", his lips quivered. The audience – mercifully my parents not amongst them – thought this exchange hilarious. Their hilarity proved too much for my fellow-actor who, overcome with hysteria managed however to retain his sang-froid. "Ha, ha, ha", he managed to gulp out with remarkable presence of mind "you can't fool me you know", leaving the audience totally bemused and the producer in despair.

My only other theatrical appearance was not much more successful. Coming from Scotland, I had considerable trouble with my double 'o's and caused Mrs RB much exasperation when coaching me for the part of a tipsy gipsy in some obscure play by a forgotten author. "Mun, mun, show me the way home", I would trill happily. "Mooon, Hazel, mooon", she would bellow from the wings, reducing me to a state of humiliation and rebellion. On *the* night, however, I reckoned there was nothing she could do about it in front of an audience, so stubbornly resorted to my more familiar version. Thereafter I was relegated to moving furniture.

I suppose I was moderately happy at school, as I made friends easily and enjoyed games – although I would much rather have been at home. The main LMS railway line used to pass the foot of the school grounds and during my first term I would sneak off to a spot behind a laurel bush, hidden from the main building and mocking eyes, and watch the trains speeding north with tears streaming down my face. At the end of term I was, to begin with, put in the charge of older girls from other schools who were also travelling to Edinburgh by train. The eight hours' journey from King's Cross to Edinburgh was a misery to me, as by then I had developed train sickness. During this ordeal I was forever going up and down the passage to the lavatory and refusing, with averted eyes, the kind offers of chocolate or cream buns that were constantly being offered to me by my fellow travellers. They, not knowing my affliction (I was far too shy to admit to my failing), no doubt thought me rather a restless and ungracious companion.

During my first term at boarding school my mother had my bedroom redecorated as a surprise for me. On arriving home for the holidays, I burst into tears when being shown my room, which upset my mother dreadfully until I explained, between sobs, that it was the thought of returning to school in four weeks' time that had induced this outburst of grief, rather than her choice of wallpaper.

We quite often spent holidays at North Berwick and then I would travel overnight in a four-berth compartment for the sum of 11/6d (57p). If one gave fair warning to the guard, who would pass on the message to the engine driver, the train would judder to a stop at 6.30am at Drem Station, an isolated halt in the middle of East Lothian farming land. Here I would descend, often the only passenger to do so, clutching lacrosse stick or tennis racquet depending on the season, thank the guard politely for his trouble, while heads poked out of carriage windows to see what was causing the delay, before being whisked away in the waiting car to a breakfast of bacon and eggs and a vociferous welcome from family and dog.

The holidays spent at our Edinburgh home, usually in winter, were normally full of social activities. Being rather slow in acquiring the art of conversation, due more to a paralysing shyness rather than the lack of anything to say, I welcomed those children's parties at which progressive games were the chief form of entertainment. These entailed 'progressing' from table to table, each set out with a different game or competition, some calling for mental skill or general knowledge and others depending on physical agility or quick reflexes. I became adept therefore at memorising objects on a tray, picking out pins from a pile of sawdust or compiling a list of animals beginning with the letter 'A' and returning home laden with prizes and complacency.

As I grew older, parties with organised games gave way to dances with organised Scottish country dancing. Here again I was quite happy, as conversation, apart from a whoop or frenzied command to or from one's partner, was virtually impossible when breath and concentration were needed to follow the intricate steps and contortions of set reels and other dances. Often enough, enflamed perhaps by the skirl of the pipe band or from some innate call from an ancestor (it certainly wasn't alcohol – nothing stronger than lemonade or an occasional shandy was ever served at these functions) our partners would lose control and fling us with wild abandon and demonic shrieks into the melée of gyrating kilted figures, from which we would eventually be hauled back into their brawny arms – seldom escaping without skirts torn by a capricious *skean dhu* or a bare arm lacerated by those lethal silver buttons which adorned our partners' velvet jackets. It was all wildly elating.

One of my mother's friends, a forceful character called Mrs. Orr, made a useful contribution to our particular community by running a badminton club during the Christmas holidays, available only to those at boarding school. Here we would whack shuttlecocks to and fro on two mornings a week, our games being ruthlessly monitored by our patron, who brooked no laxity or horseplay. The end of the holidays culminated in a competition for the boys and girls. I was rather a favourite of our sponsor. One year, when I was beaten somewhat unexpectedly in the girls' finals, she switched the first and second prizes, having ascertained beforehand my preference, so that I received the coveted brooch I had set my mind on. My mother was really shocked when I boasted of this achievement at home, although more at her friend's behaviour than at mine.

A way for my parents to ensure a peaceful sabbath afternoon in the winter holidays was to despatch all three of us to the Sunday Skating Club at Edinburgh ice rink. During the week the rink was largely used for curling matches, a sport my mother much enjoyed, with only a small section screened off for skaters. On Sundays the whole area was open to Club members for skaters only. A distinctive waft of chemically cold air greeted us as we pushed through the swing doors into the building and descended to the ice-rink proper, a long rectangular arena with vaulted roof and a raised dais at one end. Here a full-blooded band played appropriate music while skaters of every age would glide, race or waver round the stadium depending on their aptitude. Females changed into their skating boots in a little cubby-hole, garnished with lockers, presided over by a lugubrious individual called Miss Webster, dressed invariably in black, but always at hand with plaster or liniment should the need arise.

Once shod we would teeter our way to the ice to meet up with old friends or in the hope of meeting new ones. A tea interval lasted thirty minutes, to allow time for the ice to be swept and the band to be refreshed. A first priority was to ensure that one was invited to join a tea party. It obviously added greatly to one's status to be included in a party organised by a young blood or by one of the officers stationed in or about Edinburgh in the years preceding the Second World War. Inevitably there was much competition and I, for one, was thankful enough to be invited by someone more humble, or even, as a last resort, by my own brother.

After tea came the dancing interlude when the more advanced skaters had the rink to themselves and could show off their expertise. I had managed to achieve a rather wobbly figure of eight for my brownie badge at the age of eight, but had made little noticeable progress since. However I had an admirer, admittedly somewhat puny and with only one good lung but a versatile skater, who invariably asked me for the first waltz. Thanks to his prowess and remarkably stalwart arms we always managed to circumvent the rink without disaster. At six o'clock a bell would signal closing time and we would walk the short distance home beneath the stars or in the rain, as the bells of St. Mary's Cathedral summoned its congregation to evensong.

The things my father excelled in – finance and sport – he wished to see mirrored in his children. Alas! this was not to be. None of us showed any aptitude for figures and the only one who was any good at games was myself. True, George did in fact sprint for Rugby and ruptured his appendix as a result. The school's doctor diagnosed his collapse as jaundice and if it had not been for the timely intervention of my godmother's husband, an eminent surgeon who lived nearby, George would have departed this world a decade before his appointed time.

My younger brother, John, liked to look the part of whatever role he decided to play: immaculate on the tennis court in well-pressed white flannels; gun crooked under an arm protruding from a well-cut tweed jacket; plus fours or 'long bags' on the golf course with an awesome display of pullovers to match. This sartorial display I always felt was designed to attract the eye of the onlooker, preferably feminine, and never quite matched his skill at hitting the ball over the net, bringing down a grouse or keeping to a straight course on the fairway.

It was left to me, therefore, to collect athletic laurels, which I did with enthusiasm and vigour, modest though those laurels were. A fitted sewing case was my first prize, I recall, for winning the 'all round trophy' at my kindergarten's sports day – due mainly to my dexterity at leapfrog – but my prize did not encourage my life-long aversion to sewing as I would have much preferred a skipping rope. Later accolades included the captaining of various netball, cricket, lacrosse and tennis teams, which at least helped to keep my father happy and proud.

I have a snapshot of me and my brothers dressed in tennis gear, racquets across our knees, taken while holidaying at some Scottish farm. We are seated on a bench with, at our feet, an array of imposing looking trophies. On closer inspection they proved to be cups for the prize ram at the Highland Show of 1927, the champion bull at some local show of 1926 and the best milking cow in the nearby livestock fair, date unrecorded.

In the summer of 1937, because I was considered (by my family) to be above average at tennis, my mother had the unenviable task of driving me from tournament to tournament. While I battled grimly on the court in endless girls' singles, she sat on the sidelines knitting equally grimly and muttering at intervals "I'm going to be sick", whenever her daughter played a particularly puerile shot. Tempers frayed somewhat but at least it kept all the family in sweaters. It was just as well I was a very average player, as otherwise my father would have become the club bore. As it was, being a painfully self-conscious child, any adulation or indeed criticism concerning me in my presence caused me to blush hotly, an affliction which plagued me well into my teens and which was not helped by my brothers drawing attention to my fiery face by exclaiming "lobsters for lunch" or "cool off".

A game at which my father excelled and which allowed for no boasting on his children's part was that of golf. In Scotland almost everyone within easy reach of a golf course was brought up with a golf club in hand. Surrounded as we were at North Berwick by at least half-a dozen courses within walking or bicycling distance we were no exception. During our spells there we were banished almost daily to the local links where we squabbled over the rules, crowed over each other's short-comings and exulted in our few brilliant shots. On occasion the wind would be blowing so hard that it needed no help from us to propel the ball from the tee. At other times I played in my bathcap, so fierce was the rain, and it was not unusual for our clubs to slide from our near-frozen fingers. Somehow it was deemed cowardly to give up and go home, so we sought shelter in a bunker or under a tree.

A close friend at the time was Joan Donald (later Anderson), daughter of a doctor in North Berwick. I believe she became the first woman's golf pro in the UK and was twice runner-up in the Ladies Open Golf Championship, being beaten by an American, known simply as 'The Babe'. She joined the WAAF in the war and was with me at Allied HQ in Italy for some time. Endowed with a stringent sense of humour, she died as she would have wished, on her way to teeing off at the first hole at Gullane golf course.

On moving to London after the war, I thankfully donated my clubs to one of the workmen engaged in painting my flat. My mother would sometimes be heard to tell one of us that she would have been quite a good golfer if she hadn't been married to our father. My father, however, derived such blatant pleasure from our very rare golfing successes that it rather acerbated our guilt at failing to live up to his expectations all the time. For my mother it was quite enough to listen to prolonged details of each shot from one player, rather than four, and it was probably then that she took to needlework. While her husband recounted his shots, she could at least simulate interest while counting her stitches. Many a Florentine footstool or cushion cover unfolded while my father putted out the eighteenth hole.

Three

I left school at the age of sixteen, having achieved the customary School Certificate, considered adequate in those days for a girl whose destiny in my immediate circle was still considered to be marriage or the caring of elderly parents. Because it was deemed early days for either of these to occur, I was dispatched summarily to Paris for a year with the intention of being 'finished', a process shared by many of my contemporaries. As I so far lacked any mission in life, was obviously not going to be a *femme fatale*, and had no valid reason for saying "no", I went along with my parents' wishes, although I doubt if I had any choice in the matter.

The finishing school chosen for me was in Sèvres, the suburb of Paris best known for its porcelain factory and at that time with many leafy-lined streets. The house itself remains hazy in my mind but I still retain memories of some of the inmates.

The establishment was run by two single ladies, one French and the other English. Mlle Duproix was elegant with fine bone structure and a sweet smile. Nearly always dressed severely in black in high collared dresses, her hair tightly drawn into a bun, she could have stepped straight from one of the impressionist paintings of which we were to see so many during our stay in Paris. She was responsible for our lessons in French conversation and literature and accompanied us on many of our cultural excursions. Her colleague was a Miss Manson, rather ungainly and graceless but amiable and easy to please. She was in charge of our well-being and all domestic matters, which included our meals.

The school itself made curiously little impression on me. There were six other girls apart from myself, all English, bar one from Wales, which of course did not augur well for our French progress, although we were supposed to speak nothing but that language. One of my colleagues, Madeleine Griffiths, shared my love of tennis and, because we were considered to be incipient stars, we played numerous games on a covered court under the jaded eyes of a coach who had seen better days and, I guess, better players. Subsequently, on our return to England, Madeleine and I made a brief and inglorious appearance in the Girls Doubles Covered Courts Championship at Dulwich, where we were ignominiously defeated 6-0, 6-0 by the ultimate winners, Muriel Harris and Jean Nicol, future wife of Tony Mottram.

Mornings at Sèvres were devoted to classes followed by lunch. I seem to remember rather spartan meals at which globe artichokes appeared with relentless monotony, served with vinaigrette sauce. This was often followed by strips of meat, covered in an indefinable sauce, and which my fellow guests assured me was horsemeat.

The afternoons were devoted to excursions – the Louvre, Jeu de Paume, Notre-Dame, Le Jardin des Plantes, Musée Rodin and all the other countless museums and galleries which still figure in my Paris itinerary. These visits I enjoyed immensely and led to my enduring love affair with Paris.

The smells: Gauloises of course and garlic, bad drains, the catch-at-the-throat pungency of the river at night and the scent of the moment for me – Chanel No. 5. The sounds: the clanging of the tram bells passing the foot of our street, the whooshing of the water pipes used by the street cleaner outside the house, the cries of street vendors and incessant French chatter, the plop of horse chestnuts falling at our feet as we walked in the *Bois*, and the shattering noise of the iron guards to the shop windows as they were closed for the night. Sights: the kaleidoscopic heaps of produce in the markets, meat and cheese open to the elements and the flies, the tombs in Montmartre Cemetery, early morning mist over the Seine, the incongruity of the Eiffel Tower, the trousered legs protruding from the *pissoirs* that lined the streets and were *obligatoires* – and Monsieur from the house opposite who, regular as clockwork, appeared each morning, dapper in spats and checked trousers, to take a miniature Yorkshire terrier on a walk, carefully secured by a red lead.

Nearly forty years later, after conducting a party round Moscow, I had to fly directly to Paris where I had a night on my own before gathering up a group of Americans for a tour of France. After checking into my hotel near the Sacré Coeur, I went outside and stood for a moment drinking in the sight of the city spread out below me. I found myself skipping down the street like a girl let out from school, singing at the top of my voice with the sheer joy of being in this wonderful, marvellous city; exulting in the stalls and shop windows stuffed with food, smiling at strangers, listening enraptured to the laughing or grumbling pedestrians so utterly unaware of their freedom, in contrast to the restrictions and drabness of a Communist regime.

Not all our excursions were given over to culture: 1937 was the year of the Paris Exhibition of Arts and Technology and under the chaperonage of one or other of our two cicerones we would visit some of the countless pavilions, each flying its country's flag and displaying its products. Dominant over all, I recall the huge arrogant double-headed eagle and swastika of the German Reich, facing the hammer and sickle of the Soviet Union, surmounted by statues of two massive figures depicting youth and the future. Visits to the *Palais de Glace* also figured in our curriculum. At the entrance to the ice rink on the Champs Elysées stood a kiosk with striped awning, which sold a memorable caramel of huge proportions and satisfying taste. With one of those gob-stoppers distorting our cheeks we would swoop up and down the ice, often meeting up with friends or some callow but ardent youth taking time off from his studies for the '*bac*'.

I had my introduction to opera at the venerable Opera Garnier. This was a performance of Charpentier's 'Louise' and not the perfect choice for a novice to opera. I found the music uninspiring and repetitive. In fact the only line I recall is, I presume Louise, singing rather plaintively "*passe-moi le vin, Papa*", but I may have dreamt this up. By contrast, I remember almost every magical moment of '*Les Trois Valses*', starring Yvonne Printemps and Pierre Fresnay and on my return to Edinburgh used to drive my family mad by playing over and over again the lyrics from this operetta. I retained for years 78 rpm recordings of the songs, despite their becoming increasingly cracked, which I played nostalgically from time to time since, to the best of my knowledge, the operetta has never been revived. Even if it was, I doubt if I would go and see it. The disenchantment might prove too great.

By the end of my time in Paris I was fast becoming a Francophile, so prevailed upon my family to keep me across the Channel, but not at school. My mother, fondly imagining that I was turning bi-lingual and acquiring a polish I had to date been lacking, found a family in Grenoble that was willing to have me as a paying guest.

With the *famille* Magnon I found instant rapport. Apart from an English boy who stayed for a short spell, I was the sole guest in a non-English speaking household, so my French improved by leaps and bounds. Madame was widowed, much given to laughter and warmly welcoming. A married daughter lived nearby and the elder son, Pierre, was not at home, his work being at Lyon. It was therefore left to Claude, the second daughter some two years my senior, and her sixteen-year old brother Jacquie, to look after me. Claude was red-haired, vivacious and years ahead of me in the ways of the world. She must have found me a bit of a drag being younger and, as yet, not all that articulate in the French language.

She was a gregarious person and included me in most of her

activities with her numerous friends. With Jacquie I was on very good terms. His was a sweet and equable disposition and his schoolboy sense of humour made me feel instantly at home. The three of them got on very well together and seemed to take it in their stride to have a foreign stranger in their midst, although I suspect it was necessity on Madame Magnon's part. During the week we lived in a large rambling flat in the rue Pont St Jaime in the old quarter of the city, from where Jacquie went to school each day and I to the occasional class at Grenoble University.

Weekends and summer months were spent at the family's small château at Narbonne, a hamlet deep in the mountains surrounded by cherry orchards. Here we would all be put to work at the arduous but convivial task of cherry picking during the latter part of May, with warnings not to eat too many of the fruit in case of dire consequences.

Here too, we were forever being asked to take part in some form of entertainment – be it a treasure hunt by car or bicycle, games of tennis, or walks culminating in a picnic in some lush meadow near an icy stream. Claude excelled in skiing, a sport I took up far too late in life to become any good at. Some months after my return home, I received a black-bordered letter informing me of the tragic death of Claude, killed in an avalanche. After the war, I tried to trace news of the family, and to find out how they had survived the war, but to no avail.

The three Magnons were enthusiastic bridge players, so were delighted to have me at hand to make up a fourth. My mother was a good player and from an early age I had handed round plates of bridge rolls and sandwiches at her frequent bridge parties. I had so far escaped being a player despite, or perhaps because of, my mother's insistence that "bridge is a useful social asset". However, *chez* the Magnons it seemed churlish and un-cooperative not to join in and as Madame put it *"vous allez améliorer votre jeu au bridge et votre français au même temps"*. I cannot say that these sessions converted me to the game, but they certainly improved my vocabulary and they were played in such a light-hearted manner, without recriminations on anyone's part, that I really began to enjoy them.

Six months passed happily with the Magnons, but it was a life leading with little evidence to the finesse that my mother was hoping for. I had put on weight, thanks to the delicious but robust meals served by Madame, and enjoyed the wines of the region. So on being recalled to London in the autumn of 1938 to prepare for my presentation at court – to my mind a total waste of time and in any case why not Holyrood? – I looked at myself in the mirror of my little room in Grenoble and was not reassured.

Another affliction I suffered from was acne – not conducive to self-confidence – and even with the help of cosmetics and sunburn, my complexion was anything but satin-smooth and without blemish. However, during the train journey back to London I was somewhat cheered by the attentions paid me by a young Frenchman, on his way to take up a post as chef to one of London's leading hotels. He clearly enjoyed my company, spots and all, so with boosted morale I adjusted my rather too-tight skirt and powdered my ever-shining nose. I did, admittedly, have doubts about my hat (a must in London at that time) – a small green velvet beret-like object, which was the worse for wear having been crammed into a drawer, unworn, for some months.

I was really looking forward to being with my mother who, after all, I had not seen for over a year and of whom I was very fond. It was a hot day in September and late afternoon when my train steamed into Victoria Station. I joined the throng of passengers on the platform. Having secured a porter and recovered my luggage from the guard's van we battled our way to the exit, I clutching a carrier bag containing a bulb of garlic, several boxes of French chocolates and a Camembert cheese, which was, by then, making itself evident. I caught sight of my mother looking, even at a distance, decidedly drawn (I afterwards discovered she was suffering from gastric flu) but as always, beautifully dressed and elegant.

"Mummy", I yelled, with all the exuberance of an undisciplined puppy. "Darling", she cried on catching sight of me, her face alight with love and expectation. A quick glance at my figure and wardrobe could not altogether conceal her chagrin at finding her daughter not the sophisticated butterfly she had hoped for, but still very much in chrysalis form with rounded contours and lack of chic. "It's a pity hats are in fashion", she remarked as we wended our way towards the cab rank "and what is that funny smell? Oh cheese", she exclaimed with relief as I revealed its cause. "What on earth made you bring a cheese back, when we're staying at a hotel for two nights?"

What indeed, except that I thought we were to return to Edinburgh first, before taking London by storm. On arrival at Langham's Hotel my mother took to her bed for two days and duly recovered. The Camembert was banished to the kitchens and I spent quite an enjoyable time meeting friends and exploring London on my own. We then returned home, when my father asked rather petulantly whether I was going to be around for a while, and my brother John, awaiting the finished product, pronounced me underdone.

However, a brief stay at home was only a prelude to the, to me, ridiculous charade of 'coming out', a role quite unsuited to my temperament, figure or inclination. Had I been a more rebellious character, or even had had something better to do, I would have resisted. As it was, I accompanied my mother to endless appointments to her rather grand dressmaker called Selina Cross, who brushed away my mother's remarks on my figure as "puppy fat, modom, puppy fat". A further visit to a skin specialist resulted in a diet of live yeast and green vegetables.

The parties and balls in Edinburgh I enjoyed, as at least I knew many of my fellow guests and had rather more to say for myself than hitherto. Dances were programme affairs in pre-war days. On arrival at assembly hall, ballroom or private house, the hostess would greet you with a minuscule programme to which was attached with silk thread an equally minuscule pencil. The programme would list the order and type of dance – be it foxtrot, waltz, foursome reel and so on, numbering about eighteen in all. The real business of the evening was to ensure that your programme was filled in advance of the first dance – or risk the ignominy of spending the duration of a dance in the ladies' cloakroom, miserably powdering an over-powdered nose.

My mother always attempted to extract a promise from my long-suffering brother George to see that my programme was filled. How he was to fulfil this was not clear to either him or me. Was he to coerce his friends by cajolery or by bribery to dance with his sister, or worst thought of all, was he to be my partner for all eighteen dances? My brother John was never approached on these lines, it being a complete waste of time. Once he had crossed the threshold and surveyed the company, he was seldom seen again, the suspicion being that he had absconded to some more amusing or less conventional place of entertainment. My mother once told me that John, at the age of eighteen (I was seventeen months his junior) had told her that he only knew two virgins and one was his sister. "Oh dear", was her reply but it is not clear whether her reaction was consternation at the thought of all those Edinburgh mothers bringing lawsuits to her son's door, or concern that her daughter was lacking in sex appeal. In any event, George being the kind and reliable person he was, would resignedly approach me and hopefully enquire whether my programme was full. Paradoxically, if I replied that this was the case, he would become quite piqued, having kept a dance or two free. We usually agreed, however, to dance an old-fashioned waltz together as I had taught him the steps and we rather fancied ourselves as a pair.

It was when my mother and I moved to London for a short

'season' before being presented at Court that I became resentful. Back at Langham's, I was invited to a round of lunch and cocktail parties, with other 'debs', many of whom I had scarcely met or was unlikely ever to see again. I enjoyed going to the theatre or cinema with old school friends, but would have much rather been fishing with my father in Scotland.

Ironically I cannot remember much about the presentation itself. My sponsor was a friend of my mother, Lady (Evelyn) Carr, a Christian Scientist, sharp-tongued and exceedingly handsome. I liked her forthrightness and we became good friends when I later lived in London. I do remember that it was a wet night, as white-gloved and gaitered flunkeys held enormous umbrellas over us as we descended from our hired limousine.

Decked out in white tulle, blue-beribboned and ostrich-feathered (me); champagne coloured watered silk (my mother) and some very diaphanous material (our escort), we gathered our trains together and advanced inch by inch in a crush of similarly attired females up the red-carpeted staircase to the Throne Room, where Their Majesties awaited us under a canopy of chandeliers that sent a galaxy of rainbow coloured splinters into the air as they glittered on jewelled tiaras, diadem and necklaces.

Once in the presence of Their Majesties, we braced ourselves for the curtsey, practised a hundred times before our bedroom mirrors and safely executed on the night, to my mother's evident relief. I have photographs of us both in our presentation robes taken by the court photographer of the day, Lenare, whose great art was to depict his subjects rather hazily – so that even the plainest of his sitters assumed a rather romantic guise. My mother looks lovely but I have a decidedly chastened air about me.

After this Royal episode – having achieved quite what? – I was content enough to return home for most of 1939, learning the rudiments of shorthand and typing at McAdam's secretarial college in Edinburgh, which I enjoyed. I also attended, at my mother's instigation, a term at Atholl Crescent, Edinburgh's prestigious College of Domestic Art, my course being entitled, somewhat optimistically in my case at least, 'The Bride's Course'.

I may have made out my mother to be insensitive and unloving, but this was not at all the case. "It is only because I love you darling", she would exclaim, having delivered a *coup de foudre* with the words, "I must admit I've seen you in things I like better" or "I never thought of you in that colour", just as I was feeling a million dollars on my way out to meet the current youth of my dreams. "If I didn't love you, I wouldn't bother what you looked like, would I?" No use trying to explain that her criticisms did more harm than good and that she should leave me to find out my own mistakes. Or did they really do me harm? I certainly harboured no feelings of animosity or resentment towards her in later life. We enjoyed each other's company and grew increasingly close with advancing years.

The year 1939 unfolded with no clear idea as to what was to be my future or indeed the future of any of us. Germany's menace, although shelved for the time being, was ever present and neither I nor most of my contemporaries thought that the Munich agreement really meant "peace in our time". Cocooned in the security of our own little pampered world, most of my female friends still regarded marriage as being the ultimate goal, despite the fact that the majority married either to escape from home, for financial security or merely because it was expected of them.

It must have been galling for my mother to hear of other daughters' engagements or weddings. In fact she told me long after the war, in a rather perplexed tone, that it never entered her head that she would have a daughter who didn't marry and it was I who felt sorry for her, not for myself. I had a comfortable home, caring parents, many friends both male and female, and varied interests. Many of my friends were in similar circumstances. It was just that we felt rudderless. So it was hardly surprising that with the declaration of war on 3rd September 1939 (my brother George's twenty-third birthday), I discarded mufti for the anonymity of khaki uniform with as much alacrity as a starving donkey grabs a blade of grass – and embarked on a future that promised independence, responsibility and new horizons.

The war years

Four

New horizons were not in great evidence at first. Before and since Munich, Territorial Army activities had played a prominent part in many citizens' lives throughout the British Isles. Both my brothers had joined the Territorials: George with the Lothians and Border Horse, later part of the 6th Armoured Division, whose HQ was in Edinburgh, where he was at that time apprenticed to a firm of Writers to the Signet; and John with the Lanarkshire Yeomanry, for by then he was employed with a firm of papermakers, Robert Craig & Sons, whose mills and offices were in Airdrie, an unprepossessing industrial town on the outskirts of Glasgow. Greyhound racing and football were the main pursuits of its male inhabitants, while factory or mill girls with brawny arms and broad vowels constituted much of the female companionship available – neither exactly the choice of menu suited to my brother's more sophisticated appetites.

Parallel to the military bodies were the female equivalent – the ATS (Auxiliary Territorial Service), MTC (Motor Transport Company) and the First Aid Nursing Yeomanry, better known as the FANY. The original role of the latter, as envisaged by its founder, a Sergeant Baker who took part in the Sudan campaign in 1896-99, was for its members to gallop on to the field of battle on horseback to succour the sick and remove the wounded. However, the FANY was not officially formed until 1907, and by the time the First World War erupted, horses in this particular field were rapidly being replaced by mechanised transport: the first volunteers crossed to France with the British Army and their first motorised ambulances.

Between the wars the FANY continued to expand. Recruits were trained in all mechanical and other duties connected with transport – such as the driving of staff cars, ambulances, trucks and three-ton lorries, as well as map-reading, first-aid (including how to deliver a baby) and stretcher-bearing. During the spring and summer of 1938 many of my contemporaries, already FANYs, took part in weekly manoeuvres, mostly with their own or their family's cars. These ranged from an Austin Seven to a heavily-built Minerva saloon. On one occasion a newly joined recruit was driven to camp (a twice-yearly event under canvas) by her mother's chauffeur, who after handing over the keys of the family Daimler, returned home by train.

Because I had been away from home for most of 1938, I was a late enrolment and rather on the outside of these activities, but during 1939 I was admitted to the weekly training sessions in mufti, adorned with an armband bearing the letters FANY. A similar tab was worn on the sleeves of the uniforms already worn by the older members to distinguish them from what we regarded as the lesser members of the ATS. To begin with, FANYs were allowed to order their own uniforms, usually being made to measure from Scott Adie, a well-known kilt maker in George Street, in the case of the Edinburgh members. Not surprisingly these were a great improvement on the army issue uniforms, which were *de rigeur* in later years when we were amalgamated with the ATS – except for those dedicated souls who opted to remain free FANYs (usually those with bi-lingual French and English) and were dropped into occupied France for service with the Resistance forces, many of them to suffer torture or to perish in concentration camps.

I remember the pain it caused me, some years on, when I had to relinquish my tailor-made uniform for the thick serge khaki skirt of shapeless cut and battledress top, or for dressier occasions such as church parade or sergeant-mess dances, a waisted jacket. I often think the designer of those uniforms had much to answer for. The jackets had breast pockets that usually took the place of handbags and contained most of our valuables, such as money and identity cards, not to mention cosmetics for the day and family photographs. What couldn't be crammed into our already bulging pockets went into our gas mask holders, the masks themselves having being discarded in those days when gas attacks did not appear to be imminent. When I met Katie, our cook, wearing my ATS uniform, she took one look at me and said, "Oh Miss Hazel, you're in the army noo". We were always envious of the Wrens who looked immaculate and trim in their navy blue uniforms, the officers with tricorne hats and silk stockings.

So when war was finally declared, my brothers and I had our allotted roles, so to speak, while my parents were already enrolled as air raid wardens, versed in the rudiments of firefighting and how to deal with incendiary bombs. Indeed when the sirens sounded fifteen minutes after Neville Chamberlain's broadcast to the effect that we were at war with Germany, convincing us that bombs were about to rain on us, my mother bravely donned her steel hat and stood on the front steps of our house briskly blowing her whistle. A small boy passing on his bicycle with no idea that history was in the making, cheerfully called out "penalty goal". Throughout the war I doubt if she was ever to blow it again.

A telephone call to the 4th Scottish FANY headquarters in Edinburgh instructed me to report to its depot there and then. "Bring the minimum", I was told, "you'll be equipped from here and uniform is not important for the time being". So I packed my hold-all, slung my gas mask over my shoulder, kissed my emotional parents an excited farewell, and boarded the tram for Colinton, two miles up the road! On looking back, I must confess to a feeling of guilt. My brothers had already joined their units, admittedly not very far off: George to Dunbar before moving on to Bovington and armoured cars; John to Lanark and subsequently seconded with his regiment to the Royal Scots Greys at Redford Barracks, to where I was about to wend my way. My parents had just seen their three young lambs leave for the unknown and no one knew then how the war was to unfold.

"Going to do your bit, hen?", enquired my neighbour on the tram, a beshawled lady carrying a load of washing, and nodded approvingly when I grinned assent. "Good luck, mate, gi' 'em hell", called out the conductor as I got off at the terminus.

Inspired with good fellowship and patriotism, I trudged the short distance to Inchdrewer House on the perimeter of Redford Barracks and at present occupied by the FANY. The commandant in charge of us was a delightfully plain character called Betty Hunter-Cowan, inevitably known as the Hunting Cow. Largely built, with a heart to match, the war for her was, I suspect, an even greater boon than to me. She was at least a decade older than I, unmarried and the daughter of a talented and slightly eccentric artist mother, which can't have made life easy for her. She welcomed me with warmth: "Wood, good to see you", but at the same time intimated in her manner that life in future was to be no cynosure.

To begin with I slept in an attic room shared by my cousin, Jean Leared, who was shortly to leave for France, and April Watson, an old school friend with whom I shared a somewhat shameful bond. We had never had to wash clothes in our pampered lives, so watched with interest how those less fortunate mortals handled these chores. Soon after, April defected to the Wrens: perhaps she decided navy blue suited her better than khaki.

I suppose these first few months were no more than a novel and stimulating game to many of us. We were not endangered from the skies or from gunfire; we were sheltered within our own little palisade, free from responsibilities and decisions; immune from problems as to board and lodging or clothing. Companionship was at hand if required and if dormitory life and a few deprivations such as sharing ablutions with eight or ten others were not what we were used to, we only had to think of the occupied countries and count our blessings.

At first I was allotted to kitchen duties, as I had as yet no uniform and little driving experience, having passed my test six months previously. The kitchens at Inchdrewer had seen better days and were depressingly drab, but windows gave on to the barrack square, so there was always some diversion to distract us while peeling mounds of potatoes or preparing vegetables.

The two cooks in charge of the kitchens were both older than me and both had had some culinary experience. Christine Rutherford was a placid female of generous proportions with a cigarette for ever dangling from her lips. I would watch hypnotised as the ash grew longer and longer, wondering if it would join the stew she was stirring – not that it would probably have been detected. Slapdash in her ways, she was nevertheless tolerant of my shortcomings and ready to show me the art of slicing onions or rolling pastry. Her colleague, Betty Kay, had an equally tranquil nature and possibly higher standards. Her sense of humour smoothed over many a contretemps. Shortly after my arrival we were joined by Betty's younger sister, Isobel, who became a lifelong friend.

I was the general dogsbody and, with the help of a kitchen orderly who changed daily and was usually a driver whose car was out of action or relegated to kitchen duties for some mild misdemeanour, coped with the never-ending tasks necessary for the feeding of forty to fifty hungry FANYs. All non-commissioned drivers, mechanics, orderlies, secretaries and administrative staff in the FANY were classified as Drivers and bore that title as opposed to Private, with the subsequent ranks of corporal, sergeant etc. running parallel with army ranks. The Hunting Cow bore the rank of Junior Commander or it may merely have been Subaltern in those early days. Military regulations – or was it the FANY's own set of rules? – decreed that no FANY other rank was to be seen in public with any male who had officer status – except in the case of husband, father, or close relation. As most of our male friends had commissions in one of the Services, it soon came to light that we had myriad brothers, uncles or fiancés etc (broken engagements were commonplace). It did not take long before authority realised the idiocy of this regulation and the influx of 'relations' cooled off after a bit.

The intake of FANYs soon outgrew Inchdrewer and we were moved to premises in one of Edinburgh's fine terraced houses in Abercromby Place, part of the New Town plan carried out by William Playfair and James Craig in the early 19th century, and much more convenient for our off-duty pursuits.

Once kitted out in uniform, I was removed from the cookhouse and became a driver at the Headquarters of Scottish Command, housed in those early days in South Bridge, with little or no parking facilities. The Second Echelon of HQ was located in a rambling country mansion at Riccarton, some six miles from the city centre. For junior officers and other ranks who did not merit a staff car, or for the occasional visiting big-wig, a ferry-car service was provided between the two Commands. This consisted of two shooting brakes sprayed with camouflage paint, heavy steering and room for eight passengers.

The winter of 1939/40 was extremely severe and it was not uncommon for one or other of the brakes to be stuck in a snowdrift, from which it would have to be extricated with the help of its passengers and passers-by. Ten to twelve trips back and forth each day along the same route could have been monotonous, had it not been for the variety of passengers, and it proved good experience for the inexperienced driver. I had the privilege on more than one occasion of driving General Sikorski, Commander of the Polish troops in exile in Scotland. A delightful and courteous man, he would cause me considerable confusion, as after I had opened the door for him and saluted, he would in turn open the door for me, with much clicking of heels.

Early in the New Year, HQ Command was transferred to premises at John Watson's College (now the Scottish National Gallery of Modern Art), an imposing building by William Burn and formerly a school for the children of merchants. With its spacious grounds, there were no further problems over parking.

The FANYs' room was presided over by Sergeant Nan Herdman, an individual ideally suited for the job of relegating drivers to jobs, dealing with complaints, soothing ruffled feathers, fending off insistent boy-friends and chatting up 'the Brass'. She was married to an Edinburgh surgeon who was serving with the RAMC, was an avid bridge player, and with her soft Edinburgh drawl and unflappability, could turn away wrath from both sides of the fence.

In the spring of 1940 I became the proud driver of a staff car, a camouflaged Hillman that was available to any officer above the rank of lieutenant, or civil servant of equivalent rank, who requested authorised transport to any destination coming under the jurisdiction of Scottish Command. I would thus find myself at short notice leaving on a three–day tour of the Borders with a senior officer or driving a Clerk of Works to a Council Meeting in Edinburgh. On one occasion I was assigned to drive a Major in Intelligence, later to become a prominent member of the Treasury, on a visit to Highland Command. During the drive through Glencoe in the teeth of a gale, my passenger regaled me with Russian legends and cigarettes. On the return journey, perhaps as a result of the outward journey, he insisted on taking the wheel, his excuse being that he had always wanted to freewheel down the Devil's Elbow and now was his chance. One could only surmise who would have faced a court martial if there had been an accident.

Another frequent and popular passenger amongst us, also in Intelligence, was a Major Perfect. His first port of call before setting out on a journey was to stop at the Sister McCraws' sweetie shop in Morrison Street where, even in war-time, a lavish variety of tablet could be seen on display, laid out in rows in all their mouth-melting and no doubt tooth-rotting temptation: pink and white coconut ice, *eau-de-nil* confections of peppermint, chocolate fudge sprinkled with walnuts, ginger slabs, and best of all, luscious bars of Swiss Milk tablet. The choice was endless and having ascertained his driver's preference, the Major would disappear into the shop to a warm welcome from the two sisters and emerge with a box of tablet, each layer separated by oiled paper. Alas! the shop was no longer there when I returned to Edinburgh after the war and I never discovered what had become of the Misses McCraw.

Driving was not always such frivolity and pleasure. Very many signposts had been removed at the outbreak of war and others had been turned round so as to confuse the Germans, should they be dropped by parachute on some Scottish byway or take part in an invasion. We were often given short notice of our destination but were expected to find out the route and calculate the time needed to get there. Fortunately I knew Edinburgh and its environs fairly well and as a rule our passengers were co-operative. The morals of it all exercised my mother in no small way. "Do you mean you are going off for a day or two with an unknown man?" – or worse still with a man she or I knew. "Where do you sleep and does anyone know anything about him?" She was all for ringing up the War Office to check the credentials of the General commanding the Lowland Division or the Chaplain's Department to ensure that the inoffensive little padre I was conveying on a round of church parades was all that he was purported to be. If she but knew it, Colonels such as Sir Ian Colquhoun would do their best to arrange a tour of duty so that the day would finish in the vicinity of their homes – in the case of Sir Ian, on the shores of Loch Lomond – and thus spend a night with his wife and family, while I would be despatched to the Luss Arms down the road ... a practice my mother would equally have condemned as being undemocratic and unfriendly.

Once I was driving Colonel Tom Spens up to Inverness when we were hit by the swinging tail of an aircraft transporter, obviously behind schedule and oblivious to the treachery of highland roads. Luckily neither of us was hurt but the car was damaged and we had to limp into the nearest RASC depot to await a replacement. My passenger could not have been kinder and took the trouble of writing to FANY HQ exonerating me from any blame.

Because I was a willing horse and got on with most people, officers and other ranks alike, I was eventually awarded a lance-corporal's stripe, which I wore with great pride. Apart from HQ in Edinburgh, the 4th Scottish embraced several ambulance stations in outlying towns, one of them being at Dunbar, an east coast resort in peacetime and at the time the base of an OCTU (Officer Cadet Training Unit) to which was assigned one field ambulance with two FANYs to man it. To our great surprise Isobel Kay and myself were posted there in the summer of 1940 – possibly thanks to Nan Herdman – to replace my cousin Jean Leared, at last off to France after many false alarms, and her co-driver Margaret Allan, who had contracted meningitis.

We were billeted in a requisitioned boarding house, a depressing looking building of grey stone, one of many such lining the sea front. Net curtains to all the front windows were covered during black-out hours by drab coloured velvet hangings. Mottled linoleum lined the entrance hall and passage leading to our living quarters, which consisted of a bedroom and a sitting room where our meals were served. It was a dispiriting establishment run by a gorgon of a landlady, resentful and mean-spirited, by the name of Mrs. Gilhooley. She opened the door to Isobel and me, arms akimbo, and made it clear from the start that she was only putting up with us because she had no choice in the matter. Her suspicious watchful eyes viewed us as if we were a pair of vipers come to invade her precious territory. It was obvious that she viewed us with grave misgivings, if only for our being young, cheerful and delighted at having broken free from the confines of Scottish Command for the time being.

"I want no funny business here", she announced without prior greeting. "This is a respectable house and any visitors, male or female, are all to be shown the door by 9.30 pm." What heinous acts she thought could be accomplished after 9.30 that could not be achieved before that fateful hour eluded us, but in any event we were to discover that all lights in the 'common parts' were extinguished automatically at 9.30, which was the signal for "all oot". This of course was to lead to the general hilarity of our guests, who were forced to grope their way to the front door amidst a growing crescendo of noise and hubbub. Their exit culminated often enough with the appearance of our landlady, clad in woollen dressing gown and carpet slippers, who would admonish the interlopers to "gie oot the hoose quick mairch". She was also given to lurking in corners to ensure that we didn't ensnare her precious fifteen-year old son on his arrival back from school. We never discovered anything about Mr. Gilhooley, or whether indeed he existed. He may well have been fighting for his country, which might have accounted for his wife's sourness at having to hold the home front on her own.

Our tasks as ambulance drivers were not very arduous, since cadets were not supposed to go sick. We had to keep the ambulance maintained and in readiness for instant use in case of emergency. Every fortnight a FANY sergeant/mechanic would be sent from HQ to carry out an inspection and see that we were keeping things up to the mark. Our inspector would more than likely be a scion of the Clan McKenzie, arriving in dungarees that bore the grease of a hundred lorry-pits, her nails to match, and the perpetual cigarette hanging from her lip or tucked behind her ear. There was nothing she didn't know about the insides of a vehicle, however, and we learnt a lot from her. Years after the war had ended, I came upon Margaret McKenzie in a London supermarket and apart from the fact that slacks had replaced dungarees there was not much change in her appearance.

From time to time the Medical Officer would use the ambulance ostensibly to visit another hospital, but would divert down some country lane in search of farm eggs or a pub and would usually take Isobel as his driver. Isobel was round and jolly and appealed to men. Because my family had a cottage in North Berwick only a few miles away, I had many friends in the vicinity, so in our time off, I would hitch a lift to one of them for a game of golf or play spirited games of tennis with the cadets. Not surprisingly, away from the watchful eye of authority, Isobel and I grew rather lax about details such as always being in uniform – and on one hot June night this negligence caught us out.

We had been celebrating a cadet's birthday and for the occasion had donned the most alluring mufti we could muster from our rationed wardrobe. After a drink or two and a buffet supper we were comfortably installed in the local cinema with our men of the moment, watching I know not what film, when to our consternation a caption suddenly appeared on the screen asking Drivers Wood and Kay to report immediately to the MO (Medical Officer). To the disgruntlement of our companions we parted from them abruptly, raced back to our billets where we unearthed our heavy winter overcoats and donned them over our illegal finery. We reported panting in front of the MO who, apart from a raised eyebrow, made no comment on our appearance, but informed us that a cadet had inadvertently set himself alight, was badly burned and had to be transported at once to the Military Hospital at Edinburgh Castle some twenty-eight miles away. Nurse Falgate was to accompany us. Margaret Falgate, a VAD attached to the OCTU, had already become a friend as her parents lived nearby and she had invited us many times to their house. Unlike Isobel and me, she was correctly attired in VAD uniform with head dress severely in place and embroidered with a red cross. We lifted the cadet's mutilated body, mercifully well sedated, on to the stretcher and into the ambulance, where Margaret Falgate was to keep an eye on him.

Sweating profusely with heat and guilt, I clambered into the driving seat. I at least had had the nous to change my footwear from sandals into sensible shoes but Isobel in the heat – in every sense – of the moment was still teetering on high heels which appeared incongruously frivolous beneath her thick khaki coat. There was little traffic about and it was still broad daylight, being mid-June, so we were able to make good time.

Halfway there, however, the drugs began to wear off and I had to go very carefully as every jolt or bump brought forth a moan of pain from our patient. The hospital had been warned of our pending arrival so a surgical team and equipment were all on hand. Red tape being what it was, we had to procure a signature for the patient – a sort of receipt I suppose, in case he went missing between his arrival and the operating theatre, and we in turn had to sign our names. "Take off your shoes", I hissed at Isobel, "and pretend you've hurt your foot". "They'll keep me here in that case," she hissed back, while trying to disguise her silk clad (strictly illegal) very shapely legs from the admiring gaze of the two RAMC orderlies who had arrived to help. "There's a pair of my wellies on the back seat. No matter if they're too big. Pretend you were washing the ambulance when you were called out". Isobel did as she was bid and with the help of Maggie and the two orderlies we lifted the cadet, now comatose, stretcher and all on to the waiting trolley. A martinet dressed in the grey uniform of the QAIMNS (Queen Alexandra's Imperial Military Nursing Service) called to us imperiously, fortunately from a distance, "come along girls, this way".

To an accompaniment of wolf whistles and catcalls from an assortment of blue-clothed patients lining the corridors, we cowered behind the trolley as it made its way through the castle's labyrinthine corridors towards the operating theatre. A stentorian voice suddenly halted us in our tracks. "Stop," it shouted, almost stopping my heart simultaneously. "No street clothes in here, most unhygienic; out you go, quick".

"The stretcher," I cried. "We must have our stretcher back" – the thought of possible disciplinary action for losing WD property warring with my instinct to make as quick an exit as possible. "Oh very well, wait here," barked the voice.

We waited on tenterhooks while Maggie and the orderlies disappeared through the swing doors of the theatre to emerge minutes later with the empty stretcher. Isobel took the front handles while I took up the rear position and we made speedily for the outside world. After a few paces however, the back view of Isobel swam into view. The sight of her shuffling along in Wellington boots several sizes too big for her, her greatcoat incongruous on that sizzling hot June night and the two back buttons, their brass flagrantly devoid of polish, was bad enough. But the final straw was the glimpse of two pretty little pearl and diamond earrings dangling from beneath her service cap. This proved too much for my already tautened nerves. I gave vent to a strangulated snort of mirth, followed by a convulsive heaving of my shoulders. I shook with sobs; tears coursed down my cheeks about which I could do nothing, my hands being fully occupied with the stretcher. An orderly whom we had passed on the way to the theatre looked up at our approach.

"Too late, were ye?" he asked with kindly concern, noticing my contorted face. "Dinna tak it tae heart, lassie," he continued as I blindly stumbled my way past him. "Ye did a' thae a lassie could dae and if his time's come, it's come." I was relieved to learn several days later that our patient's time had not yet come and that he was making a good recovery.

Elizabeth Hanna (later Binny), a close friend from kindergarten days and a fellow FANY, was similarly caught out. Returning from a dance one winter's evening with her evening dress hitched up below her greatcoat, she checked in to the duty officer, saluted smartly and revealed a bare arm and wrist, resplendent with diamonds.

Whether our episode was reported to HQ I know not but shortly afterwards Isobel was transferred to another ambulance unit at Peebles Hydro. After a brief spell with her replacement, an older woman with a more serious outlook on life, I was recalled to HQ, where I reverted to driving staff cars and was awarded in due course my second stripe, which I took in my stride without the elation I felt at my first promotion.

Apart from driving, we were all supposed to know about the mechanics of the vehicles we were in charge of – never a strong point with me, despite Margaret McKenzie's schooling. Indeed, give me any piece of machinery and watch my incompetence at assembling it or making it work. We carried out maintenance under the tolerant or exasperated eye of an RASC corporal, depending on his attitude to the fair sex as a whole and FANYs in particular. I was going through my paces one day under the critical gaze of Jock, a patient and long-suffering corporal-mechanic. "There!", I cried in triumph, having wrestled with inept fingers on an electrical fault in the ignition of a staff car. "I think I've done it Jock, come and look." Incredulous but willing to believe in miracles, Jock strolled over and looked, as instructed. He then pushed his forage cap to the back of his head, sighed heavily and summed up the situation with the words, "Jesus wept".

The staff cars – a few dozen in all plus the ferry brakes and some trucks and lorries – were housed, when not in use, in a garage some ten minutes walk from our billets. It was one of my duties as a corporal to spend one night a week sleeping there, together with a fellow FANY. The idea was that if a fire-bomb was to fall on or near the garage, it would be the task of the duty drivers to evacuate the vehicles to safety, one by one – history doesn't relate to where. Our presence was supposed to deter intruders, not always the case as 'followers' were sometimes to be seen on the premises giving a hand with car washing, as whatever time a driver got back from an assignment, her car had to be washed and filled up with petrol, ready for the 'off'.

We slept fully clothed in our dungarees, steel helmet by our sides, on truckle beds in what was quite a cosy little box-like office overlooking the garage floor, so that any would-be marauders could easily be spotted. There was an excellent fish and chip shop round the corner, which did a thriving trade with the FANY. A newspaper load of the day's catch, either cod or flounder, and vinegar-sprinkled greasy chips became the elixir of life to us garage exiles. I suspect that the smell of these – mingling with the fumes of the paraffin stove, which we were somewhat surprisingly allowed in such cramped quarters, and stale petrol – would have repelled any unwanted visitor.

Some days at HQ were pure boredom. Hanging about in the staff room waiting to be called out, you would be congratulating yourself on a free evening when the telephone would ring and Major Lawson (halitosis) or Colonel Finch (a darling old flirt) would summon you to take him to an Ack–Ack site to sort out a problem that could take for ever. One day I drove in a cavalcade of cars to Greenock, flanked by armed outriders on motor bicycles and carrying the pay, amounting to thousands of pounds, for the men embarking on the Queen Mary, recently transformed from a luxury liner to a troop ship. Once the money was safely on board and locked in the ship's coffers, we drivers were allowed to go aboard and were given a tremendous lunch as a last culinary swan-song before a more austere menu was introduced.

There were accidents, of course. After all, the average driving experience of many of us younger ones was six months to a year or two at most. But there was surprisingly little damage to vehicles or passengers. Retribution for the infringement of the Highway Code was not too severe, although a friend of mine, Felix Breckenridge (now Keen), omitted to remove the distributor head from the ferry car which was parked in Abercromby Place prior to her taking it to the garage. In the interim someone stole the car, which was later found abandoned, having crashed through some railings further down the street. She was confined to barracks for two days for committing such a heinous crime.

In those early days, and indeed throughout the duration, Edinburgh was not visibly affected by the war. There was no bombing – Glasgow's turn was yet to come – save for a sporadic raid on the Forth Bridge from a stray German plane in the first few months. One of our members was on the ferry boat during this raid, crossing from North to South Queensferry, and proudly showed us her steel helmet dented by shrapnel. Very occasionally an air raid siren would sound in the middle of the night. We would curse and sleepily grope our way downstairs and cross the road to Heriot Row Gardens where our shelters were situated. After a period of spasmodic dozing, we would be aroused by the monotonous wail of the all-clear and would stumble back to our beds, pausing sometimes to look up at the stars and to wonder what was going on up there.

There was plenty in the shops, with little sign of rationing as far as one could see. For these reasons Edinburgh continued to be high in popularity as a leave centre. The De Guise, the night club adjoining the Caledonian Hotel, was the place most in vogue for night life. Here men and women from all the services used to foregather and dance the night away to the popular strains of 'You wouldn't believe me', 'Smoke gets in your eyes' or 'Begin the Beguine' – while Mario the head waiter attended to our needs and surely made a packet on the side.

By this time my brother George's regiment, the Lothians and Border Horse, had been split into two battalions. The first L&B duly departed for France and St. Valery where those who survived were taken prisoner and spent the rest of the war in captivity. The second battalion, to which my brother belonged, did a prolonged training in armoured cars and tanks before being drafted overseas to North Africa as part of the 6th Armoured Division.

John, on the other hand, was soon to leave with his regiment for India, from where my parents would receive a cable from time to time requesting them to send funds and on one occasion, "his worldly goods" (amounting to approximately £205.8.6), as he wished to marry a Polish ballet dancer who was performing with ENSA in Delhi. My parents, who knew their son, wisely ignored this plea and John's next letter would contain no mention of the ballet dancer, but refer several times to the perfections of his GOC's youngest daughter. It seemed so improbable that after his youthful philanderings, in due course, my younger brother was to remain happily married to Jean Bucher until his death thirty–five years later.

Five

As the war advanced so did the Germans. The Battle of Britain began in earnest and with the fall of France, the mood of the country changed. There was still an underlying frenetic gaiety, but with the disasters such as the sinking of HMS Hood and the fluctuations of the Desert War in North Africa, came the grim realisation that we were on our own and fighting for survival.

Equipment, including armaments and transport, were coming off the assembly lines twenty-four hours a day and vehicles, while awaiting shipment, were sent to vehicle reception depots for last-minute adjustments and preparation for the sea journeys ahead. One such was situated at Roukenglen on the outskirts of Glasgow, today one of Scotland's most popular pleasure parks. However, at the end of 1941, it consisted of a huge area of parkland designated for the assembly of trucks, lorries, ambulances and other service vehicles destined for the battlegrounds of North Africa or other theatres of war. The depot came under the jurisdiction of the War Office and Scottish Command and was manned by soldiers, mostly from the REME, RASC and Royal Engineers, with a smattering of signal and RAMC personnel and a platoon of FANY and ATS.

It was to Roukenglen that I was posted in the Autumn of 1941 with the rank of sergeant/mechanic, a misnomer if ever there was one. On putting up my third stripe, my father, to my acute embarrassment, boasted to anyone who cared to listen, that he had been told that being a Sergeant in the FANY was equivalent to being a Brigadier in the army. I doubt whether any Brigadier would have had to undergo some of the jobs set me and my colleagues. Although not as hazardous perhaps as a battlefield, Roukenglen was certainly no cynosure and in that bitter winter of 1941–42, our work was usually carried out in the freezing snow or squelching yellow mud. The base had been in existence for a month or two, but because of struggling somehow through a mechanics test, I was late in my posting there, so arrived on my own one raw October afternoon and made my way to the Reception area, my spirits sinking in tune with the setting sun. The FANY sergeant-major who received me reminded me of Penelope, our former housemaid, who had since gone to munitions – being small and neat, with a bun of fair hair tucked tidily above her collar. Coolly efficient, a mild exterior concealed a flinty resolve.

Her welcome, although polite, lacked warmth. She pressed a piece of paper into my hand on which was written the address of my billet – as no communal housing had yet been found for the female element – and arranged for a 15cwt truck to deliver me and my kitbag there. On leaving Reception I was heartened by meeting several of my former colleagues from 4th Scottish, most of them corporals, Isobel Kay and Felix Breckenridge amongst them. They all assured me it was utter hell, but they looked remarkably cheerful, and I was glad to know that at least we were all billeted near each other.

My home for the next four months was to be with a Mr and Mrs Mylne, a well-to-do childless couple who lived in a comfortable suburban dwelling at Whitecraigs, about a fifteen-minute walk from the depot. Standing with my kitbag on the doorstep of my new abode after the truck had deposited me on the pavement, I felt like a new girl on her first day at school. Mrs Mylne was entertaining three neighbours to tea when I arrived. They had been regaling her with tales of their own billetees and the exploits of some of the ATS housed with certain of their friends. So it was with growing trepidation that she prepared to greet me. "She can't be too bad," I heard one lady say encouragingly as the door was opened to me by Janet the maid, of Grenadier-like stature and wearing not surprisingly an apprehensive air. "She's wearing things on her arm," referring I presumed to my stripes.

The guests melted away, exchanging relieved glances at discovering I looked fairly civilised, and after a timid but friendly greeting from Mrs Mylne – we were both as nervous as the other, a new situation after all for us both – I was marched upstairs by the Grenadier, who showed me my room and in the days following disclosed a heart of gold. I was shortly summoned downstairs to meet Mr Mylne, a bluff kindly man with a schoolboy sense of humour and a touchingly protective air towards his wife. He had something to do with the Grosvenor Hotel in Glasgow and certainly I never went short of food at No.15, although the army paid them a pittance for my board and lodging.

Janet always brought me my breakfast in my room at seven, after which I would don my battledress and walk, often in pitch darkness, to Roukenglen where I would change into dungarees, leather jerkin and gumboots, the ritual garb of those working in the field. There was only one platoon of ATS on the site, of which I was the sergeant in charge. Together, we would make our way to the reception area, where row upon row of vehicles of every description stood in lines awaiting the finishing touches that would qualify them for overseas service. There we would coax stuttering life into recalcitrant engines, first having to defreeze the radiator with boiling water lugged from the men's cookhouse; enfold the lamps and more vulnerable parts of a vehicle with straw, cover the latter with hessian and fasten it securely with string, all this with fingers made numb by ice and snow, under which the truck would be half-buried.

I sometimes wondered if a soldier, sweating under some tropical sun, would ever stare in bafflement at these untidy and bizarre wrappings as he signed for his new ambulance or lorry and give thought to the packers. Much more likely to curse the knots if, indeed, they ever reached their destination intact. At other times we would lie flat on our backs under a motorised hulk of metal, while I tried to convince my girls that a nipple applied as much to the anatomy of a vehicle as it did to the human body. This of course provoked much hilarity and ribald remarks would issue forth, such as, "Jeannie, ha'e yer greased yer nipples the day"? or "Maggie, gi'e us the grease-gun, this wee bugger's awfie dry".

Many of my platoon – about twenty in all – came from Glasgow's docklands or from Durham's mining area, a tough bunch on the whole – unused to discipline and kicking against the pricks of authority. If, however, you worked alongside them and shared their discomforts and hardships, they soon developed a staunch sense of loyalty to their 'sarge' and we worked well together as a team. I was fortunate too in having my corporal FANY friends to support me as they were all on 'field' duties whereas my fellow sergeants had administrative jobs in relatively cosy offices and had little idea of the conditions outside.

It snowed pretty incessantly that winter and on many a morning we would have to dig lorries out of the drifts before we could move them. One day during a particularly fierce blizzard, I moved my squad into an empty Nissen hut, where we continued to clean and assemble spare parts and tool kits.

Suddenly the door burst open and a very junior officer with one pip on her leather greatcoat rounded upon us. "What do you think you're doing," she addressed me furiously. "Maintenance, ma'am," I answered mildly. "If you were in action you could be shot for deserting your post," she continued. I had a wild desire to laugh. She was so small and muffled up in her over-large overcoat and heaving with indignation and self-importance. But I had to show restraint in front of the platoon, who were gazing in fascination at this apparition covered in snow. One of my girls called Savage – "Savage by name and Savage by nature" she was wont to say when asked for her details – I could see was getting restive at this uncalled for interruption and I was afraid that an outburst might land her in trouble. I was able at last to convince my superior officer that work such as ours was better carried out in dry conditions than in a blizzard. As she took her leave, I managed to shut the door on Savage's muttered "and good riddance too, ye wee Nazi" – otherwise my champion might well have found herself in front of a firing squad, had our overzealous friend had anything to do with it.

I ate lunch in the Sergeants' Mess, but the evening meal was taken at our respective billets. NAAFI vans were also very much in evidence doling out cakes made with powdered egg and tasting of sawdust, which we devoured with relish. Kind soldiers, too, would appear from time to time bearing steaming mugs of bright orange very strong tea made with condensed milk. I have had an aversion to tea all my life, but naturally I would accept this offer with evidence of delight – and hope that the donor would depart or have his attention diverted, so that I could pour the contents little by little into the mud, which luckily was more or less of the same colour.

In those winter evenings, when it became too dark to carry on, blackout regulations being of necessity very strict, I would change out of my mud-encrusted boots and dungarees, complete the paperwork for the day and make my way back to the Mylnes, who soon looked upon me as the daughter they never had. At about 6pm high tea would be served – or in my case coffee, which happily for me was never rationed. This might consist of Scottish fare such as kippers, finnan haddock or herrings in oatmeal, mealie or black pudding (equivalent to the French *boudin*), haggis and the like, or lentil soup might be followed by cold meats and oatcakes with cheese. Then at nine o'clock Janet would wheel in a tea trolley on which would be piled more food and beverages: currant buns, cherry cake, chocolate biscuits and sandwiches. I never questioned where all this bounty came from and the Mylnes were so relieved not to have one of the 'troublemakers' billeted on them that they encouraged me to invite my friends from neighbouring billets to join in this spread. They would sit entranced as we regaled them with the day's events, outrageously exaggerated of course, while stuffing ourselves with sardine sandwiches and seed cake.

This happy interlude only lasted four months, as by then our requisitioned premises were ready to receive us and we all moved into a gaunt rambling Victorian building called Eastwood House, standing in a welter of overgrown laurels and sooty rhododendron bushes. However, it was close by the camp gates, so more convenient for everyone concerned. But I missed the creature comforts I had grown accustomed to.

Despite the house's recent conversion, everything was damp: walls and furnishings, such as they were. Our army issue blankets would emit a vapour of steam when subjected to the invaluable hot water bottle, its contents being jealously guarded and used for the next morning's ablutions. Hot water was scarce and my weekly bath was usually taken at the Mylnes, who continued to provide comfort and a warm welcome throughout my stay at Roukenglen.

It was about this time that my platoon and I were relegated to convoy work. This involved the collection of vehicles from the factory floor at Birmingham or Luton and driving them back to Roukenglen with a transit stop at some Midland town such as Lichfield, Wigan or Warrington. They would then be overhauled before being shipped overseas. Isobel and I were sent on a 'dummy run' with an all male crew to Lichfield, which finished late at night. I remember the strain of driving a three ton lorry with dipped headlights along unlit roads for miles in driving rain, with only the red rear light of the lorry in front to tell us if we were on the right track and keeping up with the convoy. We arrived at our destination, a bleak late 19th century barracks block and found we were sharing a bed, Isobel and I, as there was no room available in the ATS wing. After a breakfast of stewed liver and onions the next morning (politely declined by both of us) we joined the convoy once more and made our way back to camp.

The ATS was more considerate to the female sex and I and my dozen or so ATS drivers used to travel south by train. My charges were exuberant at the thought of a day or two's escape from the depot and its drudgery and I was glad to have time to catch up with my reading. On arrival at Birmingham in the late afternoon we would collect our vehicles from the factory, after a spell of tiresome paperwork on my part, and then proceed to our transit camp. Here we would be accommodated in a dormitory of another cheerless barracks and have the evening to ourselves. I never felt confident, until the actual take-off the next morning, that some of my flock might not have defected overnight in a bid for freedom or be pole-axed with a hangover induced by too many ports and lemon (a favourite tipple amongst other ranks).

Although the majority of my platoon were totally reliable and delightful company, there were one or two rebels who were never going to accept the restriction of army life. The most problematic of them was a girl called Allom – we were always addressed by our surnames – who went absent without leave whenever she got the chance. A foul-mouthed renegade from a docklands family and a broken home, it would take two Military Policemen to apprehend her and haul her back to Roukenglen to be brought before the Commandant. She was a friend of the Savage (mentioned earlier), whose wild eyes and unkempt hair – that invariably fell below the regulation collar line – suited her name admirably. Needless to say, I was glad to learn that neither would be sent on convoy work for obvious reasons.

After an unappetising breakfast – normally thin porridge and greasy sausages, although on one occasion kedgeree, when an indignant voice was heard asking the duty officer why we had to have rice pudding for breakfast – we emerged into a cold Midland dawn, quite often still dark. Cranking our vehicles was quite a heavy task for some of the less brawny girls, but there was usually a good-natured soldier on hand to help us and chat up the drivers. Sometimes it would be a batch of lorries we had to handle, at others a load of ambulances, the newly painted red cross gleaming on the canvas sides. With a grinding of gears (some of us had not yet mastered the art of double de-clutching) we would roll towards the exit and duty-sentry, where I would have to complete the inevitable forms in triplicate before climbing into the passenger seat of the leading vehicle. "Chariots of doom" was the encouraging send-off one day from the NCO in charge of our departure from the Wigan transit camp.

My role was to map read and decide where to stop for comfort stations and to ensure we reached our journey's end without incident or desertion – or, if such befell us, to cope with the situation. The driver I chose to be with was usually either new to convoy work or one of the more unreliable characters, so it was not a voyage without trauma for either of us.

By the time I had covered the same route a dozen times I had discovered the possibility of finding 'treats' along the way. One such was at the foot of Shap, where smiling WVS ladies served us with hot drinks and warm bacon sandwiches from the comparative shelter of their canteen van. Fortified by this ambrosial fare, we then set out on the harsh lap over the Pennines. So beautiful in summer with the sun shimmering on the heather, the landscape was not so inviting in winter, although the snowy peaks were admittedly impressive. If a vehicle faltered or had to give up due to a mechanical fault, there were almost always other army convoys in the vicinity manned by vociferous soldiers, only too willing to stop and show off their expertise and exchange verbal badinage with my drivers, who were equally happy for the diversion.

Considering our inexperience, it was miraculous how few bad accidents we had – although after I left Roukenglen, I heard of the death on the road of Cherry, one of my most cheerful and uncomplaining of drivers. Her mother wrote to me saying that her daughter had loved every minute she had spent in the army – so she had to be thankful for that.

Once up Shap and beyond Carlisle, the long haul over Beattock Moor was child's play, enlivened on occasion by the sight of a figure waving to us from a whitewashed crofter's cottage standing high on the hillside. This turned out to be the wife of a crofter, then serving with the KOSB (King's Own Scottish Borderers) and whose name I never learned. She considered it her war effort to alleviate as best she could the hardship or tedium of the men and women leading the convoys which passed below her cottage. On catching sight of the leading vehicle and having signalled her presence, she would disappear inside her house and emerge seconds later with trayloads of mouth-melting scones. She would then run across the moor and distribute them into our eager outstretched hands. We naturally never queried the apparently plentiful supplies of butter and flour. When I tried to press some money into her hand, she would refuse it laughingly saying: "Ye lassies are doing a great job and it's just me doing my wee bit".

One day there was not such manna from Heaven and no smoke to be seen from her chimney. I hoped she was off enjoying some leave with her tartan-trewed husband. Some miles on, however, I espied a café half-hidden by some petrol pumps which seemed a likely place for a halt, so instructed my driver to turn off the road. As soon as we did so, I could see the place was closed, so we immediately drove back on to the main highway. Looking behind me down a very straight stretch of road I watched incredulously, as every vehicle in the convoy assiduously followed suit, driving behind the petrol pumps and emerging again on the main road. If I had driven over a ravine I expect they would have all followed me. "Wheresoever you go..." A mere stripling myself, they had faith in me, they were my responsibility and I cared for them deeply.

Later in the year, when the interminable winter at last showed signs of coming to an end, I and my platoon were told to deliver a convoy of ambulances to Edinburgh and to pick up replacements for the return journey. As my driver, I was allotted a truculent, uncommunicative individual called Knight who had several times gone absent. I was given strict instructions by the duty officer not to let her out of my sight.

On arrival at the Murrayfield depot we were told our replacement load would not be ready for a couple of hours. Many of the drivers had homes or relatives in Edinburgh including Knight, and I myself was keen to pay a flying visit to my family but damned if I was going to do so with a glowering body at my elbow. "Knight," I said in what I hoped was a firm but unhectoring tone, "You've got two hours off and if you don't show up by 4.30pm you'll be a nuisance to the army, and an embarrassment to me. You'll be picked up sooner or later and land up in the glass house, so it'll save you and everyone else a lot of trouble if you're back on time". This holier than thou homily was listened to in impassive silence and we each went our way.

I dashed home, greeted my family, had a bath, kissed my parents and Puddy's successor, Susan, goodbye and reported back to Murrayfield. All present and correct, save for the Knight errant. At 28 minutes past four I was reflecting dismally that it would be me in the glasshouse for disobeying orders and letting Knight off the hook, when our friend strolls up, a self-satisfied smirk on her face. "Got yer worried did I sarge," she crowed as she took her place behind the steering wheel. "Expect yed given me up eh?", she cackled benevolently. "Ere," she said somewhat gruffly, passing me a paper bag, "Me mum made me some sausage rolls and said ye'd better have a few". She peered slyly in my direction. "I've eaten two or three already, so you can be sure they're not poisoned" and she laughed hugely at her own wit.

My relationship with my superior officers as a whole, and with my Commanding Officer in particular, was not such a happy one. Junior Commander Shearer, the CO i/c the female contingent at Roukenglen, was squat of stature with short dark curly hair and a twitch. In pre-war days she had bred cairn terriers and was a skier of international repute. The only time we met after the war, and before she contracted cancer from which she died at an early age, was on the ski slopes of the Lauberhorn in Switzerland where, given equal ground, I might have challenged her with lack of leadership at Roukenglen. However, knowing of her superior skill on skis and with a precipice looming by, I though it prudent to hold my peace.

She was a remote figure, seldom appearing on the site. An abrupt manner, possibly caused by shyness, did not endear her to the troops. Indeed many of the girls who worked on the vehicle park had no idea who she was, so consequently all their grumbles and complaints fell on my shoulders, who had in turn to pass them on to the CO. As a result, she rather naturally regarded me as a troublemaker. She also considered that I pampered my troops and was too familiar with them. Difficult not to be, when I literally shared the same mud and difficulties as they did. She had no conception apparently of the appalling conditions of the vehicle park during those early winter months, as I never once saw her there, and she did not seem to attach much importance to the welfare of the girls under her command. Indeed morale grew so increasingly low with absentees becoming a commonplace – and even the attempted suicide – that questions regarding Roukenglen were, I believe, eventually raised in the House of Commons.

By that time, however, I had become too much of a thorn in the side of authority and in order to get rid of me was recommended for a Commission in the ATS, a fate common to most of my FANY contemporaries. In different circumstances I would have been loth to accept such a course, but in the event I agreed with alacrity and was brusquely despatched to OCTU at Craigmillar, next to the Castle that was one of Mary Queen of Scots' favourite residences. From there in June 1942 I duly graduated as a commissioned officer in the Auxiliary Territorial Service, but was permitted to keep my FANY armband as a memento of the past.

Six

My first star or pip sewn on my shoulder, carrying the rank of Second Subaltern, afforded me much less satisfaction and pride than had my first stripe, nor did I have the heady power and responsibility I had enjoyed with three. It was rather like going from the sixth form at a prep school to the bottom class at a public school and just as lonely to begin with, as old friends had been posted elsewhere and new ones were yet to be discovered. My first posting also proved no more glamorous. This was to an ATS Training Depot at Glencorse, across the road from the HQ of the Royal Scots Regiment and only eight miles outside Edinburgh. At the depot, conscripted females from all walks of life were initiated into the mysterious ways of service life and kitted out accordingly. The basic issue to each conscript was an ill-fitting uniform including shoes and stockings; bedding consisting of three kapok-filled sections known as 'biscuits', which fitted together to form a mattress during the night and had to be stacked tidily at one end of the bed enfolded within two grey army blankets during the day; a mess tin in which all courses were served; and mug, knife, fork and spoon and two towels.

Bewildered and bemused because for many it was the first time away from home, the conscripts would begin a rigorous six weeks' training that included drill, learning the rudiments of army traditions and history, lectures on hygiene, fire-fighting, security, first aid, discipline and politics. The course ended with a final interview by the Commanding Officer, in order to assess the work most suited to the individual – be it as a cook, driver, clerk, signals operator, or in a more specialised role according to ability.

Instead of spending my days underneath lorries greasing nipples or on the road, I spent them in the reception room of the depot delousing heads of the new intake. Most of them came from poor homes and if one could afford a permanent wave it was far too precious to disturb, so hair was left unwashed and uncombed for weeks on end, providing a rich harvesting ground for the louse and the nit.

This attractive job of delousing was allotted to the most junior officers. We first had to wash the victim's hair in a nauseous mixture of paraffin and some viscous orange shampoo, then wrap her head in a towel and leave the wretched girl, by now either tearful or resentful, to sit and 'stew' for half an hour or so until the mixture had taken effect and the live vermin were at least extinct. There would be a dozen or so undergoing treatment at the same time, so at least they had each other's company and a bond in common, which proved the foundation for some good friendships. Then came the combing out, when each strand of hair had to be searched for nits and removed before they, in turn, could hatch out. We junior officers got very adept at the delousing game. We grew insensitive to the plight of these unfortunate girls and would vie with each other as to how many brace we could catch each day. However Nemesis struck as we grew careless and blasé about taking the necessary precautions and covering our own heads properly, and one day I encountered lice on my own head, after which I became decidedly more sympathetic with those recruits who swore they'd never had a dirty head before they joined the army.

Then there was the role of guide, mentor and friend to those in your section, some of them years older both in age and experience of life than I was. But we were supposed to know it all. One day a young corporal called Wechselman came to see me. She was a Polish refugee who had escaped to Scotland at the outbreak of war and joined the ATS. She was obviously in some distress and didn't even wait to sit down before she cried emotionally, "Ma'am, you do something, some action you must take". The more agitated she became, the more difficult it was to follow her rather fractured English. "Whatever is it, Wechselman?" I asked, my mind racing ahead with every conceivable and inconceivable possibility, "What has happened?". "I come home last night", she blurted out and paused as if it was all too much for her. "Yes," I encouraged her, "You came home?". "This soldier pleeceman he ask me to cross road. I do so to show night pass I think he want". She paused again as if what was to come was better left unsaid. I began to think so too. "Yes, then what?" I prompted. "He no want that. He offers fife shilling to go in field with him". "And what did you say to that Hazel?" asked my father when I related this tale at home. "Well", I admitted ruefully, "I had really no idea what to say but simply exclaimed in a tone of disbelief, 'Only five shillings, Wechselman?'."

The Parade Ground also took up a lot of my time. The new recruits had to learn to march in step, three abreast and in unison, if only to impress the locals at Church Parade every Sunday. Then we would march, myself or a colleague out in front, arms swinging, legs pivoting, eyes straight ahead, terrified at the thought of being hailed by a Royal Scot friend *en passant*. Luckily I have a stentorian voice if nothing else, but it was extraordinary how difficult some of those girls found it to co-ordinate their arms and legs once they began thinking about it. The left leg and arm would shoot forward at the same time, following by the right leg and arm lending a robot-like movement to the body, reminiscent of a puppet on a string. However after dint of practice and perseverance on my part, and much strain on the vocal chords, my platoon would begin to get the hang of it and finally became quite proficient. One afternoon towards the end of their training, I was putting one section through its paces when I noticed out of the corner of my eye a visiting bigwig and his entourage, accompanied by my own commanding officer.

"Left, right, left, right", I intoned crisply as the squad advanced towards the perimeter of the parade ground that was enclosed by a high brick wall. I then realised with mounting horror that the words for "about turn" had completely deserted me. As the wall loomed nearer and nearer and the platoon marched inexorably on, I gave a sort of strangled bellow which in my own ears sounded like "yobbo yahooh" and the blessed girls turned smartly in their tracks and marched serenely back to me. "A well trained platoon," congratulated the visiting general afterwards when I was presented to him. My own CO didn't look quite so convinced. When later I was dismissing the squad and passing on the General's comments, one private came up to me and confided laughingly, "You know, ma'am, when you told us to 'about turn', well it sounded just like 'yobbo yahooh'". I laughed back.

For one reason alone I am thankful for my time at Glencorse. I made a life-long friend in the guise of Barbara Hewitt (later Brownell). We were allotted a room together and it was Barbara who deloused my hair when I succumbed to nits. She wasn't a great reader and in my arrogance I took it upon myself to enrich her vocabulary each morning. I doubt if she ever listened to me, but she never complained, and rose, I believe, to be the youngest female major in the ATS.

At the beginning of 1943, the Training Centre was transferred to Newbattle Abbey, just outside Dalkeith, a former monastery founded by King David I of Scotland in 1140, whose monks were amongst the first to work the local coal seams. Little remained of the former building save for an old retaining wall and part of the old crypt, but there was an impressive solidity about the current house, used before and after the war as an adult education college. The colour of its mellow stones deluded one into thinking the sun was shining all the time.

Inside, the bare but spacious rooms were luxurious compared to the cramped wooden huts we had left behind us at Glencorse. But it was the layout of the grounds and gardens which gave me so much pleasure. Behind the house were the rather formal lawn and flowerbeds, flanked by sentinel stone obelisks, behind which a yew hedge served as a backdrop to the scene. Formality gave way to a wilder jumble of paths and shrubs, unkempt and overgrown, which led down to the river Esk, a fast-flowing stream running from the Moorfoot Hills to the Firth of Forth. Here, in fleeting moments of quiet, especially at dusk, it was possible to forget the makeshift camp of Nissen huts and other ramshackle buildings surrounding the house and to close one's ears to the mundane clatter and noise of any army depot. Instead I could imagine the monks going about their business: gathering up their garden tools and attending evensong. At more prosaic times I would wish I had my rod with me, so that I could dangle a fly over a fish that occasionally broke the surface of the river's many pools.

It was here that the news was broken to me of my brother George's death, killed in action in Tunisia on 9th May 1943. The 2nd Lothians and Border Horse had been engaged in one of the last offensives in the North African campaign – the battle for Hamman Lif in Tunisia – and it was there that George's tank received a direct hit. Four days later, the fighting in North Africa was at an end. George and I had kept up a regular correspondence since he had gone overseas. My letters apparently made him laugh and he would read out excerpts from them to his fellow officers, many of whom I knew. He himself was no narrator, but his letters conveyed an affection and a longing for news from home which I did my best to supply, however trivial. I sensed in him a need to be back in the ordered rather hum-drum life of Edinburgh law, which I suspect he would have pursued, although his girlfriends tended to be bossy females – not unlike his sister – and perhaps such a wife would have prised him out of his preferred groove. A recent letter had described a meal he had just consumed of bread, an onion and a bit of French sausage, which had made his tent smell like a souk and perhaps explained the reason he was alone at the time of writing! In his last letter to me, written three days before he died, he adjured me "to find a nice hero who could look after you, instead of the odd people you seem to prefer" and described the countryside as being "one huge cornfield with an abundance of poppies and yellow daisies – a lovely sight". He ended with the words, "the spirit in the Regiment is now marvellous and we are all in great form".

George was a gentle soul with a certain pawky humour, much loved by my mother with whom he was very close. Relations with his father were not so happy. He felt that he hadn't realised the latter's ambitions for him – few sons rarely do – and took deeply to heart his impatience and criticisms. Since the beginning of the war things had improved between them and during his embarkation leave he had confided to my mother in all humility, "I really get on quite well with pa nowadays". It was perhaps a sense of remorse or guilt that caused my father's unreasonable behaviour following George's death. He refused to talk about him except on rare occasions when he referred to him as "poor George", which infuriated me. He also refused to allow my mother to dispose of his few possessions to his close friends or even to members of his family, which hurt her deeply. She learnt to keep her grief to herself and this repression showed itself some years after the war in a near-nervous breakdown which, because of her great faith in the hereafter, she soon got over. She also took up gardening and found much solace in her two 'cabbage patches' as she called them; one being the back garden of their Edinburgh house and the other a little strip at our home in North Berwick.

I was given forty-eight hours' compassionate leave following the news of George's death and remember walking home from the bus stop on a shining May morning. On the way I met a neighbour whom I was about to greet when she lowered her eyes and hurried on. She must have heard of George's death, but with typical Scottish reserve, had not the courage or imagination to show compassion by means of a smile or a touch on the arm. But how might I have acted in a similar position? Might I have been afraid of showing sympathy only to have it rejected? A week or two later I was asked by a stranger how many brothers I had and was completely thrown by the question. "Two" immediately sprang to my lips, when I realised my error and began to stammer, "One I mean," which must have embarrassed the questioner as much as it did me.

After some fairly uneventful months at Newbattle, I was posted as Adjutant to a Holding Unit in Dunblane, Perthshire. My Company Commander was a Junior Commander Lewis – known, disrespectfully but affectionately to those under her, as 'Ma Lou'. She was much older than most of us, being well into her forties, and had worked in the millinery department of Jenners, one of Edinburgh's leading stores. Her husband had joined up and, with no children to care for, his wife had become an officer in the ATS in the early days of the war. She was an amiable but vacillating soul, given to much hand-wringing and indecision and was in no way a disciplinarian. She was well-endowed with a cumbersome, somewhat top-heavy body which did not look its best in uniform – how many did? – and a pale moonish face adorned with thick spectacles, which gave her an owlish appearance. The aim of a Holding Unit was to house personnel for brief periods while their future fates were decided upon. There was constant coming and going and plenty of administrative work, which I enjoyed. We were housed in Dunblane Hydro, formerly one of Scotland's spa hotels and later one of the Stakis chain, an imposing Victorian monstrosity perched high on a crest approached by a long, winding and very steep drive.

The Holding Unit shared these premises with an ATS Physical Training School which ran courses of several weeks' duration for those who were intent on becoming PT instructors. The Commandant of the School was a flint-eyed female with a scathing tongue called Durrant – her Christian name was never divulged since she did not believe in such familiarity. The officers of the two factions shared a mess and it was clear to me from the first day that the scions of the PT school viewed with disdain the members of the Holding Unit generally, and Ma Lou in particular. Durrant's adjutant was someone I had known in pre-war days (she had been a friend of my brother George) which stood me in good stead. Ma Lou sensed this at once and latched on to me as a means of salvation. I was given the role of Mess President, a far from enviable task since I had to issue weekly accounts for drink taken, which was on a help-yourself basis, signed for with chits. Measures were liberally interpreted and signatures often forgotten owing to 'pressure of war' or 'an emergency' which led to acrimonious arguments and incriminations. On the other hand I quite enjoyed the social activities that went with the job, such as the reception of VIPs, however modest. One of my favourites was Ronald Selby-Wright, the then Radio Padre and, in later years. the much respected Minister of the Canongate Church, in Edinburgh's Royal Mile.

The two things that dominated my days at Dunblane were cockroaches and Church Parade. The Hydro was an old building with much wainscoting, panelling and dark recesses. These proved an irresistible attraction for insect life and although during daylight hours members of the arthropod kingdom lay dormant in their snug hideouts, at night they would emerge in droves, their favourite haunt being the 'other ranks' dining hall where they would converge on any crumbs or other delectable refuse left lying about. Armed with insecticides, brush and dustpan, a team of sweepers headed usually by myself, would approach the hall from which emanated a kind of swooshing noise caused, as later discovered, by the rubbing together of myriad pairs of insect feelers. Entering cautiously by the door we would find the entire floor crawling with specimens of the beetle world, a paradise for the entomologist, many of which would be trampled underfoot emitting a dreadful but satisfying scrunching sound as we set about with our lethal spray. It was not long before the parquet was covered with corpses which then had to be swept into sacks and disposed of in the camp's incinerator. However many of these cucaracha hunts we initiated, there were just as many insects the next time round and eventually the local insecticide squad had to be called in to fumigate the entire building.

Church Parade I dreaded almost as much. Every Sunday I had to march a platoon of Holding Unit ATS from the Hydro to

Dunblane Cathedral, which was situated in the centre of the town, while Durrant and her satellites would be employed similarly with a platoon from the PT school. Marching down the steep drive presented no real problem, unless the rear batch ran away with themselves and precipitated themselves on the heels of the leading lot. It was then a fairly flat march to the Cathedral, a beautiful Gothic building with a fine interior, although I was usually too engrossed with thoughts of the return journey to devote much attention to the service or to the architectural gems of my surroundings. The march back to the Hydro proved a nightmare until I learned always to ensure that my platoon was in the rear. Before I got wise to this, my girls, who were a motley lot consisting of embryonic clerks, cooks, signals personnel, drivers etc. lacking any recent training on the parade ground, would start out in fine style with arms swinging and a look of grim determination on their faces. Turning into the drive of the hotel, which grew steeper and steeper, their marching grew slower and slower and their breathing more and more laboured while, in relentless pursuit came the PT platoon stepping out as one, until they were breathing down the necks of my vanguard. Curses and imprecations would then be hurled at the back of my sorry lot until with bursting lungs we reached the summit.

This competitive life did not affect me as much as it might have done, had I not been tipped off by a colleague in high places that my name had been put forward – I never knew by whom – for a course at the ATS Staff College, so that my days at Dunblane could well be numbered. In the meantime I found salvation with a family called Leslie, friends of my parents, who lived in Dunblane and offered me tea and sympathy on many occasions.

In due course – it was now the Spring of 1944 – I was told to report to the War Office for an interview. The pre–selection board for the Staff College presented an imposing array of brass hats: General Wimborne, Commandant of the Staff College at Camberley, Colonel Brett, Commandant of the ATS Staff College and several others whose names I never gathered but amongst them I did recognise, to my delight, my old commanding officer in FANY days, the Hunting Cow, now of elevated rank at the War Office. She greeted me with due reserve but her gaze behind the horn-rimmed glasses was benign.

I had been primed by those who had gone before that two of the stock questions might be, "Why do you want to go to the Staff College?" and "What makes you think you would be a good staff officer?". Naturally it would not do to reply to the first, "Because I'm sick of delousing heads and trampling on cockroaches," but should be more on the lines of, "I feel it would be a challenge, Sir" or, "I hope it might give me a better chance of going overseas, ma'am". To question two, I could think of no reason at all why I should make a good staff officer and in any event I was extremely vague as to what such a role would entail. I prevaricated with a short resume of my military functions to date – not a very impressive list – with emphasis on my experience in administration and welfare. After being subjected to a battery of questions, I was dismissed without being given any indication as to what the outcome might be. I had the rest of the day to myself before returning to Scotland and, as it was only my second visit to wartime London, I found it a sobering occasion. The devastation in imagination was far less awesome than in reality but I found a sense of purpose and resolve amongst the population and a certain optimistic gaiety, now that the war was going in the right direction, that was missing in the more complacent north.

After a week or two of suspense, I was informed that I had passed into the Staff College and was to report to Bagshot in ten days' time for a six week course of intensive training. Unrepentantly, I left Ma Lou lamenting the loss of a henchman and made my way south, accompanied by a fellow FANY and friend, Joyce Macgregor, who was bound for the same destination.

Bagshot Park, later housing the Royal Army Chaplains Department, and more recently home of the Earl and Countess of Wessex, lies on the outskirts of Bagshot, adjacent to Camberley.

It presented a very different spectrum from my previous lodgings. The house, formerly the home of Prince Arthur, Duke of Connaught, is an attractive 19th century building, standing in acres of glorious grounds, which in early June were ablaze with camellias, rhododendrons and azaleas. There were about forty candidates in all, for the most part subalterns like myself, about a dozen of whom had been FANYs. Some aspirants had been at training or transport depots, some with Ack–Ack brigades and others had been employed at the War Office or in Intelligence. But one thing we were all supposed to have in common, so we were told, was a degree of intelligence and common sense, which was soon to be put to the test. After a briefing by the commandant as to what we might expect during the coming weeks, we were allotted our dormitories in strict alphabetical order. My room mates were Wand–Tetley, Wild and Winterbotham.

For the first time since the war broke out I had to use my brain rather than my muscles or my wits and there were times during the next six weeks when I felt I was not going to live up to my father's confident utterance that "a Wood never fails". Considering the commonplace of the surname I had always felt this to be a singularly rash statement. I even got as far on one occasion as writing "Dear Daddy, be prepared...". Colonel Rupert Brett, whom I had already met on the Selection Panel, was our Commandant and was supported by no less than six rather reluctant army majors and a staff of four females on the administrative side. Here Joyce MacGregor and I were fortunate in finding amongst the latter, an old and much liked friend from FANY days in Edinburgh, Eileen Sanderson, who was to die tragically young soon after the war. We were divided into sections of eight, my 'administrator' being Major Malcolm Morris, in post-war days to become an eminent QC. He was a good-looking and affable man with a slightly sheepish air as if excusing himself from a job he considered beneath him.

Our daily programme varied considerably. We shared lectures from time to time with the 'real' Staff College down the road at Camberley, and even joined cadets of the Royal Military Academy at Sandhurst in their exercises, to the extent of being shown how to drive a tank on Camberley Heath and taking part in rifle practice. In the first instance I recall emerging from the driver's turret with snow-white hair, a legacy of the heath's dusty soil; and in the second, failing to hit the target more than twice out of a round of ten shots, and the agony experienced from the kick of the rifle each time I fired.

We were encouraged too, in the art of public speaking, a task I have always found painful, despite much practice at it in later life. During the second week, when I felt that my chances of success were not all that great, each of us was given a piece of paper on which were written the words "Is Education the Answer to Nazism?". Underneath, a note exhorted us to prepare a talk to last not less than ten minutes which was to be addressed to an imaginary audience of troops attending an Army Bureau of Current Affairs course. Only one out of the forty candidates would be called upon to speak, the name to be drawn out of a hat, and after the ordeal the audience would be invited to tear the talk to pieces. To me the question itself seemed incomprehensible. Obviously it all hinged on the word 'education' and that could be construed in numerous ways. We were given a week in which to prepare our talk and each day I convinced myself that a ratio of 39 to 1 made it highly unlikely for my name to come out of the hat, so why not relax and concentrate on other things?

The hour duly came, staff and pupils were assembled, the draw took place and the name 'Wood' was read out by a smirking yet faintly apprehensive Major Morris, since any performance I gave would reflect, however unfairly, on his tuition. As my name was declaimed, a gasp went up from the thirty-nine throats, partly of relief and partly, I like to think, of sympathy from those friends to whom I had confided my lack of preparedness. I remember rising slowly to my feet and walking even more slowly to the lecture dais. I thought of Charles I going to the scaffold and carried my head accordingly high. After sweeping the audience with a cold, disinterested eye born of utter despair, and seeing in return glimpses of expectation, commiseration and a wry masochistic amusement from those few who were rather revelling in my discomfort, I began to speak. Of the words I spoke I have no recollection whatsoever. I am told I delivered my talk in a calm, measured tone and stopped after the permitted 10 minutes to show I was in no hurry to finish. At the end, there was a short pause of disbelief – or perhaps disappointment – that I had not dried up altogether, followed by a modest show of applause. My colleagues were so grateful for their reprieve that they were lenient in their criticism and even the staff's less honeyed remarks were not too cutting. Malcolm Morris looked relieved if not elated.

After this undeserved acquittal, I grew more confident and began to enjoy the course. I learned the make-up of a headquarters overseas, what comprised a 'theatre of war' and how lines of communications worked. I understood how 'to appreciate a situation' and became adept at map reading, both of which have proved invaluable to me since, although my prowess at map reading is not matched by my bump of locality, which only works if the sun happens to be shining.

Across the road from the College was the Pantiles Café, where a group of us used to foregather between classes for ersatz chocolate cake and coffee. The café was run by Mrs Douglas Bader, an unwelcoming lady who I felt resented our carefree style and seldom smiled as she served us; but then she probably had little to smile about, with a legless husband currently a prisoner-of-war in German hands.

It was during my time at Bagshot that I first made acquaintance with the doodlebug, or pilotless plane, which was Hitler's latest innovation. On hearing the puttering sound of its engine, we would hang out of the window, hypnotised by the shooting flame of the machine, signifying that it was still on course but not yet ready to drop its load. Once it was overhead we would cock our ears for any change in the pattern of sound and after the robot had passed on would listen for the sudden silence, followed by what was to become a familiar "crump" as the bomb hit its target, fortunately never near enough to do more than rattle the windows. One evening a friend and I were returning to the college after some time off and were in the act of crossing a field when a doodlebug passed over our heads, not so far above us. We stood transfixed, rooted to the spot more with fascination than with fear, hoping our legs would take us to the nearest ditch should the need arise.

The course culminated in a 'Field Exercise', a *tour de force* initiated by the college staff, designed as a 'passing-out' test of our abilities, and which lasted all day. We worked under simulated stress – there was even a bogus air-raid laid on – in groups of three and had to find the answers to dozens of ingenious and improbable questions which came through on telephones especially set up for the occasion.

"Hello. This is Platoon Officer Smith from No.108 Ack–Ack Battery, Scapa Flow. A newborn baby has just been discovered in a kitbag with the CO's name on it. She is not here to advise me. What action should I take?" "Take it out of the kitbag and feed it?" "Oh, yes ma'am, that's already been done. No we don't know who the father might be, nor the mother for that matter, if it's not the CO." "Get in touch with the Military Police?" "Oh yes ma'am, I'll do that straight away. Thank you."

"Hello, Hello. Oh good afternoon. This is Lady Fearful from Crumble Moor. A suspected German spy has been sighted in the grounds; he could be armed. Whom should I contact? The Home Guard? But the head of that in this area is my gardener and he is busy with the dahlias at present. Hello, hello, I can't hear you!" Apart from this lighter relief, there were more technical questions such as, "You are at Allied HQ in North Africa. A message has just come in from 78 Division that they have run out of ammunition for their Bren .303 machine guns. Please send up replacements immediately". "What is the requisite ammunition required?" "Well you know that don't you? Yes that's right, ciao." Each member of the staff was at the other end of the telephone representing various departments. If you did not know an answer you rang what you considered to be the right department and received the correct answer. If you guessed wrong, you were liable to be told it was Mr Bones the Butcher and he wasn't expecting any more sausages until Friday, so you had to try again. I was fortunate in having two rather bright girls working with me, as we were judged as a team rather than as individuals, and our initiative at least was commended.

Our results were not published nor marks given. We either passed the course or failed (in fact there were only two who fell by the wayside on our course) and were called in one by one by the Commandant to be told the outcome and in some cases to be given an idea of what our future posting was likely to be. In a very few cases – and I suspect these were the *crème de la crème* of the course – there was an immediate posting either to the USA or to the War Office. I was told rather laconically by Colonel Brett that I had passed and would shortly be posted overseas, but no details or dates were divulged.

In the meantime I was to be despatched to Highland Division HQ in Inverness – I just couldn't get away from Scotland – where I kicked my heels during the day and fished in the Spey at nighttime with my delightful but underworked boss. I was billeted for these few weeks in the home of a charming middle-aged spinster called Miss MacBean, who suffered from Parkinson's disease. The first time I met her I shook her by the hand and seconds later her hand shot out again. Not knowing her affliction and rather at a loss I grabbed it again, whereupon she sensibly explained her dilemma and we had a good laugh about it. She cherished me during that brief spell and I was sorry to leave her.

After nearly a month of this sybaritic existence I received word that I was to go on embarkation leave prior to travelling to Allied Forces Headquarters (AFHQ) in Italy. With my promotion to Staff Captain, I felt pretty certain that I could be of enormous benefit to the Allied cause. It was therefore with supreme confidence and considerable anticipation that I set sail from Greenock for Naples on 24th August 1944, four days after my twenty-fourth birthday, in the troopship SS Orontes.

Seven

Looking back on this time I suppose I showed a marked degree of callousness where my parents were concerned. With one brother killed in action and another by that time fighting a hazardous war with the Chindits against the Japanese in Burma, many of the older generation considered it my duty to stay in my own country and were not slow in telling me so. But the young can be selfish and I was no exception. I argued that I had been in Scotland for most of the war to date and that if I was posted to London it would probably be much more dangerous than being at an HQ behind the lines in a foreign country. Not by a word or gesture did either of my parents seek to influence me from going. Indeed my father predictably went round boasting to his cronies of my posting, despite the fact that my destination was supposed to be 'hush–hush'. During my absence abroad, my parents' homes, both in Edinburgh and North Berwick, became havens of welcome and hospitality to a score of females of all ranks – mostly Women's Auxiliary Air Force – who were stationed in either vicinity, many of whom became my parents', as well as my, life-long friends. Indeed, on my return some sixteen months later, it was sometimes I who felt the outsider. A salutary lesson perhaps!

The SS Orontes had been built in 1929 as a passenger liner with a 20,097 tonnage and accommodation for 974. Conversion to a troopship allowed for 3,978, so our quarters were not exactly spacious. It took some ten days for us to reach Naples since, of necessity, our route took us past Spain, through the Straits of Gibraltar into the Mediterranean with the coast of North Africa on our right. I remember the voyage mainly for its confined quarters and for its uneventfulness. Apart from endless boat drill, day and night, and the occasional U-boat scare, life was monotonous. The ship was crammed with humanity. Men and

THE WAR YEARS 85

women from the Army and RAF, VADs, QAIMNs, nurses and civilians – all bound for the Mediterranean theatre of war, not to mention the crew. Although the fighting in North Africa had ended more than a year ago and the Italians had capitulated in September 1943, the war was still waging fiercely in Italy, where allied forces were engaged in trying to break through the German defences to the north.

We took turns at fire and mess duties and played interminable games of cards and liar dice. Our drinks ration (alcoholic) was fairly lavish as I recall, although at that time of my life I was prone to barter my drink ration for chocolate. Times change! Quarters were naturally very cramped, but I was fortunate in being allotted a tiny cabin with only two others, both of whom had been at Bagshot with me. One was my friend Joyce MacGregor, who was very small, and the other Thelma Oxnevad, who was very large. Joyce and I made a point of clambering into our bunks before Thelma's bulk squeezed round the cabin door, otherwise it was impossible to undress without fracturing our arms against the cabin walls. We managed on the whole very well, since Thelma was a gregarious soul given to hob-nobbing with all and sundry and would breeze into the cabin around midnight to keep us abreast of the ship's news and regale us with her adventures – oblivious of the fact that Joyce and I might perhaps be having our own adventures by then in dreamland.

The keeping of diaries was strictly forbidden due to security but I would none the less jot down impressions in a notebook kept under my pillow, alas!, cravenly destroyed before disembarkation. I doubt however if the enemy would have gleaned much from the scraps of information I scribbled down. That while acting as duty officer I had had three complaints about the food being (a) greasy and revolting (b) inedible and revolting and (c) revolting; that I was asked to take action with regard to bilge water seeping into someone's cabin; that I had received a gripe from one of the crew members that his lifeboats were being used for snogging parties; or that I had had an assignation (not in the lifeboat) with a starry-eyed 2nd

Lieutenant called Maurice, scarcely out of his teens, who looked upon me as a sort of mother figure and poured out his future hopes and ambitions into my bemused but sympathetic ears.

I recall vividly too the smells of those ship-bound days as we ploughed our way eastwards, mercifully on a calm sea for most of the time. The rancid smell of feet and packed humanity, the reek of wet khaki drying on deck, tobacco smoke, wafts emanating from bilge water and engine oil which grabbed at the throat making one want to puke; the mingled odours of stale food and the cloying aromas of cooking, beer, the pungency of ether and disinfectant which seeped out of the MO's surgery and the whiff of Thelma's rather heady scent. From time to time, I would try and find a spot on deck not occupied by a human being, where I could listen to the soothing sound of the ship's wake and feel the salt spray on my face and at night marvel at the nearness of the skies above our heads and the immensity and clarity of the stars. One morning I saw camels on the horizon heralding the coast of Africa. Shortly afterwards, we docked at Oran to take on supplies. Day succeeded day in routine practices and daily it grew warmer. We shed our battledress for tropical kit, still the inevitable khaki but at least less cumbersome.

Our arrival in Naples is blurred in my memory. No sharp impact but impressions of heat, hubbub and confusion on the quayside as our tin trunks were carried ashore by Italian dockworkers, followed by a surge of passengers as we struggled to disembark and at the same time defend our kitbags and equipment from the marauding bands of urchins. They were ostensibly there to act as porters, but were ready to disappear with cat-like agility into the crowds with any loot they managed to steal or which the more gullible handed to them. By this time the consignment of officers and troops destined for AFHQ at Caserta had been rounded up. We were herded into trucks with canvas flaps at the rear, where we would still have to be alert for the pair of small brown hands, which would appear through the opening, intent on grabbing anything which the unsuspecting had left on the floor.

Caserta lay some eight miles north-east of Naples, in the

middle of a fertile plain surrounded by hills. It was approached by a long straight road, lined by aloes and flax trees, but obscured that hot afternoon by the clouds of white dust caused by our convoy of trucks. After passing through a few dilapidated villages, we reached the town of Caserta, dominated by La Reggia or the Vila Reale, the palace created for Charles VII of Naples (later to become Charles III of Spain) by Luigi Vanvitelli in 1752. Charles, who had visions of his own personal Versailles, was purported to have asked the architect whether he could achieve an exact copy of the building and on receiving an answer in the affirmative exclaimed the Italian equivalent of "off with his head!".

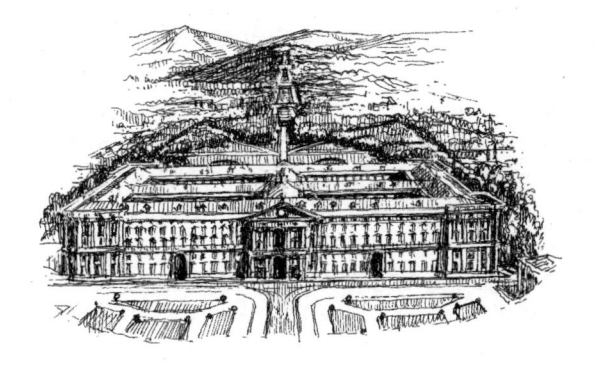

History does not make it clear whether the king was jealous at the thought of Vanvitelli's masterpiece being offered to anybody else, or whether he thought it such a monstrosity that he felt it was a kindness to do away with its perpetrator. Behind the palace stretched the park and cascades. The latter in peacetime sent a flow of water from the summit of a knoll some half a mile away, to erupt from a series of fountains emulating dolphins, caryatids and groteschi before culminating in a huge basin in front of the palace, lined by statuary and foliage. Now the cascades had ceased their gushing and all was dried up and arid.

At the crest of the hill was the 'Gold Braid Section' where many officers with the rank of colonel and above had their quarters, including the Supreme Allied Commander in the Mediterranean,

Field Marshal Lord Alexander. Also housed in this Valhalla were some of the Civil Department, presided over by Harold Macmillan, formerly Resident Minister in North Africa, subsequently British High Commissioner in Italy, soon to be the Head of the Allied Commission in Italy and later to be British Prime Minister. I was stunned by the immensity of the palace, although its total magnitude was not revealed until one tried to find one's way about its four identical buildings erected round four identical courtyards.

On arrival in Caserta, the new intake of female staff officers was conducted to temporary accommodation by a rather harassed looking adjutant. This consisted of tents erected in an orange grove and in these we installed our camp beds and canvas 'wash basins' on tripods. Water was fetched from a nearby tap, or a more thorough wash could be had at the communal ablutions hut some distance away. As it turned out this romantic setting, the overwhelming scent of orange blossom and mesmeric effect of the myriad fireflies at night-time so affected the more susceptible of us that we were soon transferred to a bug-infested billet in the town where life became more prosaic and much time each night was taken up in disinfesting our beds.

After removing the dust and grit of Caserta's highway from our persons, we were marched up to the palace to be briefed on our assignments and to meet our Commanding Officer, Poppy Thorne, who turned out to be an ATS Colonel whose father had been GOC Scottish Command at one time. She was an indeterminate soul who lacked her father's qualities of leadership and seemed to be scared of us all. Some months later her place was taken by Senior Commander Baker, a genial lady with a stubborn streak, which stood her subordinates in good stead since she was prepared to fight for the rights of those under her wing. Before learning our fate we were first invited to tea in the vast officers' mess, which must have accommodated well over a thousand people and access to which was reached by the magnificent and impressive main staircase, the steps paved with marble and lined with elaborately carved balustrading, an awe-inspiring prelude to the dining hall.

But it was the tea itself which stupefied me. I had always looked upon Scotland as being fairly lax where rationing was concerned but my former mess meals were austerity itself compared to the lavish spread which met our rather dazed eyes as we surveyed the scene before us. Sideboards were laid out with tea urns and a bewildering choice of food – shades of my Roukenglen billets – was handed round by a host of Italian waiters, brought into service following the Italian surrender. Once we had overcome our initial bemusement we set to with a will and even I, with my thrifty upbringing, was able to subdue without difficulty a rumbling of guilt and fall upon the variety of sandwiches with relish. The mess was crowded with men and women officers of all the services – including those from South Africa, the USA, Canada, and Australia – as well as civilians, foreign delegates and soldiers and airmen on leave from the front. I soon realised that any part I might play on this particular stage would be that of a very little cog in a very big wheel. The thought rather depressed me, especially as some of my colleagues had already been apprised of their appointments as Personal Assistant to some General or other and were smugly awaiting confirmation.

At the top of the Grand Staircase had once stood the Royal Apartments, a glitter of gold leaf and embellishments, now converted by plywood into a beehive of boxlike partitions where AFHQ's less spectacular staff played out their many parts.

Having been rounded up from amid the tea-urns, we were ushered into one of the ante-rooms where we were given a pep talk by our leader as to how we were to comport ourselves and keep in perspective the fact that females were out-numbered many times over by the male population. This was brought home to me a week or two later by an American Captain with whom I had become friendly, a budding opera singer in civilian life and who introduced me, to my eternal gratitude, to opera in general and to the San Carlo Opera House at Naples in particular. He had a habit of breaking into song during our walks together and one day asked me how I found my fellow women officers. "Nice enough," I replied, "but not very friendly or welcoming". "Well that's to be expected," he drawled. "When an attractive gal like you comes along, the ratio of men to women is bound to fall from two hundred to one to a hundred to one!" It was a timely reminder to keep things in perspective, as we had been warned.

Any thoughts I might have had about taking Allied Headquarters by storm were quickly dispersed on hearing that my first appointment on the operational front was to be Staff Captain (Statistics) with REME (Royal Electrical and Mechanical Engineers), a worthy branch of the army but scarcely in line with my dreams of involvement with Intelligence or the War Room. I suppose my FANY training might have had something to do with it, although I sometimes wondered if my old adversary, Shearer, knowing how much I disliked the mechanical side of life, might have had a hand in my ultimate fate. It took me several days to find my cell-like office without losing my way through a labyrinthine maze of corridors. I wished that I had been as resourceful as Hansel and Gretel and kept a pocketful of bread pellets or pebbles to scatter in my wake.

My job carried a certain amount of responsibility, no doubt, as seen through the eyes of the soldier in the field. On an enormous graph which spanned one wall of the office – 'Wood's Wall' as it became known – it was my task to complete daily the number of guns, all of different calibres and makes, tanks and armoured cars of varying designs, shells and ammunition (a) lost to the enemy, (b) just lost, (c) replacements required, and (d) estimated supplies for future offensives. Information had to be gleaned from the War Office, Company Commanders on the battle front, RASC headquarters, as well as reports submitted by prisoners of war taken with equipment – theirs and ours. Bulletins also had to be devoured daily for details of new equipment, rifles, armoured vehicles and ammunition etc. I became passionately involved with my coloured crayons, rejoicing in any upward surge depicting an adequate supply of arms and equipment and despairing should the figures take a headlong dive. Each day I had to report my findings to the head of the department, a taciturn Major Raphael with cold grey eyes, who I believe became highly regarded in legal circles in post-war days. What was he doing in REME? He obviously viewed me with grave misgiving – I was the only female in the department – rarely addressing me with more than a gruff "Good morning" and dismissing me with a curt "That'll do thank you". On one occasion, however, he castigated me in no uncertain terms for confusing two types of ammunition. "Might have cost a soldier an arm or a leg", he barked as I grovelled before him. I slunk from his presence back to my desk to be comforted by my colleagues.

We were a mixed bunch, this little posse of REME Stats, stuck away in our gloryhole at the end of a corridor near the junction with a staircase, which entailed a constant stream of passers-by, often stopping for a chat, which I rather enjoyed. My office companions were not all REME personnel. They came from various regiments and from all walks of life. It must have been irksome at times having a lone female in their midst, but they treated me with a mixture of indulgence and courtesy and at times exasperation. Staff Sergeant Jackson was my mentor and friend and saved me from many a gaffe with the graph. He had technicalities at his fingertips and, with angelic patience, initiated me into the intricacies of what ammunition was used with what machine. The nearest to me in age was a young captain of Apollo-like appearance called Peter Willard. He had a vacillating nature reflected in a weak chin and a rather apologetic laugh, but put up with my whims and proved an agreeable and willing escort to various social functions. As a contrast, the next desk to me was occupied by Jock Craig, a God-fearing teetotaller with a pear-shaped head and ill-fitting uniform who joined Unilever after the war and continued to woo me with Wall's sausages and ice-cream.

During office hours my life was pretty humdrum. After the momentum of marking up the graph and passing on the information gleaned from it, there was little to stretch the imagination or alleviate the tedium. Off duty there were limitless diversions and many companions with whom to share them. I discovered old friends and made new ones.

There were frequent visits to Naples, a restless city of poverty, craftiness and corruption at that time, but with a certain underlying cheerful acceptance from a population who had made survival their business. But most of us only caught glimpses of the squalor as we drove through back streets to the Officers' Club, overlooking the bay, which offered drinks, sex and distractions to those in need, or to the exquisite Teatro San Carlo Opera House with its six tiers of boxes and perfect acoustics. There were walks in Caserta old town with its abandoned palazzi and peeling churches and to the Roman town of Capua where, enveloped within its walls, Hannibal had rejoiced in a sybaritic existence. As the allied troops advanced northwards so our excursions extended. Rome had been taken in July of 1944 and later became a favourite leave centre, female personnel being accommodated in the YWCA, now one of the city's luxurious hotels, situated near the Borghese gardens. I recall spending one leave with officers of the Lovat Scouts, who I suppose must have been stationed somewhere in the Abruzzi Massif. At any rate I was introduced to skiing for the first time in my life – although my initiation was not on gentle nursery slopes as it is for beginners today, but what seemed to me to be a precipitous drop down a mountainside. Not surprisingly I came to grief quite soon, spraining my ankle badly. In a misguided act of chivalry, one of my companions removed my skis from me and disappeared into the blue with them, abandoning me to a WALK back to base with every footstep sinking inches beneath the snow and torturing my damaged ankle. I remember whimpering with self-pity and rage at my stupidity and longing for a St. Bernard to come bounding over the horizon with the traditional keg of brandy round its neck. However, perhaps it was the treatment my ankle needed, as although I had to hobble round Rome for the rest of my leave with it strapped up, it healed remarkably quickly.

I had an opportunity of visiting Cassino some months after the town and abbey had been captured by the allies, after weeks of desperate fighting resulting in heavy loss of life and supplies on both sides. It was late afternoon on a sullen November day as we entered the town, the approach to which was lined with gangs of Italian labourers engaged in filling in shell craters and clearing debris. The cold was intense and they were hunched into their army greatcoats looking cowed and dispirited, even if the war was over for them. The ruined monastery, dominating the hillside on which it had once so proudly stood – so many times rebuilt – was now a heap of rubble, while discarded equipment and rusting vehicles sprawled across the outskirts of the ravaged town. Despite the danger of a live mine lurking undiscovered, families of peasants were crouched in this desolation, huddled round their flickering fires while devouring their meagre evening meal. For them there was little hope of any early deliverance from a life of misery and hardship.

My job with REME ground on until the end of the year, when salvation came via friends in higher places who had been working on my behalf – and I found myself appointed as Personal Assistant to the ADAG (Assistant Deputy Adjutant General), a job I had secretly coveted for some time. To begin with, I worked for a Brigadier Ware, an unassuming figure with fussy old-maidish habits and an arch sense of humour. He was small and spare with wispy hair and an untidy moustache and reminded me of Wilfred Rabbit. He was, however, on the point of being posted back to England, which filled him with as much delight as it did me since his hobby was archaeology and he couldn't wait to get back to his latest dig for arrow-heads near Tunbridge Wells. His place was taken by his antithesis. Jack Napier was a regular soldier and a gunner. He had had what could be described as a textbook army career: Sandhurst, service overseas, Staff College and so on. He could, I suppose, be described as the salt of the earth – which makes him sound very dull, which he was not. He was the least pompous of men with an infectious ringing laugh, and treated all ranks with consideration and their idiosyncrasies with tolerance, which I found madly irritating at times. He was devoted to his wife Muriel, who clucked over him in daily letters, and to his three children at school in England. I suppose he could not have been more than in his middle forties when I first met him, but I looked upon him as a favourite uncle and he became a good friend. I was indeed fortunate in working for such a man since, because he was so universally liked, my circle of friends widened considerably.

I could at least locate my new office more easily, since on the wall outside my door was a very beautiful porphyry wall fountain enriched with ormolu taps terminating in dolphins' heads. I went searching for this lovely object on a visit to Caserta in the 1960s, but failed to locate it. Perhaps it had been looted by the victorious armies or by Neapolitan workmen employed on the rehabilitation of the palace to its former glory after the allies had moved out.

I also found that I had more in common with my new colleagues who were also working in the same department, some of whom became good and lasting friends. Jacobine Hichens, with whom I had made friends on the SS Orontes, worked for Jack's immediate superior officer, the DAG, a General MacLeod, with whom I had little contact. After the war Jacobine married Lionel Sackville-West and became chatelaine of Knole, whereafter our paths diverged. She sadly died quite young from cancer.

Another colleague I saw much of was Michael Wheeler, son of Sir Mortimer, later to become a well-known barrister and Treasurer of Lincoln's Inn. Intelligent with a witty turn of phrase, he was given to making clever puns and referred to his father from time to time with a note of resignation: "Dad's at it again". He was married to Sheila, an opthoptist whom I got to know well in post-war days and who was known as "poor Sheila" when Michael was being at his most obstreperous. Another good friend was Ursula Barclay, auburn haired and given to plumpness, like myself at that time. In after years, she was quite slender. She had an irrepressible sense of humour and became my successor as PA to Jack Napier after I left the army at the end of 1945. She later married David Lloyd-Owen, also serving in Italy at that time, and by a strange co-incidence her future daughter-in-law, Antonia, joined Specialtours, the travel company of which I was a co-founder, many years later. My friends Barbara Hewitt from Glencorse days and Joyce Macgregor, who was with me at Staff College, were also posted to Caserta but disappointingly from my point of view were both transferred to bases outside Caserta. I was, in fact, a bridesmaid at Joyce's wedding a year later to Lt. Colonel Tom Scott. The marriage, however, was not of the happiest.

There was certainly no such thing as routine in an ADAG's timetable. His duties embraced the supervision of welfare, administration and education throughout liberated Italy, with the result that we were on the road a great deal. When at base I had to attend conferences for minute-taking, meet visiting 'Brass' and other VIPs before handing them over to their equals; defend my master from inopportune visitors and liaise with other departments. It was during such a liaison that I first came across Judy Hutchinson, later to become a close friend and whose death sadly occurred in 1989. It was only after her death that it became known to many that whilst working for General Terence Airey at Caserta, she had been involved in Ultra, the code name for the deciphering of signals coded on the enemy's Enigma machines and one of the best kept secrets of the Second World War.

As far as I was aware she spent most of her time plotting with flags on a huge map the progress of the war, not unlike my graphs but on a slightly higher echelon. Strikingly handsome and generous of build, she one day toppled off her ladder and did herself considerable damage. She was carted off to hospital where I got to know her well. On one such visit she confided to me that before the stretcher bearers arrived, Fritz, General Airey's dachshund, had helpfully tried to lick up the blood but had been called to heel by his master. "Not blue enough for you," were his terse words designed, no doubt, to make the victim laugh.

On our excursions away from Caserta, the Brigadier and I used to travel in his staff car – the ubiquitous Humber Snipe sprayed with camouflage paint – with his driver, Earl, at the wheel. Earl was a man of few words, stocky and rather owlish in appearance with a gnomish sense of humour which belied his usually impassive features. He had an equable temperament and was ready to cope with any emergency. He was inordinately proud of his 'tea-urn', his own invention, which he had concocted from army surplus metal and which he boasted would bring water to the boil in three minutes flat. "Much safer to brew up here, sir", he said broodingly one day as we found ourselves parked outside one of the Borgia strongholds – as if at any moment Lucia herself might materialise and offer us refreshments laced with iron filings.

Although conscientious to a fault, Jack Napier saw no reason why business should not be combined with pleasure, if the opportunity arose. Being an insatiable fisherman like myself, it was my responsibility to see that the inflatable dinghy was lashed to the roof rack and the fishing rods stowed aboard, before setting off on any official visit, be it to inspect new billets at Sorrento, to attend an ABCA session in Perugia or to preside at a court martial at some obscure field post.

Between appointments we would hope to find some likely spot beside a lake or river and while Earl was brewing up, Jack would inflate the dinghy with my bicycle pump and we would set off with the help of a home-made oar (Earl's ingenuity again) to try our luck. It never ceased to amaze me that we occasionally caught a fish; indeed on one occasion when fishing from the bank, we came across a shoal of crayfish. Any catch was cooked on hot stones over an open fire, a legacy from Girl Guide days that proved useful in the Italian countryside.

We would sometimes be away for several days at a time and on a freezingly cold night in January of 1945 found ourselves fairly near the Front Line, within earshot of gunfire. We were to be the guests for the night of a squadron of the 6th Armoured Division and while Jack was spirited off to the CO's quarters and Earl disappeared in the direction of the NAAFI, I found myself having the party of a lifetime with men who hadn't seen a woman for weeks. Searchlights seared the sky and the distant sound of guns only added to the unreality of the situation. For the little of the night that remained I was given a choice of sleeping quarters. Either I could install myself in a barn which had been shelled the night before or accept the invitation of a war-weary major with spaniel eyes and a much darned pullover to share his couch in his cosy caravan. Thanks to my Presbyterian upbringing, I opted for the former and spent the coldest night of my life, huddled in my greatcoat, gazing at the stars through the holed roof and bitterly regretting my prudish ways. How much more generous in their emotions are the young today.

Some journeys to conferences were made by rail in the Deputy Adjutant General's private train, which carried a sprinkling of Generals and Brigadiers together with their ADGs and PAs. A fair amount of work was carried out during the actual journey but in the evenings some of the more senior officers liked to relax with a game of bridge. Unfortunately not many of the junior ranks shared their passion and it was our dread that one of us would be summoned to make up a fourth.

This may all sound like carnivalia but in truth there were many hours of tedium when one's thoughts turned to home, many more of tension and many of intensive work; depressing news of setbacks before the final breakthrough; news of the death of friends causing distress and heartache; or worrying letters from one's family. In a close packed community of several thousand men and women romances flourished, marriages were broken, friendships waxed and waned. There was intrigue, jealousy, heartbreak, cases of mental strain and nervous stress. Ambition at times over-ruled compassion and sometimes a sense of humour lost the battle against depression or despair. Because I am not a particularly emotional person, affairs of the heart passed over me lightly, except for one when I became moonstruck for months.

There was one admirer, a Southern Rhodesian captain in the Intelligence Corps, who pursued me with offers of marriage. He had an embarrassing habit of sending letters to my office marked TOP SECRET, PRIORITY which on being opened revealed happy snapshots of his numerous nephews and nieces bearing the caption "Doesn't this make you want to say yes?". I lived in fear of these documents bypassing me and being delivered direct to my General, who would no doubt have been quite amused.

Leave came round once in a while and was often spent in Positano, then a delightful little fishing village, deserted except for the local inhabitants and troops on vacation. Days were spent swimming in the Mediterranean and evenings at the Buca di Bacco, a tavern serving ambrosial meals of fresh sardines and rough red wine. The one drawback to this paradise was getting there. To reach our goal entailed a sick-making drive, usually in an open-backed truck, down the Sorrento Peninsula weaving our way round countless zigzag bends with jagged rocks above our heads and a sheer drop to the ocean below. Never a good traveller at the best of times, I rarely completed this journey without throwing up over the tailboard. I spent the Christmas of 1944 on the Island of Ischia which involved another purgatorial journey, this time by sea on a gunboat which bucketed and plunged through viscous green troughs of spume throwing us about like rag dolls as we fought to keep our balance on deck, to which we were relegated. After the war in Italy came to an end on 29th April 1945, we were able to go on leave as far afield as Millstat in Austria, where we stayed in one of Hitler's former human stud-farms – where the pillowcases were embroidered with sprouting swastikas.

During the spring and summer of that year, I was fortunate enough to accompany Jack Napier to Greece on two occasions, where he took part in peace conferences. In September he was designated to fly to Germany on a similar mission. General Bridgeman was the senior member of the party, which consisted altogether of about eight members of Headquarters staff. It had been debated as to whether PAs were to accompany the party, but we were rightly considered redundant and were sent on leave instead. I was recalled 24 hours later with the news that the aeroplane carrying the delegation had stalled over the Dolomites due to the engine freezing up and all the passengers had been ordered to bale out by parachute. They had, it transpired later, jumped strictly in order of seniority – resulting in the General and Brigadier coming to rest halfway up a very high peak. News filtered through that General Bridgeman had broken a leg and Jack his collarbone. Fortunately they landed within 'halooing' distance of each other and managed to drag themselves to the edge of the mountain where they seriously considered the possibility of launching themselves into space in the hope that their parachutes might re-inflate! Luckily for them they were spotted by shepherds on a neighbouring crest, who organised a stretcher party to bring the unfortunate pair down the mountainside and deposit them in the Military Hospital in Klagenfurt. The rest of the party landed without mishap on the plain which caused some unkind hilarity back at HQ along the broad lines of "The first shall be last ...". There is sometimes compensation for being of a lesser order.

Earl and I were summoned to our Lord and Master's bedside with any papers requiring attention and lots of whisky. We enjoyed immensely our drive to Klagenfurt, although we witnessed some grievous areas of destruction en route, which somewhat subdued our jubilation at being 'off the hook'. We crossed the frontier into Austria without difficulty and our spirits revived with the breathtaking beauty of the Dolomites on our left as we traversed the Piave valley, lush and dappled in the late afternoon sunlight. Klagenfurt was crammed with service personnel, some in administrative posts, some on leave, and other flotsam and jetsam who just seemed to have drifted there.

We located the hospital and I introduced myself to the QAIMNS matron in charge, a severe looking figure with shrewd eyes, behind which lurked a definite twinkle. She greeted me with palpable relief. "The Generals are being very trying," she said testily. "Wanting to be up and about at once. It's not as if they are young men." She herself must have been over fifty, but I murmured sympathetic acquiescence and was shown up to their room, which they were sharing. I thought this was a great mistake, as their grumbles would be twofold and, like two schoolboys, they would no doubt be hatching some form of escape.

I found them distinctly irritable, due possibly to mortification at their plight, but they cheered up at the sight of me, and even more so when I produced a couple of bottles of Johnnie Walker. I told them that they were now both eligible for membership of the Caterpillar Club, having made their debut as parachutists. This made them chortle, but I felt cheated at missing out on such a drama, although I did wonder on occasion whether, had I been the only female aboard that plane, I would have been ordered to jump first or last!

Apart from reporting twice daily to the hospital for the dictation of letters and the passing on of news received from HQ, the day was mine. The war was over now – a least as far as the fighting in Italy and Austria were concerned – and there was a distinct feeling of letting go. Klagenfurt, the capital of Carinthia, straddles the right bank of the River Glan and connects by canal to the Wörthersee, a short distance away. In those early autumn days, still warm and sunny, the leaves of the oaks and ash were already turning russet and crimson, casting their reflections on the lake which showed scarcely a ripple on the water. I would meander round its shores, sometimes with the car and Earl, to some remote corner, where I would fish from the bank (needless to say the rods and dinghy had accompanied us from Caserta) while Earl would lie nearby, smoking his vile tobacco, which at least helped to keep the midges at bay, and dreaming no doubt of Mrs Earl and life after the war.

At other times I would walk into the hills behind the town on stony tracks leading steeply uphill, until they petered out at the edge of forests of spruce and pine, which in turn gave way to undulating pastures of lush green grass giving off the pungent, aromatic scents of clover and thyme. The sound of cowbells was ever present in the distance and once, on passing a farm dwelling, I was offered a glass of milk warm from the cow and in exchange helped with the peeling of newly boiled potatoes. I remember the earthy smell of the steam that rose from the cauldron in which they had been cooked, and the waxy texture of the vegetable as the skin was pared away.

Another diversion was having my portrait painted. The artist was a young army lieutenant kicking his heels before being demobilised. His name was Jamie Drew, a misnomer if ever there was one, although his draughtsmanship may have improved since then. It was a terrible painting, but I must have been flattered at anyone wanting to paint me and eventually dragged this doubtful masterpiece home with me, filling out endless customs forms en route, ignoring raised eyebrows and jolly quips before presenting it with dubious pride to my parents.

Then it was all over. Jack recovered and we both returned to Caserta, he to receive considerable badinage from his friends, while I was given 'an honourable discharge' and succeeded in cadging a lift home in the DAG's private train. Quite a few others were equally privileged, so mercifully any games of bridge were out of the question. I reached home just before Christmas, where my mother's greeting to me after sixteen months of absence was, "Oh darling, how glorious that you are home again. You *have* put on weight". I was indeed home.

Back to the real world

Eight

Six and a half years had deluded me into thinking of life as a succession of events dictated either by fate or by one's superiors. We in the Services did not have to consider the material things of life. They were all provided free of charge: board and lodging, clothing, medical attention and even entertainment, if you counted the ENSA concerts and mess dances laid on for our distraction. However much we eschewed the camp beds and barrack walls, or looked with disgust at the food put before us; however much we despised the uniforms gracelessly covering our bodies or cringed at the sight of a syringe puncturing our skins to protect us from tropical diseases, we accepted it all as a matter of course. Civilians at home with a family to bring up were not so fortunate. They had to juggle with their rations to ensure that their children were adequately fed; stand for hours in queues for some unexpected windfall of oranges or scour the countryside in the hope of finding a private source of eggs. I know we had to think for ourselves on occasion and take decisions at a certain level, but there was always someone higher up the ladder than oneself to whom the buck could be passed.

Little wonder that after being demobilised and issued with the money considered adequate for a new outfit – I seem to recollect that mine was of serviceable grey flannel – many of us felt disorientated. The first few months of 1946 were a restless time for me. Many of my friends had married; others had moved away and those who were left did not necessarily share the same interests or outlook as myself. It became increasingly clear to me that I had to leave Edinburgh. I had had my taste of freedom and London was obviously my goal. I had to face the fact, however, that although I could drive most vehicles (including a three ton lorry), delouse heads and handle irascible generals with equanimity, these were hardly the attributes likely to impress the business world of London, who could choose from millions of aspirants with many more qualifications than myself.

One of my mother's closest friends was Dolly Scott. She had borne four children, three of whom were triplets who appeared on the Edinburgh scene three months prior to myself. Because they were premature babies and at least two of them unexpected, their first cot was the drawer of a tallboy lined with flannel, incubators being a thing of the future. All survived – two girls and a boy – although David, the last born, was mistaken at first for the afterbirth and nearly disposed of. They were healthy children and grew into stalwart adults – achieving their joint 240th birthday in 2000 – and entered the Guinness Book of Records in 2004 as being the oldest surviving set of triplets in Britain. Their mother had married a feckless Irishman who disappeared shortly after the triplets were born, leaving his wife with next to no money but an indomitable spirit, which surmounted every obstacle throughout her life. The family moved south to Haywards Heath when I was very small to live with Mrs. Scott's mother, Granny Addis, and I lost touch with them for some years, although my mother saw Dolly whenever she went south.

During the war I had had occasional meetings with one or other of the family, more especially David, who was in the Royal Navy and who visited Rosyth from time to time. His mother worked at the Rainbow Club throughout the Blitz, where she was a huge success. After peace was declared she bought a house in Abingdon Villas – in London's Kensington – which she shared with her widowed sister, Aunt Annie or Tanny as she was known, and any other member of the family or their friends who happened to be in need of accommodation. So it was that No.10 Abingdon Villas became my first home in London when I moved south in the Spring of 1946. Living there at the time, apart from myself and Dolly and her sister, were the latter's son Ronald, a doctor at St Thomas's and later to become one of its leading orthopaedic surgeons; Margery, destined to be the third wife of John Skeaping, the well-known painter and sculptor, and Sheila, a radiotherapist shortly to be married to Dickie Botterill. Michael, the eldest child, and David, being in the army and navy respectively, were present only intermittently. No.10 was a gregarious household, full of laughter and noise and I was very happy there.

Dolly Scott had a face that was a bit askew, which gave her a slightly quizzical expression. Although poor as the proverbial church mouse, she had an air of elegance about her and the most wonderful capacity for the enjoyment of life. She was one of the few people I knew who really laughed, accompanied quite often by tears of mirth coursing down her cheeks, which would reduce us all to a similar state of hilarity. She had a habit of breaking out into a parody of a music hall song which she called a 'treacly', and which earned her the name of Dolly Daydreams amongst her family, who all loved her dearly, as did her many friends.

Although as yet I had no clear idea of what I wanted to do, I had an ill-formulated plan of going into the hotel business. I envisaged a leisurely life running a fishing hotel in the Highlands during the season and relaxing in the winter months – which shows how little I knew about it. However, with this at the back of my mind I did find myself a job as a trainee in a small restaurant in Beauchamp Place, known simply as No.15. It was housed in the basement of this busy cosmopolitan street and was managed by two women partners.

Violet Wood, who was no relation of mine, must have been in her late forties and was unmarried. She was tall and angular with a precise manner of speaking and smoked a small white clay pipe. She was a strict disciplinarian but had infinite patience and I never once saw her lose her temper with any of her staff, however sorely she was tried. Her partner, Madge, was the exact opposite and I often wondered how they came to be in business together. She was handsome in a dishevelled sort of way and was attractive to men, although she had been discarded by her husband, or so one gathered. Impulsive and slapdash, she was given to bouts of generosity that she could ill afford and was besotted by her only son Donald, who was then sixteen. She alternated between periods of optimism, when everything would be viewed through rose-coloured spectacles, and days of deep depression, when she would drink too much. Although outwardly an ill-assorted pair, the partnership seemed to work quite well.

The restaurant catered only for coffee and lunches, which suited my book very well, as it left my evenings free. Both the kitchen quarters and the restaurant were somewhat cramped and we could only seat about twenty at a time. Rationing was still very much in evidence, with egg powder and ersatz foods to the fore, which restricted the choice in menus and encouraged ingenuity. Items such as stuffed hearts appeared on my horizon for the first time and it was not unusual to unpack a crate of chickens sent from some poultry farm, only to find them crawling with maggots. I dealt with these pretty much as I had dealt with my ATS' lousy heads – albeit with different ingredients – and to the best of my knowledge, they were served and consumed without complaint or ill-consequence.

I used to bicycle to and from work unless the weather proved too vile. Traffic was light in those days and I equipped myself with a spacious basket, which could accommodate any food surplus to requirements that the staff were permitted to take, especially at the weekends, and which were much appreciated by the household at No.10.

I was initiated into the art of cooking by a highlander called Mary MacDonald – and into the art of swearing by our washer-upper, a Welsh lady called Mrs Evans. A cigarette dangled perpetually from the latter's lips and never a pot or pan entered the sink without being referred to as "that bugger" or the epithet of endearment as she used to ask, "Where's that bleeding little bugger Hazel? She promised me a fag". I seem to recall that she had seven children, but of her husband I remember no mention. On the other hand, Mary was a gentle soul, decidedly fey except when under pressure, when she would become very excited and begin shouting. She was a great raconteur of tales of her childhood, which she related in a musical highland lilt. Her father had been a shepherd and she, Mary, had seen service in some of the big Scottish estates. I suppose she was no more than a very good plain cook, but under her tuition I learnt far more than the rudiments of cooking. Many tips and short cuts I gleaned from her have saved me much time in the kitchen ever since. The treat she enjoyed most in life was to drop in at the Coal Hole in the Strand, where she would indulge in two ports and lemon – never more – so now and again we would board a bus together and treat each other to a couple of rounds.

I enjoyed my time at No.15, as not only was I learning a trade and being paid for it, but I used to accompany Violet Wood to market and learned from her how to cost dishes and to keep accounts. I also got to know many of the shopkeepers in Beauchamp Place who used to lunch regularly with us: Madame Raymonde and her daughter, who were haute couturiers from next door; Mrs Hale from Tetley & Hale, antique dealers, John Flower in the same trade; and many other shopkeepers whose leases were for a short duration and who dabbled in costume jewellery, domestic agencies, toy soldiers, reject china and so on. Apart from 'trade', quite a few of my friends, visiting London for the day, would drop in for lunch on the off-chance of exchanging a word or two with me between courses.

I acted as waitress as well as cook. On one very busy day I ushered two customers to a table. Both were mannish looking females, indeed one looked exactly like Burlington Bertie without the top hat and cane and produced a monacle from her lapel with which to peruse the menu. Orders were piling up and my two clients became restive. "Mary," I pleaded, "do hurry up with the order for my two lesbians, they've been waiting for ages." Mary, flustered by the unaccustomed activity, did not look up from the stove. "I don't care if they're Scandinavians," she retorted. "They'll have to wait their turn like everyone else". Unfortunately she was getting on in years and retired before my year was up.

Her place was taken by a volatile European called Jean-Pierre who hailed, so he said, from France and whose father was Polish. In truth, it turned out that he and his mother had escaped to France just before the Germans marched into Poland and from there had found their way to England. He styled himself a chef, rather than a cook and made it plain that he considered he was doing us a favour by joining such a humble establishment and only then in a temporary capacity. In fact I think he was thankful to find any employment immediately after the war, especially one which left his evenings free for him to do some freelance work. I found I had not nearly so restful a time working for Jean-Pierre as I had had with Mary. He had a mercurial temperament and for some reason found me madly attractive, his amorous inclinations complicating my life exceedingly in such cramped quarters. His idea of playfulness was to chase me round the kitchen table with a carving knife held aloft, at the same time crooning French endearments at me. Mrs Evans called him "that wee French toad" when she wasn't calling him worse names, and threatened to castrate him with his own carving knife if he didn't leave me alone. He was, however, a superb pastry cook, so at least I learnt from him the art – and in his hands it really was an art – of creating Danish pastries and croissants. In order to augment both our incomes, we undertook, with Violet Wood's blessing and under the umbrella of No. 15, to cater for cocktail parties and sometimes dinners in private houses, where Jean-Pierre would do the cooking and I acted as waitress and general dogsbody. This arrangement worked quite well and if his amorous inclinations got out of hand I would simply threaten to walk out there and then.

We used to speed to these functions on Jean-Pierre's motor bicycle with me on the pillion and the food and equipment in the sidecar.

During my time at No.15, I had been negotiating with the Hotels, Restaurants and Caterers Association with a view to becoming a participant in its exchange scheme, whereby a trainee from a foreign country – in this instance Switzerland – would be 'swapped' for a trainee from the British Isles. The exchange would last for a year, the wage would be minimal, but board and lodging would be free and tips were purported to be munificent and should prove sufficient to live on.

This perhaps should have given me fair warning of the hours one was expected to work. My negotiations eventually bore fruit and at the beginning of 1947, I was informed that the son of an hotel proprietor in the Vaudois town of Aigle in Switzerland was to be engaged by the Savoy Hotel, while I was to take his place at his father's Hotel Victoria. Perusal of maps and books divulged the minimum of information on Aigle and what I did glean did not fill me with any great enthusiasm. I learnt that the town was situated in the Valley of the Rhône and Ormont rivers; that it was a junction town where one took the train to more well-known and attractive places such as Chamonix, Montreux and the mountain resorts of Château d'Oex and Gstaad. Aigle itself boasted a modest wine industry of the Vaudois grapes and a military depot. Of the Hotel Victoria there was no mention at all. *Tant pis*, I thought.

The Swiss have a very high reputation in the hotel world and an exchange with the Savoy must have some sort of cachet. Thus I convinced myself and duly signed the contract binding me to employment in Switzerland for one year, under the auspices of the Hotels, Restaurants and Caterers Association.

As I had a few weeks between leaving No.15 and leaving for Switzerland, I spent them in Edinburgh with my long-suffering parents, who were beginning to get used to my restless comings and goings. To keep my hand in, I took a temporary job in the kitchens of l'Aperitif, one of Edinburgh's leading restaurants at that time, run by Donald and Anne Ross. Compared to No.15 it was very up-market, with linen tablecloths, discreet lighting and excellent working conditions. A barrel of beer stood in the kitchen from which the staff could help themselves, a practice that astonished me at first, but I never saw this privilege abused.

My job was that of omelette cook (usually with tinned eggs), a role not taken very seriously by my friends who lunched or dined in the restaurant from time to time and who would issue invitations via the waiters for me to join them for coffee and brandy. This embarrassed me not a little, until I found that most of the waiters were willing to be my allies and would bring the brandy to me in the kitchen instead.

It was very early on a pearly Spring morning when I dismounted from the train at Aigle station. The mist was still hovering on the lower slopes of the mountains and after a few deep breaths of the mountain air I decided to walk to the hotel. The station master promised to send up my luggage by carrier in the next half-hour. The road I took was not unattractive, being lined with chalet type houses that spread over the hillside beyond. They were embellished with wooden galleries from which hung baskets of greenery, to be replaced later on by geraniums and petunias. Wide green valleys surrounded the town, sloping upwards to the limestone escarpment beyond which I could catch glimpses of the peaks of the Vaud Alps through the thinning mist, dominated distantly by the Dents du Midi. It was all more majestic than I had imagined.

I reached the main street where I understood my destination to be and there it was, easily identifiable by the gold lettering along its façade, proclaiming HOTEL VICTORIA***. It did not need its grading (two stars less than the Savoy) to confirm my suspicions that this was a less than equal exchange. There was no top-hatted flunkey at the door ready to direct me to the tradesmen's entrance. In fact there was no sign of life whatsoever, either outside or in, except for a dog exploring a dustbin some way up the street. Nor, when I rang the door bell was there any response – but after all it was not yet 7am and I could sense it was not the sort of establishment to boast a night porter.

My morale was at a low ebb by this time. Feeling distinctly forlorn I was about to ring again when the door suddenly inched open to reveal a Hogarthian female figure of slatternly appearance, clad in a pink padded dressing gown and with her hair in curlers. She let flow a flood of French dialect, which I had much difficulty in following but guessed the gist was to the effect that I was earlier than expected, but since I had arrived I might as well help with the breakfast.

I soon surmised that this was Madame Herzog, wife of the patron. In all fairness I have to admit that when she had completed her *toilette* and dressed herself, she turned out to be quite handsome and stylish in a bold and brassy way. Her hair was peroxide-gold with dark roots and she looked much more Teutonic than French. She regarded me appraisingly but with a marked lack of enthusiasm and showed me to my garret-like room – under the eaves but cosy enough, its one window giving on to the main street, where there was always something to watch. I washed and changed into a dark dress over which I donned an apron, and went in search of the breakfast room, hoping that I would be offered some myself.

The Hotel Victoria was essentially a commercial type hotel run by Monsieur and Madame Herzog with a minimum of staff, catering largely for overnight visitors, commercial travellers and army officers resting from manoeuvres. But the hotel was also renowned locally for its food, as the patron was a chef of considerable skill. The bar served meals and dispensed drinks throughout the day and well into the night, and was a sphere away from life at the Savoy or, for that matter, at No.15 or l'Aperitif. It also housed an infernal machine designed to inject steam into cold liquids transforming them into piping hot drinks, a great saving of time when under pressure but the intricacies of which I took several days to master. All I succeeded in doing that first morning was to scald my hand quite badly from a blast of hot air that expelled itself on to my person rather than into the milk jug. My puerile efforts were watched either expressionlessly or expectantly by what was to become my regular breakfast clientele, largely composed of local tradesmen, peasants from the nearby vineyards and *commerçants* on their way to the neighbouring town, who perched on stools surrounding the bar while reading the morning papers and dunking croissants in their coffee, accompanied quite often by a '*fine*'.

After breakfast I was introduced to Monsieur Herzog, a short stocky individual with hair *en brosse*, rather reminiscent of an aggressive wire-haired terrier. In earlier years he had been a professional boxer, which might have accounted for his occasional irrational outbursts. It did not take me long to discover that he and his wife disliked each other intensely. Right from the start it became a tug-of-war, at times physical, over for whom I was to work. If Madame wanted me for laundry work, Monsieur would order me to the kitchen; if Monsieur sent me to pick vegetables from the potager, Madame would ferret me out and require my help with the beds. I soon learned to take advantage of this battle of wits and sneak off to have a cigarette or breath of fresh air, knowing that each would think I was working for the other. When Monsieur was goaded beyond endurance by his wife's nagging, he would yell at her "*Allez-y aux montagnes, vieille vache*", and she would shrill back "*J'y vais*", and depart for several days at a time, whether indeed to the mountains or to a lover was never made clear.

Most of my mornings were spent in making beds. I remember being astounded and somewhat shocked at the unexpected discovery of hairnets lurking under the pillows of a contingent of stalwart Swiss mountain troopers who were our guests for two or three nights. Then came the preparation of the dining room for lunch and the serving of drinks from the bar, should Monsieur be otherwise engaged. This was no easy matter as I had to master the correct preparation of aperitifs hitherto unknown to me except by name. Pastis – how much water to add? *Genièvre*, neat or diluted? *Fines, cognacs, sirops* of all flavours, *marc*, Fernet–Branca and, for the more sophisticated, a vermouth *sec* or *à l'eau*. Most of my regular customers were only too happy to initiate me into the art of drink-dispensing by pouring out a generous dollop of their own particular choice and adding the minimum of water. This I was more than happy to let them do, but Monsieur's irascible appearance would quickly put an end to such laxity.

Another worrying task was the replenishing of empty liqueur bottles from the casks kept in the cellar. In the dim light I had to distinguish between a straw-covered flagon of cognac and an identical one of green Chartreuse, or identify at short notice a particular *sirop* or liqueur from the choice of cassis, peach, *framboise*, Chartreuse (green or yellow) and a host of others.

One day I was wrestling with a cask of kirsch when the cork expelled itself with enormous velocity, drenching me in a shower of potent liquid and temporarily blinding me. Luckily there remained enough in the cask to fill the bottle required for the bar, after which I groped my way upstairs to the *toilette* where I washed out my eyes and my person as best I could and presented myself in due course behind the counter. Monsieur was luckily engaged in the kitchen but from time to time would emerge to seek some liqueur for a certain dish and sniff the air suspiciously. "*Quel odeur de kirsch*", he muttered to himself on this occasion but on seeing my enflamed eyes he no doubt thought I was suffering from a bout of home-sickness and left me alone.

After a good lunch – for the staff were never stinted in their meals – I was allowed half an hour to myself. Then came the more arduous tasks – such as trundling several wheelbarrow loads of wet laundry to the drying green several hundred yards down the lane behind the hotel. Here sheets and towels had to be hung out to dry and trundled back again some hours later to be put through a huge mechanically-worked revolving iron. There was quite a knack to this task and I received several reprimands from Madame for allowing creases to appear, before finally mastering the technique. Or I might have a pile of Monsieur's socks to darn, an occupation I abhorred and did not excel at.

I was assisted in these undertakings by the three other members of staff – Lisette, Pietro and Genesia. Lisette was a cheerful Swiss girl of peasant stock who, with her generous build and brawny arms, tossed the sheets on the line as if they were gossamer threads and handled the loads of washing with consummate ease. Pietro and his sister Genesia came from

Genoa and found life all happiness, infecting those around them with a similar happiness although it was hard work at times as far as I was concerned. Although all three were totally uneducated, they shared a basic philosophy that work was their lot and that to kick against their destinies was a waste of time. They certainly made my life bearable by their camaraderie and constant offers of help.

Suzanne von Lauthen was another light in my darkness. She was the rather unlikely distant cousin of Madame Herzog and lived in Geneva, coming to the hotel sometimes to help out. She was chic and sophisticated and we enjoyed each other's company. I myself became the subject of amorous attention from a regular client called Monsieur Martin Martinique, who lived on the shores of Lake Geneva near Lausanne.

Monsieur Martinique was pure music hall. He was portly and of medium height, grew a luxuriant moustache with carefully waxed ends and invariably wore a dark suit and waistcoat, starched collar, spats and a trilby hat. He carried a fob watch and chain on his *embonpoint* and a dejected looking beagle on a lead. To myself I called him Mr Salteena. His French was flowery and his English execrable. During his absences on *'les affaires'* (I never discovered what he did) he used to bombard me with postcards and letters, some of them indecipherable, enclosing snapshots of himself. His opening address fluctuated between "To my darling" and "My dear Wood", but inevitably ended with "Good boy, my dearest, yours trully, Martin". One postcard bore the cryptic message "I hoppe to you a son", which disturbed me somewhat until I interpreted it to mean "Hope to see you soon". He never came to the Hotel Victoria without presenting me with some gift, chocolates or flowers and on one occasion a ruby ring, which I politely declined lest his intentions be misconstrued. Poor Monsieur Martinique. He got nothing from me except ridicule and gratitude for giving me something to laugh about. At least he recognised me as a human being.

Nine

It was Suzanne who rescued me from this strangely ambivalent existence by suggesting I should go and work at the Grand Hotel in Château d'Oex for the summer season, as they depended on students and casual labour. My contract stated that as long as I stayed in Switzerland for a year and worked in the hotel or catering trade, I could change my job as often as I wanted to, so I gave in my notice to the Herzogs and left without regret or apology. I felt they had had their pound of flesh.

Château d'Oex at that time was a small mountain resort above Aigle, much patronised by British and American visitors, which was the reason the Grand Hotel was glad to have an English speaking waitress in their midst. The hotel lived up to its name in rather an old fashioned way and had a reputation for attracting the same guests year after year, who stayed for at least one or two weeks – so one got to know the long term residents quite well. The staff were a mixed bunch and apart from a self-styled Don Juan from Canada called Rick, and myself, were for the most part French or Swiss. The majority were students on vacation who looked upon me as quite elderly. I luckily found favour from the start with the head waiter, a Swiss called Jean who felt he had a bond with me as he had once worked as a commis chef in the Caledonian Hotel in Edinburgh. He therefore called me Scotty for reasons of birth, except in moments of stress when he called me other names.

One day I was on my way from the dining room to the pantry, loaded with plates from wrist to chin, when I slipped on a lettuce leaf that someone had dropped on the dining room floor. Down came waitress, crockery and all. Jean loomed over me. "Call yourself a bloddy vaitress?", he snarled down at me as I lay inert amid a welter of broken china, while my fellow staff looked on in dismay tinged with delighted appreciation at this comedy act to enliven their somewhat stereotyped days. "No," I snarled back, trying to restrain tears of hurt pride and some pain. "It is the last thing I'd call myself." I finally extricated myself from my humiliating position on the floor and gathered up the debris, which I carried to the pantry to be greeted with derisive laughs from the rest of my cronies. After lunch Jean summoned me to the then deserted dining room. "We drown our sorrows, Scottie, with *un petit verre, non*?", he announced, drawing the cork from a bottle no doubt filched from the hotel cellars that he would consider his due in time of affliction.

I grew friendly with a visiting Dowager Duchess whom I discovered had been at the same school as my mother in Edinburgh, although in different years. The first time I waited upon her at table she admonished me gently for misplacing the plate in front of her. "Do remember dear," she said, "that some of us have crests on our china and it would never do to have them upside down." We were allowed off duty for an hour each afternoon – otherwise our working day was from 6.30am until midnight. Her Grace would sometimes send her Rolls for me, parked discreetly some distance from the prying eyes of my colleagues, and we would take a short drive together while she entertained me with stories of her past and I retaliated with life behind the green baize door at the Grand Hotel.

Sometimes I was relegated to duty as barmaid in the hotel's tavern – a sort of nightclub adjoining the main building – and much frequented by the local population. My uniform on these occasions was a black dress with diminutive white apron of broderie anglaise just large enough to hide the money bag that was worn, sporran-like, underneath. If asked by a customer for a dance, we were allowed to accept, on condition that we removed both our aprons and our money bags, which were left in the not altogether reliable hands of the head barman.

As the summer declined and the guests grew fewer, we were allowed the occasional day off. I sometimes spent these with Suzanne, with whom I had kept in touch, or on my own exploring the region round Lac Léman. A friend of my father lived at Vevey, a beautiful little town facing the Savoie Alpes. He was a near-recluse with a conscience who felt it incumbent to show occasional kindness to the daughter of his old friend, although he was almost inarticulate with shyness. I am sure he regarded me as a child on a day out from school and treated me accordingly. After giving me a large lunch and pressing a box of chocolates into my hands, he would see me into the train with ill-concealed relief and return to his library of rare books. These visits were not unmitigated pleasure for me, but I appreciated any escape from drudgery and the banalities of my fellow staff.

Switzerland can be a beguiling country, especially the Vaudois region with its vividly green meadows spiked with wild flowers in the spring, the blue waters of the lakes running to steely grey under storm clouds, foothills clothed in vineyards stretching up to and merging with expanses of rock and finally culminating in the majestic peaks of the Alpine range. But I found the Swiss a smug race, irritating in their conviction that the war had hit them hard resulting in a shortage of sugar. Workers they certainly were, sometimes to the exclusion of all else, as if the making of money was the be all and end all of existence. But as hoteliers they were hard to beat and if one wanted to learn this trade, they were indeed the ideal masters.

Château d'Oex was not sited at a high enough altitude to rank as a ski resort, which was why the Grand Hotel closed from the end of October until Easter of the following year. I still had five months of my contract to run so had to find another job and it was here again that Suzanne came to my aid. She had friends in Château d'Oex called Schwab who ran the chemist shop in the main street. It was they who told her of a popular patisserie/café called Le Relais, which required a waitress and general help to the young couple who owned it, a Monsieur and Madame Lenoir.

As usual, the work carried no salary but included a room owned by the Schwabs over their pharmacy and all tips were mine, since I soon discovered that I was the staff, helped out at weekends by a local girl called Josette. This was an improvement on the Grand Hotel where all tips were put in a communal *boîte aux pourboires* and were distributed by management as they thought fit. This led to endless disputes amongst the staff as to who deserved the lion's share. Occasionally I was lucky enough to find a guest who would say "this is for you" and press a note into my unresisting hand.

A reflection on the hours I slaved in my final job is shown by the healthy state of my bank balance when I left Switzerland. I had opened a Swiss bank account some months previously and this stood me in good stead when the travel allowance in the UK was still at a premium. A 'half-day' at Le Relais lasted from 8.00pm until 8.00am the following morning, as Madame Lenoir graciously undertook to do the breakfasts on these days. Perhaps she thought I would indulge in some form of nefarious night life during my time off, but in fact I was often so exhausted that all I could do was to slump on my bed and rest my aching feet.

I did have friends in Château d'Oex with whom I spent some time or had the odd meal out. The region abounded in English and American residents and the town itself boasted an internationally known, rather up-market, school run by a very determined lady called Mrs Reed. She was all for involving me in the life of the British community but soon saw that I had neither the time nor the inclination for such a commitment.

There was one very eccentric elderly American lady called Weatherburn who had a chalet half-way up a steep mountainside some way out of the town. I used to visit her occasionally since I found her entertaining, as well as being an imaginative although rather slapdash cook who concocted delicious meals for me. Her past was difficult to piece together, since her reminiscences conflicted now and again and I suspect that sometimes fact and fiction became confused in her mind. She had travelled extensively to remote outposts of the globe, producing sepia-coloured snapshots to prove that this was indeed fact, referred briefly *en passant* to a husband and hinted obscurely to an oriental lover of royal birth. Her appearance alarmed at first sight as she was very tall and angular with piercing grey eyes and large yellow teeth that were frequently bared when emitting a high cackling neigh. To reach her eyrie I used to take a bus to the foot of her mountain and, with the help of snowshoes loaned to me by Madame Schwab, trudge upwards through a wooded track to her domain. However much I protested she insisted in bringing me home by sledge – a terrifying but exhilarating experience. She revelled in speed and had an uncanny but unnerving knack of avoiding trees by a split second and on one occasion a snow plough, by inches – but we never came to actual grief.

On one visit I had taken my knitting with me, as my hostess had expressed a wish to see the rather intricate pattern I was engaged upon. It was to be a jersey and although I am no great knitter I was quite pleased with my efforts to date and was half way through the first side. On our return journey we set off as usual, both well wrapped up in sheepskin coats, myself in the rear position, clasping Mrs Weatherburn's large frame round the middle. My knitting was in a bag slung over my shoulder and from the start I had a niggling doubt that all was not quite as it should be, but had not time to investigate since we were by now travelling at breakneck speed and it took all of my concentration to stay yoked to driver and sledge.

On reaching our destination, I found my worst fears were realised and that my knitted work of art had somehow managed to unravel itself, leaving a trail of blue wool behind us down the mountainside and less than an inch of knitting on my needles.

The Lenoirs had two spoilt little boys called Georgie and Roger, apples of their mother's eye. Part of my duties was to attend to them from time to time when business was slack and to get them up in the morning. Naturally they resented such an intrusion in their lives – and a foreign one at that – and were determined to resist the discipline that I was determined to wield. Many a battle of wits was waged between us, in most of which I was the loser since they only had to go weeping and wailing to *maman* to be consoled with kisses and cakes. "*Vous devrez comprendre, mes chéris*", I would hear her murmur, mopping up their tears, "*elle est étrangère et ne connait pas nos usages*". Of course this merely made them even more rebellious and my position regarding them more tenuous.

Their father, Monsieur Lenoir, was a good looking young man and a pastry cook of real distinction, so Le Relais was very popular and nearly always busy. Light meals were served all day – of the omelette and *croque monsieur* variety, drinks of all kinds, and of course the patisseries for which the establishment was renowned: *mille feuilles*, *bateaux aux marrons*, *tartelettes* of every sort of fruit with the appropriate glazed finish, florentines, *galettes* and – my favourite – *japonnais*, a luscious concoction of macaroon, coffee cream and kirsch, dusted with crushed nuts. Luckily I had neither the time nor the opportunity under Madame's vigilant eye to avail myself of these mouth-watering wares, otherwise I would have regained all the weight I had lost – to my mother's great relief – since I had returned from Italy.

Living over the pharmacy meant at least that I could escape from Georgie and Roger and from the confines of the café premises to my own territory for the short night that remained. My room was small but comfortable and warm, although it could be noisy at times since it overlooked the main street. Soon after I moved there, I remember being awakened in the early hours of the morning by a deafening jangle of bells, urgent cries and the lowing of cattle. Looking out of my window I watched transfixed as a slow-moving mass of cows, goats and sheep progressed ponderously down the cobbled street, the great bronze bells which were attached to the necks of the cows swinging crazily from side to side while the lanterns held by the cowherds and shepherds cast monstrously distorted shadows on the surrounding walls. The barking of excited sheep dogs and the oaths of the men further contributed to the scene of bedlam below. I later learned that this was the ritual bringing down of the herds and flocks from the high mountain pastures to the byres and stables in the lower valleys for the winter months.

Monsieur Schwab, the pharmacist, was a cold fish, withdrawn and unsociable, but his wife was one of the beauties of Château d'Oex with shining gold hair tied in a chignon, her slim figure immaculately clothed in a spotless white overall when serving behind the counter. Gossip related that she was engaged in a turgid and not always discreet affair with the elder son of the Singer family, wealthy Americans who had made their money from the manufacture of sewing machines and who owned a chalet in the vicinity. David, the younger son, became a friend of mine since he was a frequent visitor to Le Relais, where he consumed vast quantities of cake and hot chocolate while keeping me *au fait* with the latest family and local gossip. The Lenoirs welcomed his visits as he spent much money and I did likewise as he was a generous tipper. He was sometimes accompanied by a girlfriend, Phyllis Hardinge, whom I also got to know well. On my very rare days off I used to go with them both on excursions to Montreux or Gruyère – and before my return to England, Phyllis and I spent a short skiing holiday in Gstaad, which proved more successful than my debut with the Lovat Scouts a few years previously.

Ten

I returned to England in March of 1948, having learned certain functions of the hotel world although admittedly in the lower, rather than the upper echelons of the trade. I still had a certain hankering to pursue this line of country, but after a few months back in London my hankerings became more and more half-hearted. I had sampled the life of plenty in Switzerland, so it was quite a shock to find Britain still in the grip of strict rationing and ersatz food. It was difficult to obtain a hotel or restaurant license necessary to establish such a project and even more difficult to procure a liquor license in order to run a bar which, after all, brought in most of the profit. I was also aware that, in order to manage a hotel, it was necessary to be on the spot and I had had enough of living-in jobs for the time being.

The Scotts took me back into their family circle when I first returned to London, but by this time Margery Scott and I were considering sharing a flat together. In the meantime I found myself a job as cook/manageress of the London Tea Centre, a company whose main function was to promote interest in tea by running a combination of museum and restaurant, the chief ingredient of both being tea. It was a job particularly ill-suited to me as I am a coffee manic and dislike tea intensely – and that beverage alone in all its myriad varieties was served at the Centre. Next door to the Tea Centre in Lower Regent Street was the Hungaria Restaurant, which was then in the process of being partially gutted and rebuilt. This resulted in a plague of rats moving from their hitherto undisturbed habitation in the rafters and cellars of the Hungaria to the neighbouring building, which happened to be us.

Outwardly I remained calm as I opened the oven doors each morning to reveal nests of newly born pink ratlets, their scarcely taken breaths to be extinguished almost at once by an emulation of the then much publicised gas chambers. To those around me I seemed unmoved by the sight of a king rat running across the skirting above the sink where I was engaged in washing up and would appear full of aplomb as I toppled it with the broom handle into the suds below. I showed too, a sangfroid to the general public as I ushered two elderly ladies to their seats in the restaurant, ensuring that they were facing in the right direction while keeping a monster rat at bay and distracting their attention with the menu until I had alerted Jack, the storekeeper, to deal with the situation. But my waking hours began to revolve around the rat kingdom and how best to outwit its residents, while my dreams became infused with their exploits and with Pied Piper images in which it was always the rodent who outwitted me. After three months of this I cravenly gave in my notice. Mr Lavender, the manager, not unexpectedly took a dim view of my defection, but cocooned in his office six storeys above the kitchens, I doubt if he had ever come face to face with a rat.

My last foray into the catering world was equally unsatisfactory. Because by this time I knew in my innermost being that I was not destined to be a star in the hotel firmament, I cast around for a part-time job that would give me sufficient time to attend a refresher secretarial course, as all my contemporaries assured me that with typing and shorthand the world was my oyster. So I applied and was accepted for the post of Dining Room Supervisor at the RAF Club in Piccadilly. This entailed a very early start each morning as I had to supervise breakfasts, but the morning shift ended at 1pm when I handed over to my afternoon counterpart. My work was not very arduous. I had to supervise the waitresses, see that the tables were laid up correctly and seat club members as they arrived in the dining room. The trouble was that many of the members had fought a hard war, had been awarded medals for bravery and leadership or had held elevated posts in the Air Ministry. Many of them were now cut down to size but had failed to recognise the fact and their arrogance and lack of courtesy astonished me. One of a pair of twins, for instance, both renowned for their exploits in the air, was terribly rude to one of the waitresses one day because he had to ask for the peppermill twice. Naturally all complaints were laid at my door.

My afternoons were spent at Pitman Secretarial College, where I was by far the oldest member on the course – and was treated with a sort of cheeky deference by my classmates who were, for the most part, school-leavers. Deliverance this time came from Judy Hutchinson, my friend from Caserta days. We met at a party one evening and between the canapés and vodka/tonics I confided to her that I was seeking new horizons, an idea until then I had hardly admitted to myself. Judy suggested that I should apply for a job at Mallett, the well-known antique dealers in Bond Street, where she knew two of the Directors. This I did and despite my rather shaky secretarial qualifications, and thanks to her recommendation, I entered the world of antiques, in which I was to remain for the next ten years.

What a different world it was! Gone were the steamy confines of hotel kitchens and smoke-laden cafés with barked commands of impatient customers. In their place was the rarified air of a Bond Street showroom; discreetly lowered voices using formal nomenclature: "Forward please, Miss Wood"; curved glass windows displaying one or two choice pieces – a unique red lacquer cabinet or amusing pair of carved wood negroes holding aloft a gilt shell; the display augmented by an exquisite flower arrangement titivated twice a week by Alex Church from Constance Spry. The street door opened into the main showroom, thick pile carpets underfoot. My mother told me she had had a strong inclination to genuflect when first she crossed the threshold of these admittedly awe-inspiring premises and I myself experienced a feeling of total inadequacy and insignificance when I reported for work that first day.

It never ceased to amaze me that there was so much money about to spend on the luxuries of life so soon after a world war, but this was an era when "investment in art" was all the rage. It was considered much wiser to put your money into an impressionist painting or a pair of Chippendale chairs, rather than in stocks and shares. And when one compares the prices paid then for such items with what they are worth today, such investments have surely proved a wise move.

Mallett, a family firm, had originated in Bath, where it not only dealt in furniture but in antique jewellery and silver. The company moved to London, where it rapidly established a reputation for the sale of high quality 18th century furniture, objets d'art, needlework and painted glass pictures and fine lamps. At the time I joined the firm, the managing director was Stanley Goodland, an elderly man of the Old School, invariably courteous to those around him and highly regarded in the antique trade. Not long after my arrival he retired, to be replaced by a much younger man who had been with the firm since the end of the war. Francis Egerton was an old Etonian, had been decorated in the war fighting with the Welsh Guards and had been passionately interested in antiques since a schoolboy. He and two colleagues of similar background, Elydr Williams and Rupert de Zoete, presented a united but somewhat arrogant front to the rather mixed fraternity that constituted this particular trade. These three, together with a rougher diamond called Roberts, and the one woman director, Sybil Tutton, daughter of one of the original members of the firm, comprised the 'higher echelon' so to speak.

On a lower level came the secretaries: myself and three others – Joanna Sampson, Penelope Clay and Miss Fisher. We were forbidden to call ourselves by our Christian names in public, good friends though we were to become. This taboo we considered rather partisan in view of the fact that the higher echelon had not such restrictions in the usage of the rather effete nomenclature of Francis, Elydr and Rupert. I was appointed secretary to Francis Egerton and positioned in the front showroom – the word 'shop' was considered infra dig – my 'counter' being behind a sort of wrought iron railing. As I was nearest to the front entrance it was my task to act as butler and greet clients as they came in before passing them on to more knowledgeable beings.

BACK TO THE REAL WORLD 129

Shortly after I joined the firm, when Stanley Goodland was still in residence, I was given the job of cataloguing a collection of snuffboxes and bonbonnières belonging to a customer. I was seated behind my 'grid', the boxes spread out around me and so busily engrossed was I with my work that I did not at first notice a long dark limousine gliding up to the front door. Out of this stepped Queen Mary who, as I was quick to learn, very rarely heralded her arrival in advance. Mr. Goodland, who had met her on several occasions previously, was duly alerted and as he passed me on his way to greet Her Royal Highness, gestured at the china and muttered "put them away or she might wish to acquire them".

During her visits to No.40, Queen Mary not only enjoyed a conducted tour of the galleries but liked to see what was going on in less hallowed quarters, and discovering the parcel room would carry on an animated discussion with Carpenter, our Foreman, on the merits of string as opposed to sealing wax.

Below stairs in the basement was the porters' domain, presided over by the said Carpenter. Every item that came into the firm was entered into the stock book with purchase price, cost of repairs if required, and selling price. A ticket was then affixed to the article with similar information, the cost price being in code. Some years after I left Mallett, I caused some consternation amongst the young men (unknown to me) on duty on Mallett's stand at the Antique Dealers' Fair at Grosvenor House, by remonstrating (in fun) over the disproportionate profit they were making on a particularly fine bureau-cabinet and quoting them the cost and sale prices, the code having remained unchanged since my departure.

I was eventually put in charge of the stockbooks, a responsible enough job since every single article had to be accounted for at the twice yearly stocktaking. One would think it difficult enough to lose track of a mammoth sized double-fronted bookcase but it was a common practice to send items out on approval, not to mention to the various cabinet makers and workshops where repairs were carried out. The practice of sending out goods on approval was a fair enough arrangement, which often paid dividends, but sometimes the reverse. On one occasion, a client asked for a set of 12 dining chairs to be sent to her Belgravia address to see how they would look round her dining table. The chairs were duly despatched and after forty-eight hours returned as being "not quite suitable". On inspection the seat covers were found to be liberally bespattered with gravy stains and other tell-tale residue of a five course dinner party at which the chairs had obviously played an important part. A not insubstantial invoice was forthwith sent to the culprit for the recovering of 12 chairs, which she paid without demur. It was at least cheaper than investing in a set of antique dining chairs at several thousand pounds.

Carpenter and I carried out these stocktakings together. He lived in a flat above the premises with his diminutive but managing wife, and their daughter. Carpenter had been with the firm for many years and was by my time beginning to be a bit stooped and grizzled. Both his movements and thoughts were unhurried and deliberate, but his integrity and loyalty were beyond question. Mrs Carpenter's chief grumble was that her husband was not getting the praise or recognition he deserved.

However, despite her shrewishness, she always treated me with friendliness and kindness. On the evenings when we worked after office hours trying to trace a missing snuffbox (finally located in a drawer) or account for thirty yards of gold damask, she would serve us with continual trays of coffee and home-baked cakes.

The stockbook itself was an enormous tome, buff coloured suede with a rich-looking spine. I lugged this 'bible' home with me twice a year in order to total up the stock figures in peace – no computers or calculators alas! in those days. On one such occasion, I was puzzled to find that the purchase price totalled more than the selling price, until I discovered that an over-zealous boyfriend who was helping me had also added in the date column at the top of every page, it still being in the days of pounds, shillings and pence.

The porters were a cheerful lot and fetched and carried with a will. The firm's van, an impressive maroon coloured vehicle, was manned by Bert the driver and his henchman Rance. For me, one of the joys of working amongst antiques was the sight and handling of the variety of woods that passed through our hands. Tables or chests of faded to rich honey-coloured walnut with oyster-shell design or intricate figuring; the mottled grain of burr woods with their lovely veneers; the infinite shades of mahogany ranging from rich chestnut to a smoky brown; the streaky sworls of rosewood and plum-pudding look of holly wood; and the silk-like texture of satinwood with delicately contrived designs depicting honeysuckle, urns and paterae etc. I was caught out one day when negotiating the sale of such a satinwood table. My client was American and was in raptures over the piece and eventually decided to have it. "I think you've made a wonderful choice," I enthused. "Those peacock feathers round the border are so original and lovely." "Peacock feathers?", exclaimed my client in horrified tones. "I couldn't possibly have anything to do with peacock feathers in my house. They are so unlucky." I learnt to keep my mouth shut after that.

All the stock on view in the showrooms was kept in pristine condition by Mabel, who every day would assiduously polish and dust each piece, enhancing their lustre and patina with tender loving care and elbow grease. In her green overall, Mabel was a self-effacing figure, speaking only if spoken to, although it was said amongst the porters that in private life she was a *femme fatale* with several children, parentage unknown.

I liked to think that some of the polish and refinement, which were the hallmarks of those exquisite pieces of furniture, might rub off on those handling them – and that during my ten years in Bond Street, I might have acquired some of the poise and confidence that my mother had hoped to see in my teens. "Hazel was a late developer", she was fond of telling her friends, although the fact that I might have been a late developer in the art of pickpocketing never seems to have occurred to her.

There was a constant coming and going of the famous and rich, as well as the less famous but equally rich. A couple came in one day, insignificant in appearance and hesitant in manner and were relegated to me, as they were deemed of insufficient importance to merit attention from a higher source. They told me they had been given short shrift from a well-known dealer across the road whose staff were rude and off-hand and that they were looking for dining room furniture. After forty minutes they had bought a three-pedestal dining table and eight chairs, a wine-cooler and urn-shaped knife box. It transpired they had enjoyed a substantial football pools win a few months previously and were able to indulge their, until then, unrequited love of antique furniture. "You can't judge by appearances", said Francis Egerton wisely after the event, but in fact we often did.

Apart from HM Queen Mary, the Royal Family were not avid collectors as far as we were concerned, although Queen Elizabeth (later the Queen Mother) came in from time to time, usually with a lady-in-waiting or with Sir Arthur Penn, her Private Secretary. Sir Arthur, normally clad in a cloak which gave him a romantic air, was a dear man with a schoolboy humour. "Trust it won't bounce!", he would chortle as he wrote out a cheque for several hundred pounds for a Chippendale mirror. "Don't know what the Treasury will say to this extravagance."

One evening, when I was grappling with the stock books after everyone else had gone home and the shop had officially closed, there was an imperious rap on the door. On going to investigate, I found the Duchess of Windsor standing impatiently on the threshold. Sweeping aside my protestations that there was no one present apart from myself, the showrooms being closed, she insisted on coming in and proceeded to make an extensive tour of the premises, although it became abundantly clear that she was 'looking' rather than 'buying'. She was polite and friendly and immaculately turned out. It was my guess that she was early for another appointment in the vicinity and was putting in time. The Duke of Windsor came in some days later and Francis Egerton always maintains that I corrected his pronunciation when taking down his address in Paris. I refute this, although his French accent was indeed execrable.

As my knowledge increased so did my clientele and I was also allowed to bid occasionally at auctions. There were crossed lines on one occasion when two of us were despatched to bid for the same lot at Sotheby's next door, unbeknown to the other. Half way through the bidding, when the price was not surprisingly rising rapidly, I was transfixed by the sight of a young colleague waving his catalogue at the auctioneer, oblivious of my doing the same on the other side of the room. The piece was finally knocked down to us but at a somewhat elevated price.

We not only supplied owners of houses – and considerable mansions at that – with furniture, but worked in close co-operation with leading interior decorators over the furnishing of their clients' houses and had close connections also with many wholesale textile firms and specialised craftsmen and craftswomen. There was a French Madame who did unimaginably fine repairs to antique needlework; Mr Baxby, an expert in 'drag' technique, then almost unheard of in wall decoration; ormolu and gesso restorers, specialists in clock repairs; and Miss Stevenson, who carried on a flourishing business of pearl-stringing, many of her clients being of royal blood. Then there were our own cabinet makers up the road, skilled in the art of replacing veneers and resurfacing damaged table tops, as well as Mr Polak, a wizard at picture framing, with impeccable taste.

Each June we took a stand at the Antique Dealers' Fair at Grosvenor House, which we all took turns in manning. I rather enjoyed these interludes, although after the first two days, business was usually fairly slack and the atmosphere close. However, it gave one a good opportunity to view works of art of great quality and learn much from so doing. There was a certain camaraderie amongst the dealers, some of whom I got to know quite well. The directors of Mallett in my day were a privileged trio inclined to keep themselves to themselves, but expert in the knowledge of the goods they were handling. They were not keen on fraternising with fellow members in the trade except on business, some of whom resented their air of superiority while respecting their reputation.

I suppose it was a pampered world that I found myself, in catering for the rich, but it was an extremely enjoyable one. After my arduous life in second-grade hotels, I found it supremely satisfying to work with a firm of high repute. It was also aesthetically agreeable to be surrounded by beautiful objects. Culture had not played much of a part in my life before this, but now I began to appreciate the vast opportunities that London offered in the way of museums, art exhibitions, auction rooms, galleries and architecture.

With experience, I gradually acquired my own personal clients, who found me less awe-inspiring than my superiors, and some of whom were to become good friends. Amongst them was a shy retired Brigadier who became a regular visitor. Francis always maintained he came to see me, rather than for his interest in 18th century furniture. Whatever the reason, he began buying a chair each time he called, which invoked Francis's remark "What an expensive wooing, Miss Wood. I hope you give him something in return". Apart from buying chairs, he used to take me to the ballet, followed by dinner at the Savoy Grill – an unchanging pattern over many months until an old childhood friend came into his life, whereupon he deserted me to marry her and the sales of chairs at Mallett declined considerably. Altogether I made many friends in those years and learnt a great deal about human nature, as well as furniture. I learnt also that men are bigger gossips than women.

By this time Margery Scott and I had bought a flat together in Sloane Street – infernally noisy and up a great many stairs – but it was very central, had character and was the first home of our own that each of us had possessed. At the back it looked on to a fire escape, up which I grew honeysuckle and morning glory, and planted herbs in pots that would have precluded any quick escape in the event of fire. A stove in the sitting room burned coal which had to be lugged up from the cellars four floors below. Until we got it alight on winter nights, we used to sit huddled in our overcoats after our return from work but revelling in our independence. The ground floor of our building housed what we guessed to be a brothel, run by two rather chic *mesdames* and their marmalade cat, Jasper. From time to time a breathless and expectant male would knock at our door and ask for Jill or Flo and we would re-direct them back down the three flights of stairs. One day an official called on us to take details for a census. As he was leaving, he asked us if we could give him any information concerning the ground floor flat. "I've knocked and rung several times", he said, "but can't get any satisfaction". "That is most unusual!", Margery and I cried in unison. Not long after, a Black Maria came and removed our two friends. I never discovered what happened to Jasper, but as we did not see him around, guess he might have done time as well.

Immediately below us on the ground floor, giving on to Sloane Street, was a successful restaurant called the Golden Bud. It was run by two powerful ladies and catered for lunches only. Over the weekend piles of garbage were piled below the well of our lift shaft – the lift itself no longer being in use – and the stench was sometimes overwhelming. On one very hot summer's day the smell was worse than usual and I was convinced a body had fallen down the well and was rotting below. As the smell increased in power, so did our alarm increase and eventually we called the police. After some delay we were visited by a phlegmatic constable to whom we confided our fears. He stood over the lift shaft and took a long deep breath, expelling it slowly to say in a strong Scottish accent "ladies, that's no corpse".

Margery had been working for some years with MI5, or the Ministry of Defence, as it is more discreetly called today. For years she had been in love with the painter and sculptor John Skeaping, first married to Barbara Hepworth and secondly to Morwenna Ward, breeder of poodles in Devon. There had never really been anyone else in Margery's life apart from a turgid siege from an Italian admirer, but she recognised John for what he was – an incurable womaniser, loaded with charm and exceedingly talented. He was in and out of the flat all the time, frequently bringing with him a pupil of his, a pretty young ingénue called Bridget Wreford, later to be married to David Astor. It was John who introduced Margery to Katharine Dunham, celebrated American anthropologist and Director of the Katharine Dunham Dance Company, with an idea that Margery could become stage manager to the company and assistant to Katharine.

At that particular time, I think perhaps John had too many involvements in his life to contemplate a further one by marrying Margery, of whom he had always been deeply fond. In any event, forever a creature of impulse, and encouraged by John, Margery found herself packing her bags and roaming the world with the Dunham Troupe for the next seven years, a role she rarely regretted, and becoming a life-long friend of the remarkable Dunham. She was eventually to have her hopes fulfilled, and in 1969 became the third wife of John, with whom she lived in France for supremely happy years until his death from cancer in 1980. She continued to live at Le Moulin de la Taillade at Castries, in the Hérault, where I had many happy visits, until her own death in 2005.

Her departure with Dunham left me holding the baby, in this instance the baby being Biddy Wreford, who was bequeathed to me more or less as a legacy by John and Margery between them.

Outwardly meek in manner, I once referred to her in John's presence as reminding me of a little mouse. "She may be a little mouse", he replied, "but a mouse that knows what's what". It must have been rather irksome for her to share a flat with someone a good deal older and a comparative stranger at that. She was certainly no trouble to cook for, as I seem to remember she was quite happy eating boiled cabbage. This legacy was wrested from me by David Astor, who began to ask her out every Tuesday and eventually married her, *deuxième noce*, and only re-entered my life briefly some fifty-odd years later.

I was now able to choose my own flat companion, also a friend of Margery's as they worked together in MI5. Jean Findlater worked for Guy Liddle, the Deputy Head of MI5, later to be branded as a traitor by Richard Deacon in his book 'The Greatest Treason'. Guy became a frequent visitor to the flat, as did his much loved daughter, who died tragically young from Hodgson's Disease. Guy reminded me always of a benevolent dormouse with a sleepy air and an infectious sense of the ridiculous, the latter shared by Jean herself. I always felt that John le Carré had Guy in mind when creating the character of Smiley in 'Smiley's People'. He became a good friend and, although who am I to say I knew the workings of his mind, nothing will convince me that he could have betrayed his country. We shared a love of early English pottery and one day each left a bid at Sotheby's, unbeknown to the other, for a Whieldon tankard. He was successful in his bidding and later learnt that I had been bidding against him. He left me the tankard in his will, so villain or not, I shall always regard him as a dear and kind man.

Jean became a close friend for many years. Never by word or sign did she ever hint at what her work signified and only long afterward, when all had been made public, did I learn she had been engrossed in the Kramer affair as well as *au fait* with the Burgess/MacLean saga. She was striking in appearance with very blue eyes – and had a keen sense of humour. Unfortunately during the latter years that we shared a flat she suffered from fierce moods, only being diagnosed much later as being caused by pernicious anaemia. Her illness was only spotted by chance during a weekend at home in Tenterden when, posting a letter before putting on her make-up, her doctor – who had known the family for years – passed her in his car and was so appalled at her colour that he ordered her to his surgery there and then.

Fortunately she got on very well with my parents, although their first meeting at the flat was not very auspicious. They had come down from Scotland bearing a dozen fresh eggs, which were still like gold dust, and had laid them down on a table in the hall. Jean, in her responsive way and eager to make a good impression, advanced with outstretched hand and welcoming smile. Unfortunately the sleeve of her jacket caught on the edge of the table, sweeping box and eggs to the floor. Luckily we all saw the funny side of it and dissolved in somewhat hysterical laughter.

Although I much enjoyed my time at Mallett and learnt much about antiques and even more about human nature, I was the first to recognise that unless one had a certain flair and inborn instinct to distinguish the genuine article from a good fake, there was never the possibility of rising much higher in the trade. I lacked these attributes and in some undefined way I was still yearning for wider horizons, so when in 1958 my parents offered me the opportunity to accompany them to South Africa, where my father had business to attend to, and where my role would be secretary, chauffeuse and general factotum, I accepted without hesitation.

Eleven

Some months previously I had been introduced by a friend to a so-called Austrian Countess who professed to cast horoscopes, and who in fact taught me the rudiments of the art of astrology. She offered to cast my horoscope and although I was born with the Sun in Venus, she also told me with some satisfaction that I had the worst sign in the zodiac, viz. the Moon in Scorpio. She never did divulge, however hard I pressed her, what dire fates I might have to undergo in future years and many decades later I am still waiting for this warning to manifest itself. However she did exclaim from time to time as the horoscope unfolded, "Movement, for ever movement"! and "I see the Eiffel Tower", (not difficult, I had already spent some time in Paris); "Here is desert sand, surely the Sahara Desert" (to my somewhat cynical mind, the beach at North Berwick was a more likely supposition); "Always packing, unpacking – so many suitcases; you will travel, travel, travel the world". As I was at that time still working at Mallett on a strictly 9-5 basis, I took this prognosis with a fairly large pinch of salt. However with the prospect of South African horizons opening up before me, dared I hope perhaps that this was to be the forerunner of the Countess's forecast?

Ships were still the most popular form of transport to and from South Africa in the late fifties, and it was in the Capetown Castle that my father, mother and myself set sail from Southampton in November 1958, a liner of 27,000 tons, owned by British & Commonwealth Shipping (formerly Union Castle).

There is a thrill about boarding a ship that cannot be matched by embarking on other forms of transport, except perhaps by an overnight journey on the original Orient Express. None of the frustrations of arriving at an airport, searching for a non-existent trolley, standing in line, inching one's way towards the check-in counter, before walking down seemingly endless corridors to the embarkation lounge and then making a wild and undignified dash across the tarmac to ensure a seat to one's liking (this prior to the introduction of seat allocation). Or, apart from the likes of the Orient Express, lurching along station platforms devoid of porters or luggage carts, before heaving heavy suitcases into luggage racks only to have them buried by mounds of other people's clobber, necessitating feverish activity at the point of destination.

True, on this occasion we began our travels with the train journey from Waterloo to Southampton, but there on the platform were uniformed porters waiting to whisk our luggage into the guard's van and further uniformed officials hovering to show us to our reserved seats. The train drew up in Southampton alongside the quay at which the Capetown Castle was anchored. Hosts of willing hands vied for – imagine! – the privilege of carrying our luggage – mounds of it – as I for one was to be away for the best part of six months and travelling light was not so easy as it is today.

As my mother and I were rather poor sailors and my father did not know the meaning of sea-sickness, it had been decided that the two females would share a cabin, so that we could heave in harmony should the need arise, leaving my father to make encouraging noises from the adjoining cabin or, as was more likely, enjoy his freedom on the upper decks. On that drab November afternoon, our cabin was awash with flowers sent by well-wishers, while a tray laid with a bottle of Veuve Clicquot and three glasses, invited us to drink to our departure. With the drawing up of the gangplank, it was as if I had finally ended a phase in my life. I turned my face towards Africa with the anticipation that has heralded almost every journey I have made ever since, and which was to become so much a part of my life over the next three decades.

At that time, although by no means in my first youth, having recently celebrated my thirty-eighth birthday, I was a totally inexperienced traveller, apart from a year's schooling in Paris, eighteen months in Italy at the British Army's expense and, more recently a few European sojourns by the cheapest means possible, so for me the comparative luxury of the Capetown Castle filled me with delight. The interior had been decorated by Jean Monro of Mrs Monro Ltd. Jean, whom I had first encountered during the war when I was a hesitant newly-fledged junior officer in the ATS and she a rebellious cadet, and later on more equal terms during my Mallett days, was to become a good and life-long friend. She had met Bernard Cayzer, a director of the shipping line, in Montego Bay some years earlier and had been helping him with the décor of his London house. In fact both Jean and Bernard Cayzer were to be at the Mount Nelson Hotel when we arrived there as guests, as Jean also was having a hand in the redecoration of the hotel.

On board we had cosily furnished cabins with portholes giving a view on to the mercifully, so far, placid sea. In the opulently furnished dining room, we shared a table with friends of my parents, Mr and Mrs Andrew McCosh, a delightful pair from Biggar, some twenty miles distance from Edinburgh where my parents still lived. Mrs McCosh, always conservatively but impeccably dressed, disguised behind a demure façade a quizzical eye and gently caustic tongue. Her husband, tall and angular, was courteous to all, with a dry humour which missed little.

Of my parents I have had more to say elsewhere. Suffice to mention here that my mother continued to embrace life enthusiastically. She was a great enjoyer of events, however trivial, and liked nothing more than to observe human nature.

As I have said earlier, my father was a more complex character. He was very gregarious and loved to strike up conversations with no matter whom, again to the discomfort of his self-conscious daughter. He had a quick wit and was a good conversationalist but he could also sulk for hours if he thought himself misjudged, which did not make him too easy a man to live with. However he was at his best with company outside the family so our meals on board were usually agreeable affairs. A drawback, to me, at any rate was the endlessly long menu offered at every meal, although both wives marvelled at the fact that their respective husbands, who scorned such fare at home, disposed of large helpings of diplomat's pudding or treacle sponge with every evidence of enjoyment.

Days took the usual routine form of life at sea – from guessing the ship's daily mileage to every form of sport and entertainment, as well as a library catering for all tastes, that saw me rather more often than the former. I did become the heroine of the ship in one respect, however. Several of us hanging over the rails at Southampton were intrigued by the sight of two middle-aged females striding up the gangplank, each of them carrying aloft what appeared to be a bunch of ping pong bats. It later transpired that these two sisters, as they turned out to be, were regular travellers on the shipping line and had hitherto always met in the finals of the ship's Table Tennis Championship, which was invariably won by one or other of them. I rather fancied myself at the more humble name of ping pong and this was a challenge I couldn't resist. Egged on by my family and some newfound friends, I went into secret training (with the ship's equipment and various members of the crew) and eventually defeated first one sister and then the other to general satisfaction all round, but to the discomfiture of the vanquished pair, who were in fact a rather disagreeable couple.

We made only one stop en route for South Africa, which was at Las Palmas, where my main recollection is of the vulgarity and crudity of the goods offered on sale from the quayside: ringleted dolls, pink plush teddy bears, the usual mish-mash of carved beads, trinkets and decorated boxes. We managed, however, to disembark for an hour or two and on our way back to the ship were fortunate enough to view the Pendennis Castle, sister ship to our own, making her majestic way on her maiden voyage to Cape Town.

Mercifully for my mother and me, the weather held good for our voyage and a fortnight after leaving Southampton we docked at Cape Town. I struggled on board at dawn in the hope of viewing Table Mountain, but this renowned landmark was shrouded in mist, only coyly emerging some hours later, its dark mass startlingly outlined against a sky of unbelievable blue, unblemished by cloud. My memory of each succeeding day was one of unbroken sunshine, which threw into stark relief the exuberant colours of foliage and vegetation which were to be the background of our journeyings. The clarity of light which silhouetted the shockingly vivid scarlet of the flame trees and vivid yellow of the cassias in bloom was almost painful in its intensity.

The Mount Nelson Hotel, to my uninitiated eye and even before its facelift by Jean Monro, was everything a hotel should be: slightly faded and shabby; friendly staff, most of them elderly, rather grizzled gentlemen, slow of movement and sometimes forgetful of our orders, but invariably courteous and well-disposed to us. Our rooms looked out on a garden ablaze with flowering shrubs, tended by more elderly gardeners moving at an equally relaxed pace. Well-tended lawns were overlooked by terraces furnished with awnings and cane furniture, a haven of rest in the midday heat on the rare occasions when one was not out and about. The food, it is true, was not much to write home about, but apart from breakfast, which was garnished with great baskets of fruit, we were out for most meals, my father having an abundance of friends and business acquaintances in the vicinity. While my father attended meetings, bringing home notes and letters for me to type on my portable typewriter, my mother and I were driven out to Hermanus and Stellenbosch to visit friends in their Dutch Colonial-style homesteads, where we would lunch on their patios, drink their own wines and exult in the summer sunshine.

We travelled too at times by train, an experience I revelled in, as it was the perfect way to observe the passing countryside: the reflection thrown from the white glare of desert, the clouds of dust tossed into the air by the lorries thundering along the highway parallel to the tracks; plantations of banana trees, fields of proteas, contorted rock formations stark against the skyline and the dense blue range of the Drakensberg Mountains, which formed a backdrop in the distance. At the various halts, there was a confusion of black bodies clad in pristine white shirts, dense crowds waiting patiently in queues or clamouring for attention at work distribution offices. Always a kaleidoscope of colour and sunshine, always sunshine, highlighting the shadows cast on the baking earth. Then there was the overnight journey in the famous Blue Train from Cape Town to Johannesburg. During daylight hours one could sit in the observation car and watch the world go by, but when night fell, there was a romanticism in being cocooned in one's sleeping compartment, mesmerised by the lights of passing trains and the muted lamps at stations which glided by in the darkness, and lulled to sleep by the intermittent blasts on the train's siren, and hiss of steam from its engines.

As expected, I found Cape Town and Johannesburg to be cities of contrast. The latter was huge and brash, vital and noisy, dominated by the Witwatersrand, a streaky semicircle of greenish-gold and white, the residue of worked goldfields stretching across the horizon, surmounted by humped mine dumps and cooling towers. The city's congested streets were overshadowed by soaring tower blocks throbbing with the frenetic hum of businesses dealing in gold, diamonds, finance and newspapers. More meals were taken with kind friends, while my father battled with more meetings, and one particularly enjoyable dinner at one of Johannesburg's most prestigious country clubs.

From Johannesburg we flew to Salisbury (now Harare) in Southern Rhodesia (now Zimbabwe). At that time the first stage of the Kariba Dam was nearing completion, under the supervision of Duncan Anderson, a dour Scot who, with his delightful wife Sally, showed us much hospitality at their home, as well as conducting us round the works in progress – an impressive and daunting project. In Salisbury we stayed at one of the city's most luxurious hotels where my mother was grievously bitten by an unidentified bug in her bed, which so mortified the charming resident head housekeeper that we were treated as royalty for the remainder of our stay – afraid of reprisals, no doubt, against the hotel! My mother's leg swelled to such dimensions that she was forced to buy and wear a pair of fleece-lined boots that looked distinctly odd below her summer dresses. Luckily, after some treatment at the city's casualty centre, her leg returned to normal and her feet to less distinctive footwear. Naturally we were honour bound to include in our itinerary a visit to the Victoria Falls. To stand, half deafened, beside those thundering untrammelled torrents was to render the viewer puny and of no account.

Flying back to Durban we hired a car, with me as chauffeur, to take us back to Cape Town via the Garden Route. Our vehicle was not in its first youth, judging from appearances, and was reluctant to go much over forty miles an hour, which suited me. We managed well enough except for one occasion when we ran out of petrol late one afternoon in the Transkei – due, I hasten to add, to a faulty petrol gauge rather than mismanagement on the driver's part. We were on our way to Port Elizabeth, where we had planned to stay the night: miles from any town on a dusty, unshaded road destitute of any form of humanity, in the heat of a summer afternoon. My mother, surprisingly philosophical on such occasions, simply unearthed her knitting from the recesses of her valise and continued to ply her pearl and plain with commendable imperturbability until such time as help would appear on the horizon. My father disappeared to relieve himself while I waited by the side of the car looking suitably helpless and expectant. Help eventually came in the form of a clapped out looking truck whose bearded driver stopped to offer assistance. On hearing of our plight he manfully proceeded to siphon by mouth sufficient petrol from the truck's tank into our own tank to enable us to reach the nearest petrol station, which thankfully for him, and for us, was not far down the road. He refused all offer of payment but accepted with gratitude an acid drop proffered by my mother who was alarmed at the thought that he might light himself a cigarette and go up in flames before our eyes.

One of the joys of travelling by car is that you can stop as the whim seizes you: to photograph, albeit discreetly, native women bearing baskets of fruit on their turbaned heads, their lithe bodies clad in coloured robes, or similarly attired engaged in picking shells from the beaches fringing the numerous little fishing villages we passed through; to follow, through binoculars, the flight of acid green parrots as they flitted between the arsenic green leaves of the banana plantations, or simply to watch the tribes passing by. Many of the main routes were lined with native fruit-sellers, who would beleaguer us with offers of freshly sliced pineapple. Taking a fruit from his heaped basket, the vendor would deftly scoop out the inside, slice it into neat rings that he would replace in the shell before passing the finished article through the car window. Eaten when one was hot and thirsty, such a delicacy was food for the Gods, but to consume such delight was the stickiest of operations and the steering wheel suffered accordingly.

It had been decided that on our return to Cape Town, I would see my parents off on the Pretoria Castle, bound for Southampton, whilst I would depart to the Kruger Park Game Reserve for a few days before joining the Durban Castle at Durban for the return voyage to England via the east coast of Africa. My duties as secretary to my father and general factotum to my parents had been derisory to say the least, and although it was never said, I had the feeling that I had been offered these terms to make it easier for me to leave Mallet. It was a benefaction on their part for which I will be eternally grateful. Although the three of us had survived our journeyings together in complete harmony for most of the time, it was with a certain feeling of emancipation that I cast off the parental yoke and turned my face towards the hills and open spaces of Pretorious Camp.

Game watching in those days was not so fashionable as it is today and it was then possible to view a lioness with her cubs without being joined within seconds by a posse of Range Rovers. To me, my sparsely furnished *rondaavel* was luxury and to sit on the verandah under a limpid sky, soon to be sequinned with stars, while listening to the maniacal laugh of a jackal or snufflings of an unseen beast (the latter eventually driving me inside) was one of the highlights of my South African visit. Later I moved on to the Hluhluwe Game Reserve, rather more sophisticated than some, in the heart of Zululand and renowned for its black and white rhino, both of which I was lucky to see. Here again I found sheer contentment in sitting on my verandah as dusk was falling, inhaling the smell of the veldt and wood smoke from the nearby kitchens. However, as likely as not, my reveries were likely to be interrupted by a visit from the camp's pet baboon, or by the braying of Jenny, the moke, which encouraged me to seek the more convivial company round the fireside in the bar.

As a contrast to the invigorating air of Natal and the Transvaal, I found Durban, where I was to spend my last few nights before embarking, soporific and steamy, but I enjoyed a mildly social round since I had friends there who ran the rather exclusive Durban Club, the facilities of which were put at my disposal. On my last night I was awakened, just as dawn was breaking, by an enormous bang which I could not distinguish at first from being part of a dream or reality. But then I felt the bed sway beneath me and heard later that there had been an earthquake in the vicinity, although mercifully of no great consequence.

The Durban Castle was one of the smaller and older ships of British & Commonwealth Shipping, lacking some of the luxuries of its newer sister ships, but none the less comfortable. Being unaccompanied on board rendered me more vulnerable a prey to the inevitable cruise ship friendships than had I been while travelling with my parents, who were the perfect alibi for protection from the dronings of the ship's bore or amorous advances from the ship's doctor. The bore in this instance was an elderly retired commercial traveller from Glasgow, who dismissed a reference to Greece with a scornful "Och, ye can have Greece, nae but ruins". Equally adhesive were a mother and daughter from Blackpool, who unfortunately I found seated at my table.

The mother was gossipy and keen for me to befriend her daughter, Christine, who was giggly and silly but easily subdued.

We had cargo on board as well as passengers, so our ports of call were many. Lourenço Marques (now Maputo) was our first stop, where I recall hanging over the ship's rail watching the dolphins leaping alongside our bows as we approached harbour. Then came the becalmed lagoon at Dar-es-Salaam in the first light of dawn, its shores fringed with palm trees reflected in the unruffled waters, glutinous as oil. We went ashore there to haggle for fruit in the market, to gaze at the Governor's Palace and to exchange banter with a small scantily clad native boy who was puffing with doubtful enjoyment at a king-size cigar. Zanzibar was our next port of call, its approach heralded by the scent of cloves borne to us on the wind while quite far out at sea, becoming quite overwhelming as we entered the harbour. Once ashore, the town's narrow streets engulfed us, lined with houses decorated with massive doors nail–studded and adorned with heavy brass or bronze knockers.

For some reason now forgotten, we had to anchor at Mombasa for two days. I took the opportunity on the first day to go ashore and explore the old town, with its impressive fort and harbour teeming with craft, and to swim from the glitteringly silver sands of Nyali Beach. The second excursion, this time by car, was to Malindi, whose beach of golden sand stretched unbroken along the coastline to the far horizon. Here, some of us, urged on by the more intrepid swimmers, ventured beyond the high-crested waves to an area of azure tranquillity where we basked and floated before plunging back through the turbulent waters that lurked between us and the safety of the beach. I prayed that a crest of the wave would deposit me there rather than suck me down into churning surf, an experience of ecstasy and pure terror. On our way back to Mombasa we stopped at Gedi, a once thriving Portuguese trading city now engulfed by the jungle, its ruined arches and portals of long-gone buildings shrouded in an entanglement of tenacious creepers, while the roots of flame trees strangled the crumbling walls of the old palace quarters. There was talk of the city being resuscitated and its ruins excavated but I for one would like to leave it to its lost dreams – a Sleeping Beauty of the African coast.

We followed the Indian Ocean into the Gulf of Aden and anchored at Aden itself where the heat embraced us like a clammy glove. I broke out in prickly heat and had to swallow loads of salt pills prescribed by the ship's doctor, who had been more than attentive over the past few days, but who obviously did not find me so alluring in my rash-like state. The pills made me feel sick, so my memories of Aden are not comfortable ones.

I seem to remember a bleakness and aridness overall but this may just have been induced by my poor state of health. For most of the journey through the Red Sea I lay like a stranded cod under awnings on deck or in my cabin – supporting heat has never been my strong point – but by the time we reached Egypt, with the desert stretching limitlessly to our left, I had recovered sufficiently to experience an unexpected awe as we entered the Suez Canal.

While the ship negotiated the Canal, we passengers were transferred to buses that drove us alongside its banks, weaving a way between throngs of Arabs jostling the bus with their baskets of cheap jewellery and ornaments and accompanying interminable cries of "bakshish, bakshish", and oblivious to the bus driver's impatient blasts on the horn and shouted expletives. Caravans of camels passed us going their own disdainful way and panier-laden donkeys were constantly being harried by their owners with hoarse cries, intent on reaching their destination before dark.

By the time we reached Cairo, night was falling. We were given a meal at a hotel – I recall not which, but we must also have passed the night there, as we were out in the bedlam of the city early the next morning. My memories are of noise and confusion, of an inferno of humanity intent on selling you something, however intent you were in refusing it; of handsome bronzed faces above startlingly white robes, contrasting vividly with the dense blackness of the women's dress, their owners' faces heavily veiled. Years later I was to visit Cairo on many occasions and was to become well acquainted with its museums and Coptic quarters. In 1959, with only two hours of liberty, I had time only for the merest glance at the Museum of Antiquities which greeted the visitor with an eruption of electric cables and live wires sprouting from flaking walls, the whole building exuding an air of dustiness and neglect. It was only in those later years that I came to appreciate the outstanding treasures that were housed within these walls. In the white heat of the afternoon we drove across the desert to Alexandria, where the Durban Castle awaited us, prior to leaving for the home stretch through the Mediterranean.

Hugging the North African coastline, we passed tantalisingly close to Tripoli, Tunis, Algiers and into the Straits of Gibraltar, stopping only at Gibraltar where we stepped briefly ashore to ensure that the apes were still in possession of the Rock. There was nothing here to make me wish to linger on these rather uninviting shores and I was glad to be on the move once more. Our last stop before Southampton was Cadiz, where we took on a load of meat as well as a boyfriend of mine, who cabled to say he was boarding the ship at Cadiz in order to spend the last three days of the journey with me. I viewed his arrival with mixed feelings. Having been away for nearly six months, I found I did not want to return to any permanent relationship and the sight of G. bounding up the gangplank with such blatant delight at seeing me again, only instilled in me a sense of guilt that I could not reciprocate his feelings.

We both found Cadiz attractive, with its gardens ablaze with cannas and semi-topical plants, but by now I was ready to exchange the torrid glare of the tropics for the greyer skies of England, and brittle seagoing acquaintances for older friends. My relationship with G. cooled considerably over those last three days and by the time the ship's sirens were heralding the docks at Southampton, our relationship had changed, although we were to remain friends. It was therefore with relief, tinged with sadness and a sense of failure, that I finally disembarked in the rain at Southampton, although I knew by then that travel in one form or another must play a major part in my future life.

Georgians at play

Twelve

As a launch into the world of travel, which was to be my goal for the next thirty years, the telegram was not particularly encouraging, or indeed, flattering. "First choice fallen through STOP job yours at £10 per week beginning soonest STOP wire decision by return." Laconic and brusque, as I had found the sender to be on an interview with him some weeks earlier. Hardly the stuff of dreams, but then I was scarcely in a position to quibble.

Since returning from South Africa some five months previously, I had been in an unsettled state, still intent on widening my horizons. But so far those horizons had only reached as far as the West End of London, where I had been taken on, in a rather shaky partnership, with a newly founded employment agency called Mary Stuart Limited, a husband and wife set up which, I suspect, needed outside financial help rather than my particular presence.

They were both worthy to the point of suffocation, finding me too frivolous when I pleaded a lunch engagement, even when I tried unconvincingly to persuade them that it could lead to the introduction of a client, be it employer or employee. Although I considered myself to be a moderately good judge of character, I was soon to discover that I lacked all aptitude for finding the right applicant for the job in question, or vice versa. After sending a seemingly capable young girl off for an interview with an affable sounding head of a company who had stipulated that efficiency and integrity were of top priority, I would be telephoned by the interviewer who would tell me in indignant tones that Miss S. was quite unsuitable, had no charisma and such an irritating laugh. Likewise a dispirited job-seeker would return for more interviews, having turned down several posts, stating that she could not possibly work with an all-women team, or that her intended office was cheek by jowl with the staff lavatories.

On the other hand, Joanna Sampson, who had worked with me at Mallet and joined me at Mary Stuart, had an instinctive flair for putting a round peg into a round hole, and even sometimes a round peg into a square hole, so persuasive was her manner, both to employer and employee. This talent led to her departure from the Pearce ménage (Mary and Stuart were their Christian names) when she personally took an applicant for an interview with John Millar, founder and owner of Avica Equipment Limited, a firm that specialised in the manufacture of refined aeronautical parts. He turned down the applicant but offered the job to Joanna with the words "You're the girl I want!". She, despite his being in the middle of a divorce, and some thirty years her senior, was so beguiled by him and perhaps by the fact that he owned a property in the south of France and a flat in Monaco, that she accepted his terms and was married to him, off and on, for nearly forty years. He was 103 when he died in 2007.

I had, however, already been given *congé* by the Pearce's, with relief on both our parts I daresay, and had been kicking my heels rather enjoyably for a month at my parents' home in Scotland. True, Mallet had offered me my old job back, which I had declined, partly I suspect because of a perverse pride that kept me from returning to a post I had rather imperiously quit some six months earlier, but more evidently because I was still in search of exploring further fields.

It was Francis Egerton, for whom I had worked at Mallet, who informed me of a job going as general amanuensis to the Honorary Treasurer and former Honorary Secretary of the Georgian Group, a society mainly concerned with the future of 18th century buildings in London, and later throughout the country. At one time it appears that Nancy Mitford had offered to chain herself to the railings in Abingdon Street, as a protest against the intended demolition of a Georgian building. Founded in 1937, the Group's first committee included as chairman the diplomat Lord Derwent, writers Douglas Goldring and Robert Byron, and the architect, Sir Albert Richardson.

I duly had an interview with Angus Acworth, the sender of the telegram, at his London flat in Eaton Square. In a purely honorary capacity, he also organised visits throughout Britain and Europe for members of the Group, so apart from acting as his secretary in connection with the Georgians, I would also be his driver on these excursions. However, in this first instance, I was pipped at the post by a glamorous and delightful lady called Diana Bleecker who was to accompany Angus Acworth and some 30 Georgians on a tour of the Veneto villas. I understand from later sources that Diana's charms had perhaps overruled her secretarial capacities. Whatever the reason, she withdrew, or was withdrawn, from the contest: hence my contemplation of the telegram on that late September afternoon in 1959. I was nearing forty, so time to get going – to wherever that might be. I duly wired back in a suitably succinct manner: "Accept offer STOP thanks STOP See you Monday".

Angus Acworth, CBE, FSA, was a complex character, as most clever men are. He had an unprepossessing manner, being brusque and offhand, brought about perhaps by an innate shyness, but more likely caused by an absentmindedness that excluded people from his immediate awareness when his brain was occupied with, to him, more important matters. His rather ungainly frame was further encumbered by a lame leg due, I believe, to a defective hip joint dating from his youth that caused him almost constant pain, but about which he very rarely complained.

However, if his demeanour was against him, determination, the courage of his own convictions and intellect largely made up for these shortcomings. Oxford saw him take a second class degree in Maths, Mods; a first in Modern History and a B.Litt in Finance and Banking. He was called to the Bar in 1929 but found himself much more attuned to the financial world, becoming Finance Officer at the Ministry of Supply during the Second World War, when he also played an active role in civil defence in his then London Borough of Kensington. After the war he worked unstintingly, with no financial reward, for the Georgian Group, then as it is now, one of the most active pressure groups in the country, bringing influence to bear on Government and local authorities to save from neglect or demolition Georgian buildings or monuments of historic or architectural importance to restore them, wherever possible or desirable, to their former glory. Acworth was, in fact, one of those most involved in the introduction of the "listing" of buildings, which was made official in a clause passed in the Town and Country Planning Act 1944, but only became operative in 1946.

His other great interest was the Leche Trust, a charitable organisation that he had founded and personally funded some years previously. This donated considerable sums of money to charities connected with the arts, architecture and music in particular. In conjunction with the British Council, it also donated grants to students, oblivious of nationality, colour or creed, to enable them to complete their course of studies which, for reasons of hardship, would otherwise have to be curtailed. Beneficiaries included Jacqueline du Pré, for studying under Tortellier in Paris; the foundation of the Beecham Scholarship for young singers; and Richard Gill, who started a puppet theatre in a garage in Westminster, and then transferred it to Wimbledon as the well-known Polka Children's Theatre, opened by Queen Elizabeth the Queen Mother in 1979. In 1946, he was invited by the Colonial Office to prepare a report on the Georgian buildings in the West Indies, which was published by HM Stationery Office. He was later to set up the English Harbour Repair Fund for the restoration of Nelson's harbour in Antigua.

In many ways my employer and I were an ill-assorted pair. I liked meeting new people – he preferred his old friends, few though they might be; I could put up with fools – he could not; I had been brought up to be polite to those in all walks of life, however hypocritical one's feelings – he opted for honesty to the point of rudeness; I could drive – he could not. We did, however, share common interests. We both enjoyed travelling, the poring over of maps, the planning of itineraries and all the research that went into the exploration of an unknown destination. We both appreciated good food and wine and both were reasonably imaginative cooks. We could put up with primitive conditions without fuss should the need arise, although we were not averse to luxurious living if it came our way. His was a meticulous mind that allowed for no shortcuts or sloppiness and, although I found his obsession with detail burdensome at times, this perfectionism in paperwork was to stand me in good stead in the years ahead.

Each year, the Georgian Group organised a number of excursions in the British Isles as well as one, or sometimes two, visits abroad – in order to provoke interest among its members and to swell its coffers in some small measure. My role was to assist Angus in the setting up of the foreign visits, as well as to participate in the day excursions, which were organised by the Georgian Group office staff – at that time Mrs Rowe, Mary Shapland and Gillian Wagner, wife of the future Garter King of Arms.

To ensure the smooth running of these visits, it was Angus's policy to carry out by car a protracted and detailed reconnaissance of the places to be included in the programme – and to persuade, bully or cajole bemused custodians of derelict buildings, National Trust curators or local authorities to allow us to visit outside the usual opening times, as well as owners of private houses to open their doors to a group of thirty or so members. It was important, too, to cover the ground beforehand – if only to safeguard against any pitfalls that might arise on the appointed day: Georgians would not be best pleased if they were to find that their fifty-one-seater coach could not pass through the pillared gates leading to some country estate, necessitating a long walk up a muddy drive, possibly in the rain.

Forty-five years ago it was much more of an innovation for owners of houses to receive parties of strangers into their homes than it is today, when it is fairly normal for a group to be charged a not insignificant amount for a cup of tea and a glimpse of the family's Meissen collection or impressionist paintings. An even more exorbitant fee can also now be asked for provision of a meal – with the crested silver brought out for the occasion and hastily cleaned, usually by the lady of the manor, and help supplied by locals from the village, or perhaps an ageing butler. In those days it never ceased to amaze me that owners were so ready to offer hospitality to groups such as ours, and even seemed gratified at the chance of receiving us, often gratuitously or for a modest sum donated to their favourite charity.

Difficult as it sometimes was to obtain access to certain country mansions, chateaux or palazzi, it was sometimes even harder to extricate ourselves from a commitment when the house or building in question proved to be unworthy of inclusion in the programme. It was not unusual for an impoverished owner of a down-at-heel house to issue an invitation for the group to pay him a visit – in the hope that he could then apply for a tax reduction on the grounds that he opened the said house to the public for so many days in the year. Then, the tactful thing was to decline the invitation on grounds of logistics or lack of time, and refer the building to the Case Department of the Group for its investigation.

My employer worked and lived on the ground floor of No.47 Eaton Square, one of the terraced houses of impressive frontage that faced north on the communal gardens across the road. Although the building was divided into flats, No.47 had its own front door, painted a sober black and embellished with a handsome brass door knocker that was kept glisteningly clean by Angus's housekeeper, Miss Stevenson. The latter, a tight-lipped individual, viewed me with deep suspicion and obviously resented another female entering what she considered to be her domain. Thankfully she took herself off every day at lunchtime, as otherwise the atmosphere was frosty, to say the least.

The interior of the flat was what I might have expected from an elderly man on his own who was more concerned with books and financial matters than with home comforts or embellishments. My office was the sparsely furnished guest room, which to the best of my knowledge during all the eight years spent with Angus, never received a guest. The kitchen, which lacked most modern adornments, was barely large enough to accommodate the two of us when I was pressed to stay for lunch so that Angus could try out one or other of his new culinary ideas on me – usually, I must admit, being rather good. The rather austere dining room featured the only incongruous item in the entire flat. Over the dining table was suspended a hoop on which was perched a gaudy-coloured plastic – or possibly ceramic – parrot, which sometimes swayed in the cooking-scented draught emanating from the kitchen next door and which drew somewhat startled looks from the guests assembled round the table below. I only discovered much later, from his daughter, that it was a present from his son.

These dinner parties, which Angus liked to give every month or so when he was at home, were a sore trial to me. Inevitably I played the role of hostess, usually to guests connected with the arts or academia such as Dame Marie Rambert, Klop Ustinov and Sir John Betjeman – some of whom may have wondered what other role I played in that household, although I could have assured them that my role was strictly professional.

I was sometimes entrusted with a shopping list that usually included modest commodities such as a chump chop or four pork sausages, but he preferred to buy his own vegetables – a handful of potatoes, some onions and carrots which he carried home in a string bag. He was well-known in Elizabeth Street, round the corner from Eaton Square, and an especial favourite of Mr Wood, the butcher, (no relation) who had the bluest eyes of any man I have ever known, bar Desmond Guinness, and had the greatest admiration for Mr Acworth, whom he considered to be "one of the old school".

After I had been working for Angus for about three months, he called me into his office for the day's dictation. "I'm thinking of buying a new car," he announced without preamble. His manner was somewhat defiant, rather as a small boy might put forward a bright idea but is uncertain as to its reception. "Oh good." I spoke encouragingly then, more cautiously, added "What make are you considering?" "I thought we might go this afternoon and have a look at something I have in mind." This time he sounded as coy as a lover suggesting a visit to his mistress. "Not a caravan?" I enquired jocularly, although with thrift coming high on Angus's priorities I would not have ruled the idea out of hand. Think of all the hotel bills saved!

"No, not a caravan." He spoke dismissively and left it at that.

My questioning was far from rhetorical, as I was to be the sole chauffeur of any vehicle my employer chose to buy, since he himself did not drive. So I hoped to be brought into the act and not merely presented with a fait accompli. His current car was a Standard of ancient lineage with an impressive mileage, but so hearse-like in appearance that I expected men to doff their hats as we went on our stately way. Admittedly reliable despite its age, we usually reached our destination without breaking down, but the chassis was cumbersome, the steering unyielding and altogether not a chariot of fire.

We took a taxi to Park Lane. En route I pondered the possibilities. Something in the limousine style with an interior spacious enough to accommodate Angus's stiff leg – the reason he did not drive. We drew up outside a glossy motor showroom whose windows reflected a gleaming chromium opulence. A sleek-haired salesman approached, literally rubbing his hands in anticipation. "Ah, Mr Acworth, good afternoon. Good to see you. I have the car ready for inspection."

Clearly Angus had been engaged in secret homework. We weaved our way between rows of streamlined models, mostly

Mercedes. I was impressed. A car of this standing would give definite status. I hesitated expectantly in front of a likely four door model with roomy interior, leather fauteuil type seats and expansive boot, but the vanguard pushed relentlessly on. We finally stopped in front of a low-slung Mercedes sports car, gun-metal in colour with a collapsible roof and two doors opening on to bucket seats, with the minimum of passenger space behind. The entire elegant line from bonnet to boot spelt speed. My employer's usually impassive face was pink with excitement.

"Well, what do you think?" he cried.

"She's beautiful," I breathed. He looked gratified.

"But will you manage to get in and out?" I asked. Angus frowned. "Perfectly well," he answered tersely. "It's just a matter of practice".

"Perhaps you should start practicing now," I ventured. "Just to make sure you'll feel comfortable for long journeys," I added hastily as he looked increasingly cross. Petulantly he threw me his stick and without more ado applied himself to the job in hand. After some negotiating he was able to lift his bad leg over the door jamb and minutes later to hump himself into a half-lying position against the dark green leather seat. This achieved, he settled back with the happy grin of a satisfied schoolboy. Obviously it was to be a deal.

Secretly I was terrified at the thought of being responsible for this lethal length of loveliness. True, I had driven pretty well everything from three-ton lorries to ambulances and staff cars during the war, but in this instance any damage incurred would not automatically be written off as a war casualty.

I managed to draw the salesman aside, who airily assured me that the car was a dream to drive, the steering light with an excellent lock and acceleration responsive to the merest touch. "And," he added enviously, "imagine the joy of driving such a car on the continent with the hood down!" (his client had obviously been expounding on his future travels abroad). This observation only added to my worries. I am cursed with a complexion which turns brick-red when exposed to sun or wind and am plagued with hair that requires constant entamement. How Angus would manage his scant but blow-away locks when exposed to the elements remained to be seen. These problems were to come. In the meantime I was relieved to hear that the car was to be delivered to Eaton Square. The thought of emerging into the maelstrom of Park Lane traffic unnerved me considerably.

Away from the owner's critical eye I duly put "my new possession" through its paces: hill-starting, reversing in all but its length and testing its acceleration on the open road. The salesman was right. The car was indeed a dream to drive and the effortless ease with which it sailed past lesser vehicles rendered me power-conscious. Only returning to my own Mini-Minor cut me down to size.

Thirteen

The Georgian Group, I believe, was one of the earliest societies of its kind to promote visits both at home (and abroad) for its members, now a commonplace activity for the majority of museums and organisations connected with the arts. Because such visits were novel, the Georgians travelling *en bloc* were inclined to be considered the *crème de la crème* – a sort of 20th century Grand Tourist *en masse* – a view in large part shared by themselves. Indeed, a small minority were apt to forget that they were no longer rulers of an Empire and behaved abroad with an arrogance which I found embarrassing, and the local inhabitants offensive. For the most part, however, my fellow travellers were knowledgeable, interested in what they were seeing, considerate to those in charge and fun to be with, many of them becoming good and lasting friends.

Foreign visits were usually confined to one or two a year. The destination having been decided upon, Angus and I would set off by car for a protracted reconnaissance of the places we hoped to include in the programme.

The ritual of packing up the car prior to leaving Eaton Square, for a journey lasting anything from two or three days to a fortnight, could be a lengthy affair. Although the boot of the car was spacious compared with the backseat passenger accommodation (which was redundant in any case as we never had any), by the time we had packed our suitcases (limited to one each of modest size), several haversacks containing photographic equipment, another couple holding maps and guidebooks, one shooting stick, sundry items of clothing such as jackets, waterproofs and a best suit for formal occasions (encased in a plastic bag topped by a coat hanger), space still had to be left for any likely contraband acquired along the route – such as wine, cooking pots, salami sausages and potent smelling cheeses to be crammed into the picnic basket at our last point of return.

Then there was the installation of the passenger himself in the front seat – a fairly laborious procedure, culminating in his spectacles placed on his nose and the relevant map spread before him. My allotted tasks, apart from driving, were to ensure that the petrol tank was full, to check the mileage, and, if we were to cross the Channel, to have travel tickets and passports at the ready.

We must have presented an incongruous sight setting out from the sequestered precincts of Eaton Square. Only a force nine gale or torrential rain would deter Angus from putting down the convertible hood (actually it was my job to do this single-handed – there were no automatic buttons in those days). So there we sat, exposed to the elements: I with my head bound in a hooded scarf tied securely round my neck and my neighbour with his spare locks secured in a hairnet that somehow emphasised his not insignificant nose.

One thing to be said in his favour was that he was no backseat driver. Each of us had our role: I to drive and he to navigate. He was an admirable map reader but, not being a driver himself, did not always appreciate that directions should be given well in advance and should be announced clearly and briefly. There were moments when, fumbling for the right map page or groping for his magnifying glass, I would have to circumvent a roundabout several times before he decided in which direction he wished to go.

On one occasion in Paris we were approaching the Place de l'Etoile from the Champs Elysées when it became apparent to me that the navigator had lost his place and was dithering. It was equally apparent that no French driver intent on getting to his destination ahead of all others was going to allow a foreigner, much less a female foreigner in a flashy car, to stand in his way. "Which exit do you want me to take?" I hissed tensely, knowing that there was a choice of at least twelve exits open to me. "Let me see," he mumbled as exit after exit loomed up. "Neuilly, I think". "Too late," I snapped having just seen Porte Maillot and Neuilly signposted and unnerved by the ever increasing hooting of horns behind me as I dillied and dallied at each exit. With the sight of a huge camion converging on me, I chickened out and shot down the Avenue Wagram leading to anywhere but Neuilly, before my companion emerged from his map and had time to be cross.

These 'recces' were not, I suspect, undiluted joy for either of us. In England at least, the Georgian Group was recognised as playing a useful role in the preservation and conservation of buildings and Angus himself did command respect on account of his knowledge and intellect. Even so, some of our would-be hosts might have been mildly astonished had they witnessed our arrival at their stately homes.

I recall an occasion in Yorkshire when we had a rendezvous with the titled owners of an impressive 18th century mansion, with a view to seeking permission for a future visit by the Group's members. Driving up to the porticoed front door ("added mid-19th century," muttered Angus), I parked before divesting myself of my headscarf and attending to my wind-swept face. While Angus extricated himself from the car, I went ahead to ring the bell – one of those wrought-iron affairs that set off a prolonged jangling in the nethermost regions of the house. After an interval we were admitted by a wide-eyed maid who handed us over reluctantly to the butler, who greeted us impassively. We followed him across the marbled floor and down a corridor lined with family portraits. I was by then bringing up the rear and it was only as the butler was flinging open the door to the salon, intoning our names, that I realised that Angus was still besporting his hairnet.

"Hairnet Angus," I whispered urgently.

"What?" he asked impatiently.

"Hairnet," I hissed again even more urgently.

He looked at me crossly but took no action to remove the offending article, which remained on his head throughout our visit. I can only suspect that our hosts, who were courtesy itself and graciously gave consent to a visit by members of the Group, were so bemused by the sight of this ill-assorted pair advancing over their Aubusson carpet that they did not quite realise what they were about.

In the early sixties it was possible to put the car on a flight from Lydd to Le Touquet, a painless and rapid way of crossing the Channel, alas! now discontinued. On other occasions we crossed by ferry and boarded an overnight train at either Boulogne or Calais, which conveyed us to Avignon or Nice. At first I was inwardly scared at loading the precious Mercedes on to the train. There were no willing railway officials at that time offering to do this for you and there was only one level, which seemed very high and far from the platform to which one had to descend, hand over fist by means of iron rungs – the whole operation to be carried out in reverse at our destination the next morning.

Sometimes our travels covered several countries, with routes varying from mountain passes with corkscrew bends and precipitous verges, to monotonous stretches of highway in the Lombardy plains or flatlands of the Low Countries. Usually, when exploring a region, we would aim to reach our overnight stop by the late afternoon. Angus would then have his siesta while I, armed with map and guidebook, would be despatched on foot to pinpoint places of interest in the city or surroundings and arrange them in sequence geographically, so that we could both visit them the following day and make copious notes embellished with much photographing. The latter became a thorn in my flesh. I was frequently called upon to act as a screen against the sun or to stand in a certain position to introduce a human element into an architectural background. I then had to record meticulously in a notebook the subject matter, time of day, exposure number and so on. I am not good at walking slowly, my companion could not do otherwise so it sometimes happened that I would be round a corner and heading for the next item on our agenda when a furious bellow would resound behind me, calling me to heel to record the detailed relief on a Renaissance doorway. The end results were, I have to admit, first-class.

Not being a driver himself, my passenger was immune from the concentration and responsibility required in driving on the continent. On one occasion we arrived in Brussels from France, having driven some three hundred miles.

"Angus," I said firmly, "I think I'll have a rest myself before exploring the town."

He looked at me with real surprise. "You can't be tired surely?" he asked. "We've been on the motorway all day."

My nerves somewhat stretched with the strain of ceaseless vigilance on a highway busy with speeding cars and unpredictable lorries, I snapped back: "You shouldn't talk of things you know nothing about".

Often enough we would stop for a picnic lunch, with produce culled from a local market, but Angus enjoyed his food and would think nothing of making a detour of several miles if he discovered from a search through the Michelin guide a restaurant that merited an additional mile or two. After a delicious lunch and several glasses of wine he would have his siesta while we continued on our way, but for the driver – even without wine – it was sometimes an agony to stay awake on a hot summer's afternoon, and at the same time make sure we did not lose our way with the navigator *hors de combat*.

Luckily we both had strong constitutions, but Angus was not always sympathetic with the occasional frailty of others, as I was to discover. Once I awoke with a stomach upset while driving through France. This necessitated constant stops, when I would leap from the car and disappear into the nearest ditch or any cover that presented itself. Apart from looking increasingly impatient, he proffered no words of commiseration and insisted on stopping for lunch at some *auberge* famous for its offal, recounting in details the gastronomic delights that awaited us there. He seemed genuinely astonished and rather disgruntled when, on reaching our goal, I opted to stay in the car and go to sleep.

One point on which we did not see eye to eye was that of tipping. Generous in many ways, he considered tipping a degradation and totally superfluous if the person in question was being paid to do the job. Although largely agreeing with him, he did not realise that many of the staff depended on tips for their livelihood. It was useless to protest as he turned his back with a mumbled word of thanks on a sweating but expectant lackey, who had hauled his luggage along endless corridors. It was usually I who took the coward's way out and delved into my own purse.

Our travels in Europe were not always without drama. One year, we were planning a tour to Austria for the Georgians and on our way to Vienna decided to visit Czechoslovakia to look into the possibility of a future visit to Prague. The country was then under strict Communist rule and there had been much press publicity of late about the fate of Czechs trying to escape across the border in to Austria. Armed with the necessary documents, we approached the frontier – the hood of the car down as usual – to be confronted by two armed guards stationed on a bridge overlooking the road. Their rifles were at the ready and seemed to be trained directly on us. I felt a *frisson* pass up my spine at the thought of our total vulnerability as we prudently stopped within their range, and even the hairnet seemed to stiffen a little in readiness for the over-hasty bullet.

Another guard appeared from the customs building and unsmilingly gestured us both out of the car, requesting me by signs to open the boot. Although it was stuffed to the brim with our luggage and other clobber, I could not stifle an irrational fear that some desperate fugitive might have squeezed himself between our cases unbeknown to ourselves, or was even clinging on like grim death to the underside of the Mercedes. A vision of all three of us being marched off to a firing squad passed briefly through my mind – which was, however, diverted by a curt request to empty the boot. Every item was taken out and examined minutely. We then handed over our documents, which disappeared with the guard into the office.

"Do you think he'd like a piece of chocolate," I enquired of Angus "or would that constitute bribery?"

"A cigarette might be more acceptable."

I did not smoke myself but always carried cigarettes on me, as it sometimes helped to break the ice with certain officials or guardians of buildings. After an interminable wait, with the guns still trained on us, the guard returned with our papers intact and indicated that we could proceed. He ignored the proffered cigarette but took the pack. Angus laughed. "You can pay for the next lot," I muttered crossly. We duly drove off, the chilling gaze of the frontier police following our departure until we were out of sight. We entered Prague as dusk was falling. It had been an October day of exceptional beauty and the wooded countryside through which we drove was aflame with autumn colouring. The golden spires of St Vitus Cathedral were gilded by the setting sun and reflected in the waters of the Vtlava river below.

Prague for me has always been the loveliest of European capitals but in the early sixties the city wore a cloak of drab apathy. I felt embarrassed at being behind the wheel of such an opulent vehicle when, apart from a tank or two and military trucks, there was hardly a civilian car in sight. But the moment we parked in front of our hotel we were surrounded by a large crowd, mostly young, whose uncovetous and ungrudging admiration of this capitalistic symbol, was both touching and sad.

I fell from grace the next day by landing the car in a ditch while driving along a remote country lane. The verges were treacherous and I was, admittedly, admiring the beauties of the countryside rather than concentrating on my driving. By good fortune we were within hailing distance of a couple of hefty farm workers who were engaged in hoeing beet in a nearby field. They were only too happy to down tools and come to the rescue of such a splendid vehicle and its odd-looking occupants. More cigarettes were handed out with a lot of laughter and handshakes. The owner was the one who, quite rightly, was not amused, although there was mercifully not a scratch on his beloved Mercedes.

Another occasion on which I lost face was during an exploratory visit to Yugoslavia. Again we were in a remote region, not so far from Bled, but in totally uninhabited country. The road along which we were driving was obviously under repair but seemed to have been abandoned with the work half done. The verges were strewn with boulders as well as the road itself, and it was quite a feat steering between the obstacles. Crawling along as we were, I inadvertently dislodged a large stone that crashed down in front of us and which I was unable to avoid. The impact was considerable and on looking behind me I could see the ground awash with good viscous British oil that was dripping in a steady flow from the sump, which was obviously cracked. The set expression on my passenger's face ruled out the possibility that he considered it bad luck as opposed to incompetence and I was about to set off on foot for the unknown when, like some fairy-tale pumpkin coach, a lumbering repair van appeared round a bend with winking light and complete with a stout rope and equipment necessary to tow us the twelve miles to Bled.

It turned out that the road was closed to traffic but no sign to tell us so, so I felt to some extent exonerated. Our saviour was a jolly individual who seemed to think it quite normal to find a stranded European car and passengers in the midst of nowhere. The rope was tied firmly to the Mercedes' bumper and we set off on what was a fairly harrowing experience, as the road continued with sundry boulders, untarred sections and hairpin bends. It took all the strength in my arms and total concentration to follow the gyrations of the vehicle in front of me.

Angus, relieved no doubt at not having to spend a night in the wilds of Yugoslavia and having been reassured that the damage could be easily repaired, became quite expansive on our way to salvation. My Serbo-Croat was unfortunately not advanced enough to discover how this miracle rescue operation had come about, but my admiration for the tower, and for the Bled garage mechanics who welded a patch to the sump overnight and had the car ready for the road by 8.30am the next morning, knew no bounds. I might add that the same patch remained in perfect order for as long as the car belonged to Angus.

Fourteen

Returning to London from these 'discovery trips' we would compile the finalised itinerary and advertise the tour in the Georgian Group's news bulletin. Invariably a ballot would have to be held since the number of applicants exceeded the number of places available. This inevitably resulted in bad feeling among those who failed to get a place and who were convinced the ballot was rigged, a conviction not always without foundation, I regret to say.

In the early 1960s, 'package tours' were not so much in evidence as they are today, so in order to suit all pockets, members of the party were given a choice of hotels and were responsible for making their own travel arrangements to the place of rendezvous. The actual technical details were therefore not very arduous and my main role was to give general advice in regard to flights and accommodation. Angus and I would then proceed by car to our place of assembly – be it Rome, Lisbon, Vienna or Fontainebleau – where we would meet up with the rest of the group. The programme would usually open with a reception by some bewildered Mayor or preservation official leading to interminable speeches (with translations) and the drinking of indifferent wine. Each member of the party would be given a very comprehensive booklet of notes compiled by the maestro on the places to be visited and were expected to have done their homework.

At a pre-arranged time each morning we would set off by coach or on foot. There was no waiting for laggards. At the appointed hour the coach left and that was that. So imbued in me was this maxim that it proved my undoing at Vaux-le-Vicomte, the chateau where Fouquet, Finance Minister to Louis XIV, also met his downfall. The time came to leave. I ran a practised eye – as I thought then – over the occupants of the coach. No seat appeared unoccupied. The gravelled *parterre* and levelled lawns laid out before us showed no sign of scurrying Georgian figures. So we left. Some twenty minutes later one of my flock came to the front of the bus to enquire whether I was aware that Miss Cecily Fenwick and Mrs Dent-Brocklehurst were not with us. There was nothing to do but to continue to our next destination where we were awaited. I spent a miserable day in Paris, oblivious to the treasures unfolding before us and dreading my return to Fontainebleau and the wrath of the two ladies involved. It turned out that Miss F. was resigned and forgiving and had spent a happy day on her own. Mrs D-B. never forgave me, more I think for the fact that she had not been missed by any of her fellow passengers for half an hour, than because she had been left behind. It never seemed to occur to either of them that they might have been to blame by not being on time, but it certainly taught me to count my chickens before future departures. Angus, needless to say, washed his hands of the whole affair. It had nothing to do with him.

One year the Georgian Group chartered a boat for its members, The Sea Queen, for a trip through the Adriatic. The captain was a charming but slightly raffish individual who brought aboard his girl-friend, Katie, to look after the catering and generally cherish both her passengers and the skipper. We numbered fourteen in all, apart from the crew, and for some reason sailed under the Panamanian flag, which might have explained the change of direction from time to time when, instead of docking at a scheduled port we would move further down the coast where we would obtain entry – sometimes after prolonged haranguing between captain and customs.

The joy of being on board a small craft was that we could instruct the crew to stop when we felt like it, put the ladder over the side and plunge, or in the majority of cases climb gingerly, into the Adriatic which, far from shore, was translucent and invigorating. Some years later it was the Aleksis Santic that we commandeered for a similar journey. This was a much larger vessel carrying thirty Georgians and not so manoeuvrable as the

Sea Queen. Sometimes we would put into a craggy inlet on one of the many islands littering the sea. Here the crew would kindle a fire on which they would broil the fresh sardines for which they had haggled at a fish market earlier in the day. These, when accompanied with the coarse rye bread of the region and local red wine, were indeed the food of the gods.

The islands themselves we visited in detail. Trogir, no more than four hundred metres long by one hundred and fifty metres wide, was one of my favourite places in Yugoslavia. First settled by the Greeks, it had been vanquished in turn by the Romans, Byzantines and Croats and captured by the Venetians in 1420. Sheep grazed on the cropped green grass surrounding the Castello Camerlengo while the Loggia Piccola, a diminutive fish market dating from the 15th century, stands as a reminder of one of the island's chief livelihoods, as well as being the spot where strangers were interrogated before entering the town. The importance and grandeur of this little island in its heyday is reflected in its 13th century cathedral, entered through splendid Radovan doors which lead to an interior awash with richly sculpted putti, cavorting and cascading in abandoned exuberance over columns and pulpit.

Hvar, another island steeped in history, seemed to be the perfect stage setting for an opera, perhaps by Bartok or Smetana. The town is dominated by fortifications erected by Spaniola in 1551 and contains a wealth of buildings, several of them bearing the emblem of the twin lions of St Mark.

Dubrovnik, the loveliest of Adriatic cities, embraced on three sides by the sea, seems impregnable, girt as it is by its ancient walls – although later history was to show its vulnerability to bombardment from the air. Here in the colourful market place I bought a beautifully modelled bird made of coloured clay which, once filled with water, trills and warbles in a most realistic fashion and has served through the years to keep many a small visitor wondering and happy. Here too, one of my party, Geoffrey Huskisson, set up his easel and found himself the willing portraitist of a ravishing small girl with dark curls and shy smile who stood and posed for him with no more reward than the occasional piece of barley sugar and the finished portrait at the end of her 'sittings'.

Another evening we docked at Split where we were to be berthed for two nights. Formerly Spalatro, the town owes its fame to the great palace built by the Emperor Diocletian in AD 305, who died there some eight years later. Robert Adam's remarkable work "The Palace of Diocletian at Spalatro" contains a fascinating reconstruction of the palace, with delightful sketches of its appearance in 1764, the date of the book's publication. With the decline of the Holy Roman Empire, the town fell on evil days and more recent war damage further destroyed many of its buildings. The four gates, corner towers and most of the walls remain, although much of the interior has not survived. But the atmosphere lingers, and after dinner on the night of our arrival, some of us left the bawdy roisterings of a harbour-side café and entered the palace precincts through the underground passage, where an impromptu choir of Yugoslav youths was giving voice to a selection of native songs, some lively and some heart-rending in their intensity. We continued to the vestibule, which in Roman times had formed the entrance to the imperial apartments. Flanking these is the mausoleum, converted to a Christian church in the seventh century. Its massive doors were approached by a flight of stone steps, which were almost obscured by a crowd of hippies of all nationalities, reclining, smoking or playing on various musical instruments.

The Georgians visited France on several occasions. On one such tour to Provence, Angus was anxious to include in the programme a visit to the Chateau de Castille, home of the art historian and art collector, Douglas Cooper, an unpredictable character, whose house outside Uzès contained an outstanding collection of paintings and drawings – notably by Picasso, Léger and Braque. Angus, who had some slight acquaintance with the owner, wrote to him to ask whether he would allow members of the Georgian Group to view his collection. The answer came back on an open postcard saying that such a visit was highly unlikely since he was bound to know some of the party – who were probably the reason he was now living in France. He did relent to the extent of allowing Angus and myself to view the collection in his absence, the quality of which made me sympathise with his reluctance to have the general public over his threshold. He also added the proviso that we should get in touch with his secretary at a later date for a final decision. This we did by letter only to receive no reply.

On arriving in France I telephoned the house to be told in no uncertain manner that Mr Cooper would not receive us. The Chateau de Castille, inspired by Italian architecture of the 1780s stands just off the main road from the Pont du Gard to Uzès and is visible from the road. The house is approached by a very fine colonnaded driveway, ingeniously narrowed in trompe l'oeil fashion to give the impression of greater length. Abutting on the road is an elliptical forecourt also colonnaded, flanked by wrought iron gates. Since nothing prevented a coach in those days from stopping on the road, I asked the driver to draw up. This he did, allowing us all to pile out and peer through the gates at this very beautiful architectural feature, beyond which the house is clearly visible. As we were engaged in taking photographs amid much speculation as to the owner, there came a roar like an angry bull and on one of the balconies of the chateau appeared a menacing figure, with what looked like a gun in his hand and two belligerent dogs at his side intent on denying us entry as if we were the mob of 14th July, battering at the gates of the Bastille.

Discretion being the better part of valour, I gave the crisp command "Georgians retreat," whereupon we all scrambled aboard the bus in some haste, in case a stray pellet might wing our rearguard. I often wonder if the trigger really would have been pulled, if indeed it was a gun trained on us.

Our visits abroad were confined to Europe. Spain seemed to be a country we missed out on, although Portugal figured on several occasions, with visits to the Factory House in Oporto and enjoyable tastings at various wine lodges. The Gulbenkian Museum in Lisbon is, in my opinion, one of the finest small museums of Europe and the Church and Convent of Madre de Deus, one of Lisbon's loveliest buildings.

I remember having experienced a particularly trying morning during a tour when everything had gone wrong: the coach had failed to turn up, since the company had gone on strike overnight; my local guide had turned bolshie, being convinced for some reason that I deemed it to be her fault, and the lunch turned out to be a particularly poor one. Mercifully we had a free afternoon, so I took myself off to the convent to lick my wounds in solitude. Azullejos, brilliantly blue in colour, outlined panels depicting pastoral scenes and formal landscapes. The interior of the church was dominated by a life-size canvas of St. Francis by André Goncalves. The exquisite little sacristy is decorated with further tiled panels and another painting by Goncalves. A placid and friendly nun led me to the cloisters surrounded by tiles enclosing a little Manueline courtyard. Above the cloister are more rooms, each as enchanting as the next, with painted panels set in gold, more azullejos and a fine lectern. By the time I emerged from this little jewel of a convent, all friction of spirit had evaporated and I felt ready to face the most exigeant of my group with equanimity and forbearance.

In 1960 the travel allowance in foreign currency had been reduced to £50 per person, so it was necessary for a holiday of any length to combine visits in a foreign exchange country with others in a sterling area. It was mainly for this reason that it was decided to plan a tour to Sicily, Malta and Libya. Sterling was still viable in the latter two countries and Gaddafi had not yet entered the scene in Libya. The tour duly materialised and having successfully conducted the party round Sicily and Malta, we arrived at Luqa airport outside Valetta for the last leg to Libya, only to find that the flight had been cancelled owing to a sudden sandstorm that had closed down the airport at Tripoli.

One of the group, Cornish Torbock – noted for his sartorial elegance: a yellow tussore jacket with orange trousers and a paler orange shirt was the outfit on this occasion – not satisfied with the airline's excuses, took it upon himself to create a scene with the authorities in which the Queen's name was invoked and those of several peers. This so confused the luckless Maltese official that I am sure he was sorely tempted to bribe any airline to take us off in the hope that the sandstorm might engulf us all. After an unscheduled additional night in Valetta, we eventually touched down twenty-four hours later at Idris Airport in Libya and the next day set off by coach for Leptis Magna, which was to be the culmination of our tour.

The Phoenician city has vanished but the Roman city emerges clear cut with its 8th century BC market, its arches and palaestra adjoining the Hadrianic baths dating from about 127 AD with the usual layout of cold and warm baths, swimming pool, sweat rooms, gymnasia and changing rooms, scarcely altered over some 2,000 years. Having explored the Severan Forum and Basilica, gazed down on the now silted up harbour, visited the colonnaded Temple of Rome and Augustus and imagined ourselves haggling for fish in the market, we were strolling down the Colonnaded Street, pausing from time to time to take photographs or drink in the view, when Marjorie Hawkes, a delightful and enthusiastic sightseer, asked me if we were to return to the site after lunch. Of course, I answered, rashly as it turned out.

At this announcement Marjorie skipped for joy and disappeared from sight. The ground had literally swallowed her up. There was a moment of petrified silence when we all seemed to have been turned to stone like the ruins around us and then

from somewhere beneath our feet there came a muffled and somewhat hysterical cry, halfway between a sob and a giggle.

She was at least still alive. Later it transpired that Marjorie had been standing on a dry well, which had given way under her exuberance. We succeeded in pulling her out of what was a fairly deep hole, at the same time trying to reassure her husband, Neville, who was in almost as bad a state of shock as his wife. The latter's leg was in a sorry state, badly lacerated and bleeding. I managed to locate an Arab gentleman who professed to be a doctor and who produced a dubious looking needle and gut with which he carried out a first-aid job of sorts. Marjorie was heroic throughout but was obviously in pain, so needless to say she did not return to the site after lunch but, in a commandeered vehicle, sped back to Tripoli. A brand new hospital had just been opened in the city centre at which we deposited our injured passenger, where a rather more professional team took over. Angus and the rest of the party duly returned by coach and the next day we all flew back to England. Marjorie, I understand, bore the scars of Leptis Magna until the day she died.

Fifteen

France was the country I never tired of but Angus's passion was Italy. I had always been a Roman rather than a Florentine, a preference shared by my employer – so Rome and its environs was a popular base for more than one Georgian Group visit. The two of us would go ahead by car to tie up any loose ends and be there to greet members on their arrival two or three days later.

Once installed in our hotel, which lay in the shadow of the Pantheon, resting place of Raphael and burial place of Kings of Italy since the 19th century, I would stow away the car in an underground *parcheggio* and undertake the rest of sightseeing on foot.

"Imagine yourself as a Grand Tourist," adjured the maestro, "with Rome as the Bourn and the sighting of St Peter's dome the climax".

Having explored on foot what seemed to be all seven hills of the city, I was only too happy to concede the great church as being the apogée of our visit and to rest my weary feet in contemplation of this architectural gem, as seen through Bernini's splendid colonnade that frames the forecourt.

Once the tour proper began, we proceeded by coach to places of note outside the city's boundaries. These would include the Villa Farnese at Caprarola, then the summer residence of the Italian President, with its superb frescoed apartments and extensive grounds leading to the exquisite *giardino segreto* with its cascades, fountains and amphitheatre; the Villa Lante, one of the *chef-d'oeuvres* of renaissance garden design; and the Villa Aldobrandini where, on one occasion, a Georgian got mislaid and was finally discovered supine in one of its grottoes, having suffered a slight stroke. Also included was the famous Villa d'Este at Tivoli, where I lived in hopes that the romantic setting by moonlight, with a display of fireworks in the background, might encourage two of the group who invariably travelled together to break free from their platonic friendship and call the banns, so allowing for two additional single rooms to become available. It took a further ten years before they finally took the plunge, but continued their practice of single rooms.

Once the tour ended, I would unearth the Mercedes from its underground purdah and be ready for the next port of call. Having dismissed Rome from his mind, Angus was now intent on planning a visit to Emilia, which entailed a long and arduous drive alongside the Appenine Range. The fact that the countryside between the two regions covered some of the loveliest scenery in Italy and included the historic towns of Siena, Assisi and Perugia meant nothing to him, and even Florence was dismissed as being "medieval". Being at the wheel did give me a certain advantage and on one occasion I was able to steer him in the direction of Lucca, with the lure that it was the birthplace of Pompeo Batoni, the 18th century painter of many a Grand Tourist, and also contained a number of stately homes in the vicinity such as the Villas Marlia and Mansi and Villa Garzoni at Collodi, with its superb gardens and trick fountains. Lucca, however, was a frolicsome prelude for the sterner stuff of the next few days. The Emilian tour was to include the towns of Bologna, Modena, Mantua, Ravenna and Parma – not to mention a few others on the side such as Sabbioneta with its delightful Teatro Olimpico by Scamozzi, and Cremona.

To reach our base at Modena we had a fairly strenuous drive through rugged country before debauching in to the southern valley of the Po. There is no doubt that driving in an open car brings a feeling of exhilaration and exuberance that is missing when cocooned within the confines of a saloon. One feels much more part of the landscape and as we left Rome to follow the Tiber valley on our way north, the warm breezes of the Umbrian countryside brushed our somewhat sunburnt faces, bringing the honeyed scent of broom and mimosa to our appreciative senses. There was a carefree air about our journeying which was missing under a closed hood, and even the occasional missed turning could not dim the light heartedness of our progress. To our right massed the steep hills of the Marche. After Terni the road began to climb and the landscape became impregnated with the hilltop towns which were of such strategic importance against the barbarian invasions that swept the region during the decline of the Roman Empire.

Once in Emilia itself, there followed four days of intense sightseeing, during which we photographed the mosaics of Ravenna from every angle, committed to memory the treasures in the great palaces of Mantua and Modena, exclaimed at the architectural beauties of the Teatri Farnese and Regio at Parma, not forgetting to stock up with its famous ham and cheese for our picnic basket. The weather had suddenly turned warm and after a particularly gruelling day spent largely on our feet, we managed to dispose of a couple of bottles of Lambrusco, the local effervescent and refreshing wine that seemed to have as little effect on us as iced water, accompanied as it was with platefuls of *zampone* and *salsa verde* for which the region's restaurants are renowned.

We had been given an introduction to a very decorative and delightful Italian Contessa, recently widowed, who Angus found beguiling, and who was prevailed upon at a later date to entice her brother to receive some thirty Georgians at his *casa della campagna*. Both brother and sister received us with true hospitality, with the proffering of wine and refreshments. Amongst the latter were some tempting looking *biscotti*, upon which the Georgians pounced in their uninhibited way – only to find, after one bite, that the cook must have confused her ingredients and were solid with salt. Not wishing to appear too rude, we disposed of them as best we could in the decorative urns and flower pots that adorned the terrace. History does not relate what were the gardeners' thoughts when they next came to water the plants, and although the Contessa has since become a good friend I have never dared mention this episode.

However, the zenith of our Grand Tour was yet to come. Angus's great hero amongst Italian architects was Andrea

Palladio. On a past occasion, and before I joined the Group, he was to lay a wreath at the foot of the great man's statue in Vicenza, to the mild astonishment of the local inhabitants who happened to be passing by. However, waiting in pouring rain for the ceremony to begin, it was realised that the tour bus had left with the wreath still on board. This was eventually retrieved by tour leader Eleanor Murray, with the help of Lady Berwick, one of the few Italian speakers on the trip.

Angus's bibles were the *Antichita di Roma*, first published in Rome in 1554, and the *Quattro Libri*, the last volume of which saw publication in 1570. We were to follow the Brenta and feast our eyes on the wealth of imposing villas lining its banks, before stopping for a few days of 'rest and relaxation' in Venice.

Rest and relaxation for Angus meant sitting contentedly in a café in the Piazza di San Marco writing his notes with a bottle of beer at his elbow. I, his acolyte, was dispatched each morning to put the forthcoming tour together and carry out the necessary negotiations for so doing. This suited me down to the ground, as apart from cajoling hotel managers into allotting us an exorbitant ratio of single rooms as opposed to doubles (since our groups largely consisted of single travellers, be they bachelors or widows), I also had the task of choosing suitable restaurants and discussing menus, usually over a glass of wine, and making sure churches and museums etc. were to be open at the appointed time. Otherwise, the day was my own. I was totally happy from the time we parked the car in a multi-storey car park in the Piazzale di Roma, took a *vaporetto* down the Grand Canal to the staging post at San Marco and handed our not inconsiderable luggage to a willing porter who carried it at a running pace to our *pensione*, which was tucked away behind the Piazza San Marco. My room overlooked a canal that appeared to be the meeting place of every gondolier (plus his gondola) in Venice, and although the ensuing hubbub was not inducive to sleep, the pantomime enacted beneath my window afforded me much entertainment.

Since my first visit to Venice during the war, when I was stationed at Caserta, the city has never ceased to cast its spell on me. The Hotel Luna, a former YWCA where I had spent many a wartime leave, is today amongst the city's 4***** establishments. In the short grey days of winter I like to stand on one of Venice's countless bridges watching the petrol-green water lapping sluggishly at the foundations of a brave new house under construction, and to savour the streets devoid of tourists. With the coming of Spring windows are flung open and bedding and carpets aired from balconies; fugitive gusts of wind blow in across the lagoon from the open sea, rippling the water and tossing into the air the tasselled fringes of the curtained gondolas being brought to life for the coming season.

I tried to avoid Venice in the heat of summer, when the city lies supine behind drawn blinds, awnings hang limply over the heads of yawning waiters and concierges knit slumbrously on their porches. Only with the decline of the sun's rays would the shutters open with a deafening clatter and animation return to the hitherto deserted streets. My favourite time of all perhaps was early autumn, heralded by the yellowing of a leaf plopping into a canal, the thick white mists rising from the lagoon, giving way to a crisp golden day perfumed by a pungent whiff of wood smoke.

But now it was Spring and time for action! I enjoyed these solitary sorties as I could go at my own pace, unhampered by interminable stops for photograph-taking, and at a whim disappear down any inviting looking alleyway that took my fancy. In this way I discovered some unexpected treasures; a crumbling doorway emblazoned with the remnants of some faded coat of arms denoting more affluent times for the building in question; an itinerant busker offering some spontaneous form of street entertainment to an enthusiastic audience of urchins and housewives; a flower seller perched on the steps of a church proferring bunches of violets from a wicker basket; and on losing my way one day, I stumbled across the Scala di Borolo, a folly-like spiral staircase, hidden away in a back alley.

High in my favours comes the Scuola di San Giorgio degli Schiavoni, its walls hung with an endearing series of paintings by the Carpaccio brothers depicting the lives of the Saints Jerome,

Tryphon and George. There is a particularly lively panel showing St. George despatching with a certain detached panache a rather jolly looking dragon, and another of St. Jerome absorbed in his studies with a small Battersea Dog's Home type of mongrel sitting sentinel at his feet.

One of my favourite churches in Venice is Santa Maria dei Miracoli, the beautifully proportioned façade adorned with a lunette bearing a Madonna by Giorgio Lascaris. Inside, the grey and rose coloured walls are like watered silk and covered with a riot of prophets and saints. Steep steps lead to the altar, which I was contemplating on that first visit of mine when a feather duster suddenly appeared from behind a putti's head, followed by a smiling custodian who told me she was preparing the church for a wedding that afternoon and invited me to come back and take part in its celebration.

But Angus's passions lay across the water – on the Islands of the Giudecca and San Giorgio Maggiore, where two of Palladio's masterpieces are to be found. On each group visit we took a launch across the Guedecca to the Church of Il Redentore, built in thanksgiving for the relief of the plague that ravaged Venice in the years 1575-76. The interior is austere but harmonious and contains an Ascension by Tintoretto. A short ride took us on to the Isola di San Giorgio Maggiore where the church stands beside the former monastic buildings that now house the Giorgio Cini Foundation, established as a cultural, artistic and educational centre. A cloister designed by Palladio leads to what was the guest wing, which in turn faces the entrance to the Refectory and is flanked by a handsome pair of 16th century red marble washbasins. A later staircase mounts to the library, both by Baldassare Longhena, and to the Dormitory whose immense vaulted corridor is lined at regular intervals with doorways to the cells.

Our homage paid to the great man, we would then make our way down the lagoon by private launch to Torcello, which deposited us at the little landing stage, a short walk away through flower-filled meadows from the main piazza of this rather remote village that is dominated by its famous Cathedral.

There were always surprisingly few visitors about and little to disturb the tranquillity of this Christian sanctuary. The sun shone through the windows highlighting the marble columns and the mosaic floor and illuminating the iconastasis. Here, mosaic peacocks drink from a chalice, said to represent the incorruptibility of humanity through participation in the Eucharist.

A walk took us to the neighbouring church of Santa Fosca, a Byzantine jewel, octagonal in form with a simple interior. Our launch took us on to Murano to see the glass-blowing. On a previous occasion, Angus and I had called in there to see the church of Santa Maria and Donata. After several minutes of futile hammering at the west door (according to a notice, it was closed for restoration but we were urged on by a posse of local fishermen sitting outside mending their nets), we were beckoned round the corner by a bibulous looking fellow who led us by way of the sacristy into the body of the church, where the entire 12th century mosaic floor was being replaced.

So carried away were we by the fascination and complexity of this mammoth task, which entailed every minuscule fragment of mosaic having to be matched and re-positioned, that we nearly missed the last direct launch back to the Riva Schiavoni. On the way we saw in the distance the cypresses and spires of the church of San Francesco del Deserto. Walking back to our *pensione* from the launch terminal, we passed the Palazzo Mastelli with an amusing relief over a doorway of a man leading a camel; and further on came across a funeral parlour outside of which stone steps led down to the canal on which were moored a fleet of gilded gondolas, their interiors upholstered in black velvet with purple covered bier rests.

Our work in Venice completed, we fortified ourselves that evening with platters of seafood at one of the numerous fish restaurants in which Venice abounds and next day set off, on my part reluctantly, for the Veneto.

The Mercedes had survived four days of inactivity and, like the well-bred car it was, purred into action at the first touch of its starter. Along the Brenta stand the country estates and villas built for the Venetian gentry, who sought respite from the scorching heat of summer, with pride of place going perhaps to the Villa Foscari at Mira, better known perhaps as the Malcontenta, its name reflected in its rather melancholy setting on the banks of the canal. This was our first port of call, since Angus knew the then occupants, Mr and Mrs Landsberg from the United States, who had invited us to 'drop in' and be shown over the house. We entered through a noble portico, severe and classical, differing somewhat from Palladio's more unorthodox treatment of the windows on the rear of the building. Frescoes of mythological subjects decorate the walls of the central hall.

Declining a cup of coffee, we surged on to the Villa Pisani at Stra, one of the most magnificent of all the villas and now the property of the state. In 1934 it served as a meeting place between Mussolini and Hitler. The house stands in a large park and is faced at the opposite end of a long canal by a vast stable block with an untouched and original interior. The 18th century maze still survives.

Angus began to grow rather restive at this stage, since we had the car and ourselves booked on the auto-train back to Boulogne, which was due to leave Milan in two days' time, although admittedly not until the evening. Our programme therefore became a contest of stamina and quick-fire timing. We stopped at Padua, not without considerable difficulty in parking, and while Angus sat in the car to ward off any *carabinieri*, I did scant justice to Giotto's outstanding frescoes in the Scrovegni Chapel, and gatecrashed a lecture taking place in that architectural gem, the Teatro Anatomico in the University. Thankfully for me, the lecture, although on anatomy, was not accompanied by a cadaver, otherwise Angus might have had his problems.

There were some villas about which we had read but were uncertain as to their present state and whether they rated inclusion in the programme. We therefore trudged around the ruins of abandoned mansions, part of them inhabited by *contadini* and hens scratching amongst the stubbled grass; we braved the interior of a villa whose faded frescoes framed the walls of a home for mentally retarded children and debated the merits of arranging for the group to picnic on the steps of another *palazzo*, empty of humanity, but offering the perfect background for an *alfresco* meal.

We savoured the sublime again when we visited the Villa Valmarana dei Nani at Vicenza which includes three buildings – the *palazzino*, *foresteria* or guest house, and the stables, attributed to Antonio Muttoni and his son Francesco. But the great glory of the villa is the interior decoration by Giambattista Tiepolo and his son Giandomenico. From there we walked along a grass path that led to perhaps the most famous of all Palladio's villas, the Rotonda, which formed the basis of Burlington's villa at Chiswick and Colen Campbell's Mereworth in Kent.

We stayed the night at a fairly nondescript Jolly Hotel in order to be able to visit the Teatro Olimpico early the next morning. This was opened in 1585 with a gala performance of Sophocles' Oedipus Tyrannus and one of the most lasting impressions of that entire visit to Italy was my first view of the amphitheatre with its richly simulated perspective and triumph of trompe l'oeil.

There was a slight contretemps in Verona where I mistook an underground parking place for a turning place and found ourselves descending into the bowels of the earth without any known means of getting out. A kindly attendant at last came to our aid, not before the air was heavily charged with silent recriminations.

Leaving Angus in the Piazza Bar to make enquiries about opera performances in the Arena later in the season, and to regain his calm with a glass of wine, I made my usual perambulations around the main points of interest in the town: the Piazza del Erbe, formerly the Roman forum and now a general market from where I bought bread, prosciutto and cheese for our picnic lunch; the Piazza dei Signori crowned with a monument of Dante and the graceful Loggia del Consiglio. Because I knew Angus was anxious to visit the Church of San Zeno on the way out of the town, and midday was not far off when everything in Italy shuts down more or less till three o'clock, I had time for no more than a restrained gallop round the Duomo and Church of Sant' Anastasia with a few scribbled notes on each, before finding the car and scooping up my passenger.

We made San Zeno with minutes to spare, but fortunately Angus was more concerned with taking innumerable photographs of the exterior including the two rather splendid lions that support the portico. We ate our picnic on the shores of Lake Garda in the shade of an orange grove while wild fowl flew around our heads or skimmed the water for insects or weeds. It was an agreeable finale to exchange for an hour or so stones and culture for flora and fauna.

These years were, I suppose, an overture to what was to come. In 1968 Angus was in his early seventies and growing weary. His leg was causing him increasing pain that led in due course to him having first one, then a second hip operation, the latter leading to complications. He had resigned from the Executive Committee of the Georgian Group, which was giving more of its time to case work under the efficient secretaryship of Eleanor Murray, and he himself was giving more and more of his time and his money to the Leche Trust. I could have remained with him as his assistant in this capacity and as general factotum, but

I was by now in my forties and travel had become part of my lifestyle. We therefore took an amicable leave of each other in the spring of 1968, although we were to keep in touch until his death twelve years later. I still acted as his chauffeur on occasion with jaunts to the hairdresser or to Glyndebourne or Covent Garden, as music was to remain one of his chief pleasures all his life.

Methodical throughout the years, he had never thrown anything away. On his death I was appointed an executor, together with Jean Monro and Sylvia Fletcher-Moulton, and had to go through the contents of his flat in Eaton Square. I couldn't help smiling on coming across a large parcel tied up in brown paper and pink ribbon marked "Row with Barkers 1934". A fitting epitaph perhaps to someone who was cantankerous, tenacious and intent on fair play.

The three of us were left his wine cellar, which contained some notable bottles – a Chateau d'Yquem 1921, Petrus, Tokay etc – all of which were sold at Christie's for a not inconsiderable sum. The rest of his wines were kept in a cellar in the basement of Eaton Square, and thanks to the dampness of the walls, had lost all their labels. Dinner parties in future became a so-called guessing game for guests who considered themselves wine experts.

Those eight years, spent working with a perfectionist who brooked no shortcuts or sloppiness – with an impeccable eye to detail and who stood his ground against opposition or criticism if he thought fit – gave me an invaluable grounding for the years ahead, when running my own business. The Georgian Group itself must also feel indebted to someone who unstintedly contributed so much, largely without any financial remuneration, in promoting the importance of the Group's aims and the conservation of 18th century architecture as a whole.

A *special* kind of travel

Sixteen

What to do now? I had always worked for someone, a role probably better suited to my temperament. Although I had learned to be strict in detail under Angus's "no short-cut" principles and considered myself to be a good organiser, I lacked the necessary conviction in my own ability and competence to launch out on my own. Or perhaps it was merely lack of willpower, due to the fact that it was not absolutely necessary for me to earn my own living.

I did, in fact, apply for a job shortly after leaving Angus and the Georgian Group. According to the advertisement, the job offered "an attractive salary and good prospects", entailing much evening work in the management of a chain of wine bars across central London. Liking both wine and people, I applied for the post and was duly called for an interview with the General Manager of the company. This took place in the early evening at one of his wine bars, situated in a cul-de-sac, just off Oxford Street.

I arrived, suitably clad I hoped, in a smart but unflashy suit to find my would-be employer seated at a table in a corner of the bar with a bottle of wine and two glasses in front of him, his own being already half-filled. I had a surreptitious look at the label on the bottle in case I was quizzed on its contents. A Côte-de-Rhône of modest vintage. The room was low-key, rather old-fashioned with panelled walls and soft lighting. Several tables were occupied already, although it was barely six pm so obviously it was a popular rendezvous for West End office workers en route for home.

From our conversation it transpired that my interviewer was clearly a man of ambition. "Expansion" and "class" featured largely in his vocabulary and there was an air of rather self-conscious affability about him which came to the fore when greeting his customers, but did not always extend to his staff.

Small in stature but large in self-esteem, I got the impression that I was privileged to be there and even more privileged to be offered the job. When I declined his offer he immediately raised the salary. When I replied rather loftily that it was not the money which interested me, so much as the hours involved, since I was leading a fairly social life at that time, he erupted into a tirade of contempt. "Comfortably off, I presume," he sneered, pouring himself another glass of wine but declining to offer me any. "I always maintain that a private income is a scourge to ambition". I refrained from pointing out that in this instance ambition would probably not have taken me much further than the confines of wine bars in central London under the management of someone with whom I had little rapport. I pondered his words, however, on the way home on a No.137 bus. No doubt there was some truth in what he said, although our ultimate goals might vary widely in substance.

Although package tours were well into their stride by the late 1960s – indeed they could be traced as far back as Roman times if not before – many of them catering for activities such as winter sports or general sightseeing, there were still comparatively few travel companies specialising in purely cultural pursuits, now a commonplace, and even fewer whose tours were sponsored by museums or organisations connected with the arts. One company with leanings in that direction was International Travel, one of its directors being a forceful lady called Miss Ena Molesworth. Majestic of bearing, she had been making overtures to me for some time and could not understand my reluctance to join her firm – which was certainly well thought of in the travel world and ran the sort of tours in which I was interested. But I could see myself being engulfed by a rather more assertive personality than my own and swallowed up in an already successful enterprise, whereas I hankered to create something, however ill-defined at this stage, of my own. When I eventually succeeded, my thwarted would-be employer was heard to say that we would be but "a flash in a pan". "A bloody big flash" was our rejoinder.

I did seek a partner, however, and a dynamic one at that, with similar leanings towards the travel scene. The solution came in the form of a Mrs Cicely Severne, a Georgian Group member who had travelled under my wing on several occasions. Although critical and outspoken at times, she clearly appreciated efficiency and tolerance when she was at her most trying. She had also given her patronage to another well-established tour operating company called Cadogan Travel, run by Patrick Crichton-Stuart, Aubrey Nye and Sybil Uniacke, sometimes under the guiding hand of Diana Skene. This company was the first to conduct members of the National Art Collections Fund to the USA and USSR, but was eventually taken over by Blands (a larger organisation from Gibraltar) while retaining its name, and with the consequent retirement of some of the senior staff. Diana had been told categorically by the new owner that there would be no future place on the board for her as she had once hoped. She was therefore as concerned with the future as I was.

Diana, a fellow Scot, had worked as a courier since she had moved to London following a divorce. She was large both in build and personality and had, as more than one of our future clients was to exclaim, "a presence". Where I was bossy, Diana was autocratic; where I took time to ponder over things, Diana was decisive. She might dispute my assertion that I was the more tolerant of the two but I certainly suffered fools more gladly than she did. She had warmth, much compassion, an infectious sense of humour and an intelligent mind, which grasped the more salient points of a discussion more quickly than mine. She had also developed considerable healing powers over the years and had an unexpected vulnerability, which I was later to discover belied her somewhat imperious manner. Some of our less sophisticated American clients were to find her too stringent and required more cosseting and patience than Diana was prepared to give.

Cicely Severne had decided in her own mind that Diana and I would make a good business combination and arranged for us to meet with her for lunch. I recall wearing for the occasion a not very becoming russet-coloured velvet hat and feeling overdressed and bourgeois when Diana billowed in, enveloped in a voluminous cloak, abrim as it seemed to me with poise and self-confidence. Our hostess, delighted to bring her two "protegées" together, was convinced that we only had to meet once for us both to agree that there was definitely a future for us jointly in travel. It could so easily have had the opposite effect, but fortunately Diana and I sensed an instant rapport. She rather disarmingly admitted to having had no real business experience and that her grammar and spelling were not up to much, but she had chaired council meetings in Fife and was, at least, used to public speaking. "With common sense and acumen", she stated confidently, "I am convinced that there is plenty of scope for a travel company specialising in tours for museums and organisations connected with the arts as part of their fundraising programmes". I was impressed by such self-expression. "After all", she continued, "you have the Georgian Group backing" (this was endorsed by murmurings of assent from Cicely) "and I have many contacts in the art world".

Thinking it was time that I contributed something to the meeting, apart from ordering cannelloni, I brought up the matter of finances rather tentatively. "Well, naturally we'll need capital and for that reason I think it would be a good idea to bring in a third partner and I think I know just the person". It turned out that 'the person' had also been a part-time courier for Cadogan Travel, was a widow with two sons and was, according to Diana, well read with considerable business and travel experience, an imperturbable nature and attractive to men. Diana had already sounded out this paragon of virtues who appeared to be mildly enthusiastic about the whole idea. Her name was Doreen McLaren.

Over the pasta, Diana further confided that she had been donated a spacious flat in Royal Avenue by her ex-husband's trustees, from where we could operate for the time being. "The greatest problem is to find an existing travel agent, courageous and gullible enough to take us under his wing as a specialised department for the years necessary before we can apply for our own license. I have in fact been put in touch with someone who seems possible", she laughed somewhat deprecatingly, "he is very keen to arrange a meeting with the three of us as soon as possible, if you agree". She swallowed some of the *vino della casa* with which our hostess had been plying us, the latter meanwhile listening indulgently as a teacher might to favourite pupils who were living up to her expectations; the one at least; the other was rather stupefied by pasta, wine and her would-be partner's eloquence, but able to interject what she hoped to be a succinct word from time to time. Obviously Diana was away ahead of me. Whereas I had vague and woolly ideas about setting up a business, she had done her homework and had at least laid ground foundations. I looked across at her with admiration. She leaned over the table and seized my hand. "Oh do say yes", she cried, "it would be such fun".

By the end of lunch, encouraged by Cicely, fired by Diana's enthusiasm and somewhat bemused by the sheer speed of events, I had agreed to take up the challenge and go into partnership with Diana and Doreen.

After that, events moved swiftly. I was introduced to Doreen – easygoing, self-assured and even taller than Diana. Her sons were both married, since when she had visited many far-flung countries on her own under fairly primitive conditions, so her experience of distant lands was to be invaluable to us, although she was apt to scoff at lesser mortals who opted for a more luxurious form of travel. She had many friends, both male and female, was a good bridge player and had, to my mind, a man's way of thinking. She was one of those rare persons who gave the impression of being contented, with herself, her family and her mode of life, which made her a pleasant if at times rather irritating person to be with. My first instinct was that I might appear inadequate beside those two slightly overpowering women and on our first working day together had an almost irresistible desire to pack in the whole scheme and abscond. However inherent Scottish pride and the thought of Cicely's contempt won the day. In any event, it soon became evident that as far as office administration and the actual setting up of tours were concerned

– after all, our main object – I was streets ahead of either of them, thanks to the tuition of my late employer.

The next stepping stone was our meeting with Bruce Lyons of Twickenham Travel who, like me, was so overwhelmed by Diana's blandishments that he agreed to take us under his wing. This I suspect was due, partly, to the novelty of being challenged by three middle-aged women – he himself must have been in his early thirties at most – who were obviously totally inexperienced in the intricacies of commercial travel and the complexities of airline ticketing and regulations that were to govern our lives for the next twenty years. He was intrigued too, by the type of tours we envisaged. The cultural aspect of itineraries had played little part in his business, which operated from Twickenham and dealt largely in package holidays to popular resorts.

We were to begin in a modest enough manner, with four tours planned for 1969 (it was by now October 1968) which were to be set up by the three of us while Bruce and his staff would do our air bookings. Book-keeping was not the strong point of any of us three. I remembered the Mallet stock books and kept an eye on the date column, although by February 1971, mercifully we were into decimal coinage. Admittedly life was at a much slower tempo than it is today and competition, especially in our field, was not fierce, but for how long? There were no faxes or computers in those days and if a photocopy was required or notes to be written, we had to take ourselves off to the other end of Sloane Street, where an obliging lady called Miss Cohen ran a stencilling and photocopy business.

The 28th October 1968 saw us at last in business with the title of Twickenham Travel Specialised Tours, based at Diana Skene's flat at 5 Royal Avenue, Chelsea. In those early days, when all three of us were working at our portable typewriters in a pretty confined space, life was pretty chaotic to say the least. The telephone rang non-stop and as No.5 was Diana's home as well as our office, there was a constant stream of friends and relations, would-be clients, as well as workmen installing electric sockets and putting up shelves. Quite often, however, one or other of us would be out touting for business, visiting Bruce at Twickenham to be instructed in the intricacies of air bookings and how best to deal with airline authorities and officials.

It was our policy from the start that whoever was to take the tour was to set it up and be responsible for its every aspect, including leading the groups on a "follow my leader" principle, much as Angus and I had done for the Georgians, and where necessary we carried out a recce to the places to be visited. Obviously when our travels took us further afield than Europe, agents had to be invoked. In the case of the Eastern Bloc or those countries behind the Iron Curtain, it was usually compulsory and certainly advisable to use the official tourist company: Intourist in the USSR, IBUSZ in Hungary, ORBUS in Poland. The equivalent in Czechoslovakia was CEDOK, although we were able somehow to deal direct with a firm called Sporturist, run by a gentle but overworked soul called Mr Jelinek.

Most of our initial expenditure went on publicising ourselves and building up a mailing list. As luck would have it, the publication of our initial leaflet coincided with a very prolonged postal strike. By dint of securing the help of kind friends all over the country, and maintaining a delivery service by our own cars in London, we somehow managed to make ourselves known. At one Scottish ancestral home, the owner was somewhat surprised to see a horse galloping down her drive, its rider dismounting with a flourish to press into her hands the latest bulletin from our firm. So impressed was she by such enterprise that she signed up for the Italian tour while the equestrian courier was being revived with a cup of tea in the servants' hall and her mount having a drink of water in the stable yard. Another recipient, on seeing my signature on the brochure, announced to her husband that she had been at school with a Hazel Wood many years earlier. After rummaging in the attic she unearthed an old school photograph of some thirty schoolgirls dressed in Greek tunics, each of them with her signature on the reverse. After scrutiny, she decided that the signatures tallied, which proves that either I had developed my pot hooks early on, or had made little progress since. I remembered her as a very tall, angular 'older girl' and thus rather beyond my ken. She subsequently enrolled for the Swedish/Russian tour together with her husband, son and daughter, all of whom topped six feet. Their name was Pettit and they remained faithful clients and good friends for many years.

Of course, more important than anything else was to find museums and organisations willing to sponsor us, so that we could travel under their nomenclature, as it were. We had therefore to convince the curators, presidents and secretaries of the Friends of various societies, that we could make money for them by devising a tour specifically designed for its members, possibly with the theme of a forthcoming exhibition. It was essential to visit all of these illustrious bodies and, because we were one of the first off the ground, managed to enlist the patronage of the British Museum Society and the Victoria and Albert Museum – where the then Director, Roy Strong, was cajoled into accompanying visits for the V&A's Friends, and later as lecturer for other groups. We also enlisted Friends of the Ashmolean Museum in Oxford, the Courtauld Institute and the Royal Academy. At the latter I just managed to edge ahead of Serena Fass and Richenda Gurney, later to be our chief rival under the name of Serenissima Travel. The Georgian Group was also kind enough to give us its support and Diana had a following from the National Art Collections Fund. Only the National Trust remained oblivious to our charms and indeed we were severely censured by the then Secretary, Edward Fawcett, for using its name in vain.

A lucky break which led to opening our doors to overseas associations was due to Alys Acworth, daughter of my late employer, later married to John Rickett, who worked in the modern Art Department at Sotheby's, where she herself worked. She happened to be visiting Providence, Rhode Island on rather a cold winter's day and sought some warmth in the headquarters of the Providence Preservation Society, where she got into conversation with the director, Mrs Eleanor Monahan. The Members of the Society had visited the UK on several occasions but were not satisfied with their British travel agent. Could Alys suggest anyone? The latter was kind enough to recommend ourselves, the outcome being a lasting and happy relationship with an annual visit to Britain for a number of years. Eleanor Monahan, who became a good friend, was a retired teacher and lecturer, an ardent historian with a lively sense of humour that was disguised behind a very solemn and rather owl-like countenance, emphasised by spectacles with very thick lenses. Her husband, Monty, accompanied the group on every occasion and spent most of the time while travelling by coach doing petit-point needlework, usually bargello, the first piece of work I recall being a typewriter cover. On a later occasion in France, I was rather shocked to hear that he would prefer to remain in the coach to finish a cushion cover, rather than to view the magnificent tapestries of the Apocalypse in the Chateau at Angers.

Thanks to Eleanor, word took flight across the United States, which led to tours for SPNEA (Society for the Preservation of New England Antiquities) with the blessing of its delightful chief, Abbot Cumming; the Nelson Gallery Foundation from Kansas City, led by Mr Ross Taggart, which followed Doreen on several occasions; Smith Alumnae, which came year after year to Europe with Virginia Eley who, with relentless stubbornness, wore down my sales resistance until she got what she wanted, and became a lifelong friend until her untimely death many years later. Garden Societies followed such as the Morris Arboretum society, Tradescant Gardeners of America amongst others, but I suppose my favourites were the Guides of Winterthur Museum from

Delaware who, after their eighth or ninth tour with me, invited me on a fortnight's visit to Delaware, where I was fêted night and day, entertained to breakfast, lunch, tea and dinner, accommodated in private homes and clubs until I cried for mercy, when they said "now the boot is on the other foot".

We were also naïve enough at first to take on individual bookings, thinking this would bring in a little income while setting up our group tours. I undertook to send someone round the world and, having set up her itinerary, found to my horror that I had somehow missed out a day until Doreen put me right rather scoffingly with the words "well of course you lose a day if you go round the world." After this we stuck to group visits.

We decided that our first tours should be to the countries we knew best. Diana to Rome in Italy, Doreen to Provence in France and myself to Scotland with a more ambitious follow-up to Stockholm and Leningrad. The latter was an act of sheer bravado on my part, undertaken with a total unawareness of the problems which might lie ahead, and based on a working holiday in Stockholm and a four-day visit to Moscow and Leningrad with Angus. It is an interesting fact that over the next two decades, tours to these countries, with the exception of Sweden, proved consistently the most popular and well booked of all our tours.

Once the tour was under way, we did everything except drive the coach and cook the meals: luggage handling when failed by promised hotel porters or bolshie drivers, ticket and visa handling, money changing, placating or bribing the management – headwaiters in particular – soothing ruffled feathers of clients should the need arise, knowing when to give commentaries in the coach and when to leave sleeping clients lie, writing notes on places to be visited, coping with any crisis involving cancelled flights, the breakdown of the coach, civil uprisings, illness, accident or death. All in all, nurse-maiding for the greater part of twenty-four hours a day. Sometimes we were to take a lecturer with us, purporting to be an expert on the sites to be visited, sometimes a success, sometimes not. Diana would not travel without one. I found the local guides more satisfactory on many occasions and certainly saved us much money. What became a thorn in my side was, on returning from a tour, for my friends to telephone and enquire if I had enjoyed my holiday.

Somehow our bookings began to accumulate, with ensuing pressures building up. I recall spending a weekend with Isobel Kay, my wartime friend and now married to Harry Clarke, a maltster, at their home in Mayfield with their four children. D-Day was approaching for my Leningrad tour, for which I had to write copious notes. I was relegated to the Clarke's spare bedroom, which was decorated with a particularly busy Paisley patterned wallpaper in strong purples and greens, and here I sat typing furiously while Isobel cooked delicious meals and Harry kept me supplied with well-laced vodkas and tonics. Friends indeed, what would we have done without them. They rallied round, signed on for a tour that was at best a gamble and could well be a disaster.

Diana and I were invited to a dance at the Royal Academy on one occasion and were both dressed in shades of green. A mutual friend, Douglas Pirie, approached us to greet us warmly. "*Vert pour l'éspèrance*, I see" he said. Hope indeed was the one thing we had to hold on to. As business began to build up, it looked increasingly obvious that we would not only have to find alternative premises but also find an office manager who could run the day-to-day tedium of bookings, timetables, telephone calls etc. and eventually take on the airline bookings, once we had launched ourselves as a separate enterprise from Twickenham Travel and when at times we would all three be away on tour. We managed to find fairly cramped quarters in Pimlico Road, which at least looked more professional – and it was Diana who finally persuaded John Winser to enter our lives.

A man in his thirties, married to Nell in 1972, who bred Chinchilla cats, and with three small daughters, John did not seem unduly fazed at the idea of working with three more females, all considerably older than himself, which must have been of some comfort to his wife. John was good looking, given to chubbiness with rather a lower form of schoolboy humour, unflappable, stubborn and unfailingly reliable. He had worked with P&O and Pan American Airways so knew the pitfalls in that direction and had also worked with travel companies for a number of years, including Cadogan Travel. He had a remarkably good telephone manner, which seduced many a wavering client to sign up or to turn down someone not considered suitable owing "to no more single rooms being available". Before the age of computers, his passion was graphs and at times drove us to distraction by the hours spent on these creations, albeit to good results. What he lacked in art and architectural knowledge, which was minimal, was made up for by his managerial skills, attention to detail and financial knowhow.

It was also in 1972 that Diana dropped her bombshell, by announcing that she was going to make her home in Florence for the time being and would carry on her side of the business from there. Admittedly the bomb had been ticking for some time as there had been a lot of to-ing and fro-ing from Italy – although Doreen and I assumed it was largely for the setting up of her Italian tours. She spoke good Italian, had many friends in Florence, including the British Consul, and had been carrying on a liaison with a married man whose identity remained undisclosed until much later, the main reason of course for her abduction. She also had many Italian contacts in the art world, including curators of museums, owners of important houses and garden societies. Members of the latter usually consisted almost entirely of Principessas, Contessas and Marchesas with a sprinkling of their husbands thrown in.

In many ways her departure was a blessing in disguise. Not only did her absence give us more space if we were to expand our staff but, despite the fact that she was to be a much treasured and life-long friend, we were both rather dictatorial and strong-minded, and sharing close confines over the years might well have put our friendship at risk. It was also evident that Doreen, being older with sons and grandchildren taking up much of her time, as well as many other interests in life including bridge, was not going to be as dedicated to the future of the company for as long as Diana and myself. We had therefore to find new blood and this we discovered thanks to John Winser's mother. The latter put us in touch with Kay Turnbull, who was looking to move on from Lammin Tours, a very well-known and long established firm, for whom she had worked for many years, setting up her own tours and travelling extensively. Kay was way above us all intellectually, having a degree in English at Edinburgh University and being fluent in five languages. Some years younger than the rest of us, she was of pleasing appearance and although she always professed that her love of books, art and places came before personalities, dogs excepted, she commanded a very faithful following, who travelled with her consistently over the years we worked together. As Lady Bannerman, a client, told me "Kay has a thirst for knowledge which she is only too happy to impart to others, which makes her a great person to travel with".

Our final member of the team in those early days was Jean Neilson, formerly a staff nurse and ward sister at Great Ormond Street and Charing Cross Hospitals respectively, followed by a degree in hotel and catering, and qualifying as a London Blue Guide. Tall and angular, she wore her clothes with a certain panache and liked to describe herself as a "free spirit" an exact definition of which sometimes baffled me. A gregarious soul she endeared herself to those who travelled under her wing by her humour, warmth and enthusiasm, although at times presenting rather a nonchalant approach to life, shrugging off any mishap with insouciance. She spoke Italian and, having been brought up in the Argentine, her Spanish also stood us in good stead. Americans loved travelling with her and between the two of us we took over the majority of their tours. In those early days she needed some supervision, as map-reading and timings were not her strong points, and her keenness to include as many places of interest in her itineraries was apt to land her in trouble, when she found she had to cover some 60 odd miles in 15 minutes, or else keep an irate hostess waiting for lunch. No mobile telephones in those days to pave the way if running late.

Meanwhile in Florence, Diana was engaged in putting her

protégée Susie Orso through her paces with a view to her following in Diana's footsteps and eventually conducting tours on her own, a goal which succeeded beyond our wildest dreams – but that was still some years ahead. She had been brought up mainly in England but was now married to Nicolo Orso, an Italian banker, with a small son, Francesco. Susie was all gold, deeply caring of her flocks and meticulous in her planning, thanks to Diana's grounding.

Seventeen

Although it was sensible to choose as our inaugural tours destinations we knew, it was also necessary to widen our horizons to include countries that were more difficult of access to the individual and to make it preferable for them to join an organised visit. This was possibly the reason I had chosen Stockholm and Leningrad as my debut.

In the 1970s, the Soviet Union was not inundated with tourists in the same way it is today. Groups were strictly vetted and arrangements were made direct with Intourist Moscow, who dictated terms regarding hotels, itineraries and all other aspects of the forthcoming visit. Some twenty years later, with as many visits behind me, of course I was to learn that it was useless to take anything for granted or to believe any promises. You could only grit your teeth and enter into a battle of wills, exhausting and not even morally rewarding on the rare occasions when you won. It was the blind bureaucracy which ground you down and the assumption that what Intourist dictates cannot be contested. If the sun is better in the morning for photographing the Kremlin can we change round the order of the programme? Nyet. After the sixth consecutive day of being served tomatoes and cucumber with sour cream (rather delicious on the first day), could we have a change of menu please? Nyet.

In those early days, the head of the British travel section at Intourist in Moscow was Taya Nosakova, a vivacious but inflexible lady, later christened "*La Tigressa*" by one of our Italian travellers on account of her personality and her penchant for wearing dresses sporting a simulated tiger skin design. With a face like a Madonna and a will of steel, Taya would promise me the moon – and at first I was gullible enough to believe her – until she had me and my group safely behind the Iron Curtain, when I would find that the entire programme had been changed without my having been consulted. Once I was accustomed to this behaviour I used to stand my ground, resulting in a clash of personalities.

"You are no longer the sweet girl I knew when first we did business together Hazel," she would say grittily. "Success has corrupted you."

I forbore to mention that the only success I enjoyed was when I managed to wrest from Intourist the promises they had made me in the first place and which I, in turn, had promised my trusting group. I often felt that given different circumstances, Taya and I could have become good friends. She had a striking vitality and a certain racy humour which appealed to me, but as the reasons for our meetings were usually to argue some unacceptable programme change (on my part) or to accuse me of arrogance or stubbornness (on hers), any chance for a better relationship faded in recriminations or, at best, ended in a frosty truce.

After each visit, exhausted and discouraged by a particular brush with Soviet bureaucracy, I vowed not to go back. However in those comparatively early days, most of our clients considered it more prudent to go under the auspices of an organised tour, rather than on their own, so visits to Iron Curtain countries proved to be popular in our repertoire.

Perforce I had to return. Even as I deplored the rigidity of the Communist regime, so I experienced a sort of love-hate relationship with the country as a whole, based perhaps on its ruthless but holy past. When bureaucracy and non-cooperation became too much for me I tried, wherever possible, to enter one of the few practising Orthodox churches when a service was in progress. There I would mingle, for as long as time allowed, with a congregation consisting largely of an older generation – lined and careworn *babushkas*, their heads covered by shawls – and their grizzled men-folk. The priest in his robes would move amongst his flock who, now prostrate at his feet, now kneeling before the candlelit iconostasis, returned his deep-toned invocations with a pouring forth of heart-rending chants. The bass notes of the priest and the plaintive responses from his congregation seemed to embrace, in their lamentations and supplications, an acceptance of the persecution and troubled history of the entire Slavonic race. Seduced by the smell of incense and those nostalgic cadences, I would leave this sanctuary in a humbled state of mind, to face once more the obduracy of my host country and the idiosyncrasies of certain members of my group.

So much depended on the Intourist guide allotted to us. He or she (in fact, I was never given a male guide) could be co-operative, informative, cheerful, hardworking, impassive, indifferent, or an implacable party member determined to be the one in charge. On certain points they could not be faulted: their English was usually first-class and they would be impeccably well grounded in Russian history and in Soviet bureaucracy. Inevitably some renderings of historical facts were delivered parrot-fashion, rather like a well-oiled gramophone record, and could not be deflected with questions, however relevant. On the other hand, a dissertation, say, on the Siege of Leningrad, delivered with real pride and panache by Irena Baegeva, one of the most fluent guides I ever had, would bring forth a sincere and spontaneous round of applause from her audience.

Although she pushed out the Red Flag on occasion, Irena did everything in her power to make my lot an easy one, not always the case. Unfortunately for me she married a Bulgarian and went out of my life. In any case it was most unlikely I would be allotted the same guide twice, although in the early years I was fortunate to be given Olga Nazarova on three consecutive visits.

Olga was a twin (her sister was also an Intourist guide), married to a Muscovite with one small boy. Even at our first meeting it was disclosed that the marriage was foundering, although solace was apparently at hand in the form of a Georgian engineer. Typically Slav in looks and outlook, she was given to extremes of mood, one moment cast in deep gloom and the next laughing with an almost frenetic gaiety. How she had succeeded in becoming an Intourist guide was a puzzlement, as her outlook was distinctly westward looking and she was outspoken to an alarming degree, especially after several glasses of vodka. I feared that the hand of big brother might descend at any moment on her not insubstantial shoulder – or on mine – and lead us away on a charge of over-fraternisation.

Mercifully Olga kept most of her political outbursts until we were air-bound, when the judderings and shudderings of intercity Aeroflights made it impossible for any but her closest neighbour to hear her views on the Party. Of course it may have been an act put on to encourage indiscretions on my part, but I know that the sight of Olga flying across the tarmac (for in those days guides were allowed to greet groups as they got off the plane) with arms outstretched, a hand clutching a single carnation and her beautiful grey eyes shining with pleasure, gave me a feeling of security and confidence that there was at least someone in this inflexible country who would fight for our desires. I was even led into the hotel's kitchen by her on occasion in order to discuss the menu with the catering staff as the food served to groups was invariably monotonous at best, and unappetising at worst.

As already said, I had decided that my first tour abroad was to be to Stockholm and Leningrad, a choice that still bemuses me to this day. I had just returned from a reconnaissance to both cities and was well aware of the problems that lay ahead in regard to the latter. I can only suppose that the Soviet Union, with all its difficulties, offered a challenge which, if overcome, would lend us enough confidence to promote tours to pretty well anywhere. On the other hand, if things did prove thorny, it was only what we led our clients to expect at that time, so blame could hopefully be laid at the Party's door, rather than to our own.

I am endowed with a nature that faced with diversity or calamity tends to become more and more calm – no doubt the calm of desperation. True, this impassivity has been known to give way to remonstration, anger or even invective, but usually the only outward signs of inquietude are a certain bleakness of regard – although according to Sheila Pettit, a regular fellow-traveller, "my toes tend to turn up under stress".

In September 1969, I set off for Sweden with twenty-eight passengers under my wing, the majority being trustful members of the Georgian Group anxious to show their allegiance to me and therefore an added responsibility. Our few days in Stockholm passed without incident, except for the first nail-biting half-hour at Arlanda airport when my coach failed to turn up, having broken down en route from the city. Luckily it coincided with two pieces of luggage being temporarily mislaid, so the delay passed almost unnoticed. However, pre-occupation with what lay ahead of me somewhat detracted from my enjoyment of this lovely city.

My troubles began with our arrival back at Arlanda Airport, four days later, to check-in for our flight to Leningrad by SAS airlines. We were ahead of check-in time, having confirmed our bookings well in advance. Even so, we were told regretfully but categorically that the flight was overbooked and that I would have to off-load seven of my passengers who would follow on several hours later. Cajolery, threats, induced tears and even bribery would not move the harassed official in charge of bookings who seemed to be turning away dozens of other stranded passengers. Finally I had the unenviable task of explaining the situation to my party. My plea for volunteers to stay behind brought forth an immediate response from three blessed men, Ian Grant, Paul Taylor and Tony Roper, travelling together, and the family of four Pettits, already mentioned. It was obvious that the seven looked forward to a free afternoon in Stockholm. It was not so much the idea of leaving them behind in Stockholm that worried me, but of their arrival on their own in Leningrad later that night. I exhorted them to go and have the best lunch they could find and to present the bill to SAS. They carried out my instructions to the letter, so that when they did finally arrive in Leningrad at 10.15pm they were still in a state of euphoria, induced by a lucullan feast of *smørrebrød*, meat balls and unlimited schnapps. When confronted with the bill of £72 (a lot of money in those days), SAS paid the refund without demur.

In the meantime I had taken off with the remainder of my flock, plunged in anxiety as to what might lie ahead. I have always been happy in an aeroplane, since it is the one time I can hand over the responsibility for my travellers to the captain and air crew. It is only with the adjunct before landing "to fasten your seat belts" that my stomach muscles retract, accompanied by a sinking feeling that has nothing to do with our descent. On this occasion, just as we were coming in to land, I was diverted by an urgent shriek from one of my younger members sitting across the aisle from me.

"One of my contact lenses has dropped out," she cried hysterically. "I can see nothing without them."

Within seconds, several of us were on our hands and knees grovelling in the aisle for this minuscule object, oblivious to the increasingly urgent demands for us to regain our seats and fasten our seat belts. Ignoring the commotion around us and while the plane precipitated landwards, we continued our search and miraculously enough eventually located the offending article, which was restored with relief and gratitude to the right eye of its owner. Panic then nearly took over as I convinced myself that my documents were out of order, that I had insufficient money for emergencies, that we were arriving on the wrong day with no coach or guide to meet us and that the hotel accommodation, although rechecked a hundred times, would be wrongly allotted or inadequate. All the ghastly possibilities of things that might go wrong went through my head, even though I knew I was behaving irrationally and needlessly (although it must be said that some of those fears have been justified over the years!).

Leningrad airport that afternoon resembled Dante's inferno. One brawny female seemed to be dealing single-handed with crowds of arrivals from varying destinations, all demanding control forms. I made a point of grabbing a pile which would do for my next visit if, indeed, there was ever to be one. Somehow amidst this melée, I managed to locate the Intourist desk where I was eventually delivered into the not particularly welcoming arms of Nina, our allotted Intourist guide whom, it transpired much later, was suffering the tortures of an abscessed tooth.

"Control forms to be filled in triplicate," I commanded briskly as I handed them out to the outstretched hands of my party. "And for goodness sake and yours, keep the third copy with you at all times, otherwise you will not be able to leave the country."

Some of my group looked ready to depart there and then, but applied themselves instead to completing their questionnaires. It always surprised me that so many of my clients, cultured, privileged, educated and holders of high positions, seemed incapable of filling in the simplest of forms, even to the point sometimes of scarcely knowing their own names. It was explained to me that once under the wing of a tour leader, even the cleverest and most independent of individuals ceased to think for themselves. I was their nanny, their sheep-dog (although I preferred the title shepherdess), their serf and all their responsibilities became mine.

Control forms duly completed, we joined the queues for customs clearance. A few cases were opened and searched at random and one unfortunate – the youngest member of the group travelling with her American grandmother – had her hand luggage searched. This revealed a copy of Leon Goure's "Siege of Leningrad", which she had been reading on the flight over.

"Not allowed," intoned the customs officer, confiscating not only the book but the wretched girl's passport.

"But why?" moaned my outraged client, "the citizens of Leningrad should be proud of their endurance".

"It is not because the book is subversive," I explained patiently, "It is because they want to read it themselves and it is not procurable over here." After half an hour, Phoebe's passport was returned but the book never.

Nearly two hours from touching down, we finally emerged into the arrivals hall where we were greeted by Professor Veronica Doubaskaya, an ebullient representative from the House of Friendship, who thrust into my already overburdened arms a massive bouquet of carnations.

"Welcome to Leningrad from the House of Friendship", she shouted, enfolding me in a powerful embrace to which, impeded as I was with customs clearance forms, files and luggage, I could only respond with exclamations of delight and by blowing kisses into the air behind her right ear.

"Well now," sighing with relief I turned to Nina. "To the Europeyskeya Hotel."

"Nyet," she responded dourly. "To the Sovietskeya Hotel".

An ominous glint appeared in my eye. "We were promised the Europeyskeya."

"It is now the Sovietskeya."

"Why has the hotel been changed?" "No reason given. This is the hotel appointed to you."

An equally obstinate glint had now appeared on Nina's face, while the Professor engaged herself in animated conversation with members of my party.

During the hour-long run into the city, I gazed gloomily at the drab environs, block upon block of concrete apartment houses doing nothing to enliven my spirits. I spent some of the journey in renewed protestations to Nina who merely shrugged her narrow shoulders.

"It is the responsibility of Intourist Head Office," she announced flatly. "You must argue with them."

The Sovietskeya Hotel turned out to be a modern skyscraper, uninviting in its stark symmetry, its baleful windows outlined in harsh blue paint. "The newest hotel in Leningrad," boasted the Professor proudly, but on seeing my look of hostility hastily turned her attention elsewhere. The hotel foyer rather resembled Leningrad Airport, with a seething mass of humanity queuing up for their room keys. Our rooms were on the eighteenth floor, adequately equipped but depressing in their anonymity. The lifts were intermittent. A warning buzz heralded their arrival and having manoeuvred oneself in front of the door, it was only to watch them sail past and disappear into the void, leaving one fuming impotently for the next arrival which could take anything up to ten minutes. A further disadvantage was that the hotel was situated well outside the city centre, resulting in only the most courageous braving public transport, the one means of reaching civilisation, apart from our own coach.

The next day the beauties of Russia's former capital passed me by while I struggled with Intourist bureaucracy. Taya had prudently taken herself off, so I was left to do battle with her deputy – a bear-like gentleman who obviously thought I should be in my seventh heaven staying at the Sovietskeya. Nina's grumpiness I put down to sheer cussedness, unaware of her physical agony.

After two nights in our concrete barracks, the final straw came when our promised opera tickets were replaced, out of hand, with tickets for the circus. I erupted in a tirade of recriminations against all things Soviet.

"If the USSR wants tourists it had better comply with its promises," I shouted. I threw the offending tickets on the reception counter and retired to my eighteenth storey eyrie. Later, on the second night, Nina announced impassively that we were moving the next morning to the Europeyskeya Hotel. No reason given.

The next morning a completely transformed Nina arrived at our breakfast table, her face wreathed in smiles. The abscess had burst! She also brought the news that we were not, after all, going to the Europeyskeya, but as my face froze, she added hastily, "It is to the Astoria that you go".

I felt even happier. This was the hotel at which Hitler was to have celebrated Germany's victory over the three year struggle for Leningrad and had even got so far as having invitations printed. It was the hotel which most visitors coveted. Sited in the heart of the city, close to St. Isaac's Cathedral and within easy walking distance to the Hermitage Museum, our move was greeted with expressions of joy by my flock who nonetheless had been stoic and supportive in our trials and tribulations.

We left the Sovietskeya unreluctantly and drove to our new destination. The Astoria was at that time one of the most old-fashioned hotels in Leningrad (I understand it has recently been revamped), full of gilt and painted furniture. A smiling receptionist greeted us warmly – on later visits she was to become a close ally – and took for granted that we would want theatre tickets which she undertook to procure for me. An ornately embellished turquoise and gilt lift wheezed its way up to the second floor, where a "house mother" produced intricately carved keys for the panelled double doors. These led in turn to a boudoir which preceded the bedroom proper. Plush furnishings and heavy mahogany furniture dominated the scene and a curtained alcove disclosed an Empire style bed. An adjoining bathroom housed a "period" bath standing on high legs, the taps ornately gilded, from which issued a sluggish trickle of peat-coloured water. It was imperative to forewarn the traveller to the Soviet Union to include a bath plug in their luggage since these were non-existent. Judging however by the number I have left behind over the years, this problem may by now have been solved!

One of the suites allotted to Dr Barnes, later Dame Josephine and her son, a competent pianist in his teens, contained a huge grand piano, round which we all congregated one evening for a rather rowdy sing-song. This did not meet with the approval of our house-mother who was, however, placated with a pair of nylons – gold dust in these days.

I sometimes wonder if our change of treatment was in any way due to the inclusion in our group of the Baron and Baroness Dimsdale. The first Baron had had the title conferred on him by

Catherine the Great for his services as a doctor to her court and for the introduction to Russia of the vaccine against smallpox. Although the Tsarist regime had been swept away, the great palaces in and around Leningrad were in the throes of being reconstructed down to the most meticulous details to their pristine splendour and many members of the present regime were not averse to being conversant with a Russian title or two. The current Baron was a kindly soul, much engrossed in his ancestral background and with a keen knowledge of Russian history. His wife was a delightfully fey lady who invariably wore a striped football jersey and gave the impression of not being quite in this world. Also with us was the actor, Alan Wheatley, now alas! dead. He had a deliciously mischievous sense of humour and won much acclaim at a party given for us at the House of Friendship, by courtesy of the Professor, when he was recognised as having played the role of the Sheriff in the television series of Robin Hood.

These parties were designed to give us the opportunity to meet Soviet citizens with the same interests as ourselves, in this instance mostly art historians, architects and those connected with the theatre. I enjoyed these occasions – not least because the food was so much better than that served at the hotels, and accompanied by much sweet champagne, vodka and Georgian wine. At one such event, however, I did notice that, as the evening progressed – and it was still comparatively early around 8pm – our hosts became increasingly fidgety with frequent glances at their watches. It was obviously time to go. Intrigued by their relieved faces as we trooped out, I could not refrain from asking the Professor what they would do with the rest of the evening.

"Oh," she replied somewhat sheepishly, "it's the final instalment of the Forsyte Saga on television tonight and we do not wish to miss it."

"Who is your favourite character" I asked.

"Soames, of course" she replied.

With domestic problems solved on that first visit, I was able to relax and participate in the glories of Leningrad and the great palaces of Tsarkoye Selo and Pavlovsk, still undergoing repair. The Professor accompanied us on several expeditions and by the end of the week we were on Veronica/Hazel terms.

Later visits to the Soviet Union often included a reception at the House of Friendship where Veronica, by then a welcoming friend, acted as hostess. She was in fact a bit of a devil but great fun. Black and red caviar was unstintingly served and after several glasses of vodka or Georgian wine, a number of my party usually became sufficiently uninhibited to give speeches or a vote of thanks, the general theme being 'eternal friendship'.

On the day of our departure from Leningrad on that first visit, I had arranged breakfast at the airport, since we had an early flight. We were assembled in the coach ready to leave the hotel when one of my party, Neville Hawke, launched into a speech of thanks to Nina and to myself, whom he described a "a true leader of men". I was then called outside by the driver to identify a piece of luggage, after which we left for the airport. Being nicely deserted at that hour of the morning we were quickly through customs, but I found to my puzzlement that I was still clutching two boarding passes in my hand. No doubt the counter clerk had miscounted or perhaps the missing pair had headed for the '*tualyet*'. The former I admitted to myself was highly improbable. Somewhat disquieted I led my party into the dining room and sat them down. Two places remained unoccupied. The cold truth dawned on me that the true leader of men had somehow mislaid two of her flock. A frantic call to the hotel confirmed my suspicions, but I was informed that the couple were on their way to the airport by taxi. It transpired that while I had been checking the luggage, they had got off the coach to spend a final penny. Their subsequent arrival at the airport was greeted with derisive cheers and whistles by their fellow travellers, but I was mortified. The Soviet Union was not a place at that time to be left behind with an expired visa.

I suppose it was inevitable that, after embarking successfully on one visit behind the Iron Curtain, others would be passed on to my somewhat reluctant and at that time comparatively inexperienced shoulders. Over the next two decades therefore, I was to lead tours to Czechoslovakia, Poland, Yugoslavia and Hungary, not to mention many more to the Soviet Union, including the Caucasus and Soviet Central Asia. Sometimes this was happily with Tamara Talbot Rice as our much respected and delightful lecturer and interpreter. Tamara was widow of David Talbot Rice – after whom the Talbot Rice Gallery is named at the University of Edinburgh – and her involvement made my task so much easier and contributed to everyone's enjoyment.

Because of the difficulties encountered in Communist countries, compared with visits nearer home, more dramatic, rather than merely frustrating, happenings were liable to take place, which is perhaps why Russia plays rather a large part in these narratives.

Eighteen

Was it really bravado that prompted us to plan the most ambitious of tours to far-flung destinations in those early days, infrequently mounted except by the larger internationally well-known firms? Was it perhaps to show the world and convince ourselves that we were ready and able to take on any challenge? Or was it merely the desire to visit territories hitherto unvisited by ourselves, an act of bravado in itself, although our rivals might have called it foolhardiness and our guinea-pig clients irresponsible. Ignorance, although not always bliss, at time overcomes obstacles which, if apparent or analysed beforehand, would deter the fainthearted and which were often overcome by the simple fact that we did not recognise or were unaware of their existence.

The success of my initial tour abroad, that to Stockholm and Leningrad (for despite certain setbacks it had been a success according to my fellow travellers, who had pronounced it totally enjoyable) must have gone to my head. Earlier in the year the three of us had discussed the number of tours and their destinations for 1970. I at the time was engrossed in Paul Scott's Quartet and the re-reading of E.M. Forster's 'Passage to India', so my thoughts were turning eastwards. I was further inspired by the introduction into our lives of an Indian gentleman called Aycee Anand, who was posted to London as representative of the Indian Tourist Board and who ran a tour operating agency in Delhi. He was naturally anxious to capture new clientele and promised me every assistance, treats undreamed of in the common package tour. He also promised to honour his every promise, all of which I was only too happy to believe, not yet having got the measure of the Indian mentality – which is to say only what you want to hear. Not that their promises are not meant in all sincerity; they really believe in them themselves but somehow there is always a third party, usually of a divine nature, that steps in and ruins everything.

Shortly after the inaugural trip, my imagination was further kindled by articles appearing in the Sunday supplements, extolling the marvels to be discovered in the more distant realms of India, Thailand and Cambodia, accompanied by tempting photographs of the jungle-entwined Angkor Wat and the Golden Buddha of Bangkok. A tour embracing all three countries seemed irresistible, a splendid opportunity to put ourselves on the map as an enterprising company. We would offer an optional three days' finale in Hong Kong, the only country of the four that I had already visited, as a climax for relaxation and shopping. Such arrogance appals me now, but in those early days I must have had a sublime faith in myself and trust in those who were credulous enough to sign up.

Even after many years' experience of guiding groups, I was never to outgrow that sinking sensation on arrival at the airport. Checking in my own luggage and identifying my flock helped to occupy my mind to some extent. I grew adept at the latter and scarcely had need of the puce-coloured labels which adorned their luggage for easy identification at our destinations. In any event, our clients could usually be distinguished on two counts. For the most part elderly, they either carried with them an indescribable air of assurance, declaiming themselves as the accomplished traveller knowing all the ropes, or they diffused an aura of uncertainty at the thought of breaking new ground and wondering if they were going to regret it. By the time I had checked them all in, deferring to the first and reassuring the second, I had usually regained my equilibrium and, like an actor going on stage, knew that I had to remember my lines and deliver them accordingly.

So here I was on a bleak mid-January day in 1970 at Heathrow Airport, taking off for Paris en route for Bombay, with a group of sixteen including myself. Quite a few were known to me from Georgian Group days, but the rest were an unknown entity. By the time we had dined together at the Hotel Littré, it was clear that I was faced with a dauntingly versatile party. My audacity was challenged from the start when I was to discover that the oldest member of the group, Mrs Goldberg – nearer eighty than seventy – had lived in India for twenty-two years as the wife of a high-powered official in Indian Railways. Admittedly she had not been back since independence, but even so, I guessed that her knowledge of the country might be somewhat greater than my own, although she never showed me up for the sham I was.

With me too were Eliot Hodgkin, a well-known artist and his delightful Swiss wife, Mimi, with her unfettered laugh and enquiring mind. Her husband, although a champion of our venture from the start, was apt to make sardonic asides at any shortcomings, intended more to keep me on my mettle rather than to wound. His paintings were of such meticulous detail that the object became almost tangible; the feel of the bloom on a peach or the scent of a Blanc Double de Courbet rose. He would entreat me to keep for him a certain plaited roll served for breakfast at the Auberge des Temples in Siem Reap; or to search for the more spectacular rarities which could be found along the shell-encrusted shores that fringed the Temples of Mahabalipuram; or in the baskets carried on the hips of small bare-footed girls who, with their enormous brown eyes alight with anticipation and mischief, dangled a necklace of cowries or monster iridescent shells before our eyes, enticing us to part with a rupee or two in exchange. A slight thorn in my flesh was a vegetarian lady barrister, who proclaimed before every mealtime, "Not forgetting little me, Hazel, are you?" "As if you could," muttered a rebellious fellow traveller.

Another Georgian friend was Jean Monro, who I had met during the war and whose work I had so admired on my trip to South Africa in 1958. She was one of London's better-known interior designers and was recovering from a rather turbulent time in her life. Large-hearted of voice and generous in spirit, she could give censure when too hard pressed by adversity but her full support in time of trouble. Travelling with the Hodgkins was a former actress, Peggy Ross, elderly but still lovely with faded red/gold hair and a serene manner. Somewhat eccentric in dress and quite unconscious of the curiosity of passers-by, she would kneel in front of a temple praying to whatever God she worshipped for a trouble-free day. I supported her wholeheartedly.

Already a friend was a former Mallett customer, Doreen Wood, who had recently lost her husband. We had met by chance in Sloane Street just before Christmas when she had asked me if I had any long tours planned.

"Yes, I've one of four weeks starting in late January," I replied.

"Sign me up for a single room please."

"But Doreen, don't you want to know where you will be going or the cost?"

"As long as it is warm and with you, I couldn't care less!"

Used to luxurious living, by the time she reached Bombay some six weeks later, she was beginning to have second thoughts about the entire enterprise, but luckily met up with Jean Monro, in whom she found an ally and they became close friends. She usually enlivened her journeys by targeting a fellow traveller in order, as she explained, "to get her adrenalin going". In this instance she chose a rather flaccid lady whose name escapes me. Ponderous in movement and in thought, she carried a parasol at all times and wore white cotton gloves reminding me of Frances Cornford's "Why do you walk through the fields in gloves".

She was the subject of much interest in India to schoolboys, especially when mounted on an elephant.

Another participant was Cecil (Sam) Clutton, of the property family, a rally driver of veteran cars, organist and collector of clocks and barometers. An impatient character, he brooked no laxity and was apt sometimes to kick against the pricks of group travel and of having to wait for the slower members of the party, but was also to become a good friend. Two couples kept themselves very much to themselves and caused me no anxiety, except towards the end of the tour, when Mr Randall's health became a cause for concern. Protracted constipation led him to fear that he might be suffering from a bowel constriction, so the whole party awaited his daily bulletins with bated breath and when, at last, about the eighth day, the dam burst so to speak, there was a general sense of relief all round. India seems to me to be a country which either repels or enthrals. It is not a country of half measures.

On that first visit, as I set foot on Indian soil at Bombay airport, by the time I had inhaled that indefinable scent of cow-dung, sweat, curry and *patchouli*, and had been adorned with the welcoming garland placed over our heads, I was hooked for all time. Some visitors find too repugnant the squalor, the dirt, the poverty, the incessant cries for *bakshi*, the harassment by beggars thrusting their severed stumps in front of one and the maddening habit of promising you what they think you want to hear, rather than the more unpalatable truth. But look at the inherent dignity of the Indian women and the grace with which they wear their saris; their deportment and the flashing white of their teeth; the politeness of the Indian official in spotless white shirt or *dhoti* who at times put our own manners to shame; the hospitality and friendliness of museum directors and owners of houses we were privileged to visit, with no malice of things past. Indeed the naïve pleasure – or was it revenge – in serving us with remembered dishes of tapioca or Cabinet pudding instead of a dish of lychees or mangoes which we would have preferred. But it is the beauty of the countryside and richness of its cultures and civilisations which assail the senses most vividly.

These were to follow. My first memory of India was our drive into Bombay from the airport after midnight and feeling a foolish surprise at the number of what I took to be refuse sacks lining the road, until I realised that each sack contained a sleeping body – comprising a large percentage of the city's homeless. A week or so later we were to experience a similar journey, this time from Dum Dum Airport into the centre of Calcutta, as dusk was falling. Hordes of Indians were returning 'home' from work on foot, by bicycle, in rickshaws and pousse-bicyclettes (a three-wheeled tricycle-like vehicle), buggies, cars, and buses piled high with humanity and luggage, their sides alive with bodies clinging to whatever support they could find.

Cows lumbered in front of our wheels or ambled amongst the strolling crowds while on the pavements numerous families were lighting up their wood fires prior to cooking their evening meal. The smoke from these fires, mingling with the sulphuric glare of the illuminated hoardings lining the highway – together with the blaring of horns, cries of street vendors and the hawking and spitting from a thousand throats – conjured up a vision of Dante's inferno, was it not for the fact that the crowds looked surprisingly resigned to their lot.

The days in India passed in visits to myriad temples: the intertwined designs in honey-coloured stone at Halebid and Belur, the caves at Ajanta, the stunning architectural creations and reliefs at Mahabalipuram and Kanchipuram, the cylindrical buildings at Bhubeneshwar and the unique erotic wheel at Koronak. Our visit to Elephanta Island coincided with a public holiday. Our pathway up the hillside to the caves was impeded by the local population intent in hindering our progress in the jokiest way possible, especially for one or two of my group who elected to be carried both ways by litter.

Apart from a few pinpricks such as delayed flights (no reason given), minor breakdowns to a car or bus, and eternal promises by our guides, not always materialised, our remaining days in India passed without mishap. For me it was enough to absorb the every day scenes which met our eyes while journeying by road: a biblical-like figure of a child guarding flock of goats and sheep; a sari-clad woman proudly bearing a water jar on her head or a turbaned elder astride a donkey, its panniers crammed with greenstuffs and market produce while his womenfolk trudged alongside on foot, equally burdened.

We spent our last two days at Puri, a picturesque fishing village on the shores of the Indian Ocean, where most of the inhabitants were fishermen living in thatched huts along the palm-fringed beach. Because of the huge waves and treacherous currents, no one was permitted to bathe without being accompanied by a lifeguard clad in a loincloth and yellow pointed hat. Rather disdaining the offer of a proffered hand by my life-saver, I found myself dragged under water by the vicious undertow, only to be plucked out by the scruff of the neck, and shaken like a terrier before being deposited on the shore, spluttering and discomfited, much to the amusement of my party.

Our next destination on that same tour was Cambodia. I have never ceased to be grateful for the opportunity of visiting this ancient kingdom only a month before it was occupied by the Khmer Rouge, with their ensuing desecration of the country and the carnage of its people. Our hotel, the Auberge des Temples at Siem Reap, was French-owned and delightfully situated in view of the great pyramidal pile of stone which signalled Angkor Wat itself, on the edge of the jungle. Here we were greeted by smiling staff offering warm scented towels and fresh lime juice in a garden full of aromatic plants and sweet-smelling flowers. The food was good and the hotel's elephant put at our disposal to convey visitors to and from the temples if so desired. Geckoes ran up and down the walls, inside and out, and over all was the brooding silence of the jungle.

Most of the temples and monuments we were to visit over the next five days had been left untouched for centuries and only discovered by chance by a French hunting party. Although much of the encroaching vegetation had been cut away to expose the breath-taking beauty of the stone carving beneath, nature was still much in evidence. Tortured branches tangled with chiselled lintels and from the fissured foundations of a building, the twisted roots of a giant banyan tree would emerge snakelike, to be smothered by the entwining creepers of a trumpet vine.

Rounding a corner we would stumble on a moss-covered gargoyle or some grinning stone satyr, while above our heads a family of monkeys chattered away on a canopy of densely interlaced branches, cutting off the sunlight and leaving one with a sense of unease and oppression.

Angkor Wat itself stuns with its sheer immensity. The best renowned of the Khmer relics, it is approached by the great exterior staircase rising in stages, culminating in the pyramidal tower containing the sanctuary. One is mesmerised too by the colour of the stone, which changes from honeyed to darker tones as the sun goes down. Angkor Thom, the ancient capital built at the end of the 12th century, is approached by the famous snake balustrade. Close by is the exquisite little temple of Banteay Srei, perhaps my favourite of all.

One afternoon I escaped the clutches of my group and set off on a hired pousse-bicyclette, driven by an elderly but agile local who introduced me to some of the lesser known temples – all but hidden by dense undergrowth. With a sudden shock of surprise we were confronted with a crumbling pile of red sandstone that still retained some lovely and intricate carving to window and door surrounds. Most were the home of bats, judging by the droppings and ammoniacal stench emanating from them. Gaudily winged butterflies flitted around us or alighted on the heady-scented honeysuckle, which draped itself across the ruined remains of buildings. Occasionally we would come across a saffron-robed monk who smiled and clasped his hands in blessing as we passed. Otherwise the peace was only broken by the whirring of our wheels, the monotonous melancholy peep of some bird and the song of the cicadas. Nearing civilisation once more, we drove through villages of thatched huts, in front of which squatted women preparing their evening meal – and once we waved at a small naked boy guarding a couple of black, white-socked piglets. As dusk fell, fireflies twinkled in and out of the trees like so many flickering miniature candles and I duly arrived back at the hotel refreshed in mind and body. And yet only weeks away this tranquillity was to be torn asunder by war, and the richness and fertility of the countryside transformed into killing fields.

Our last port of call before the optional three days in Hong Kong was Bangkok in Thailand, our arrival coinciding with Chinese New Year, a not auspicious day as it turned out. We touched down on a very hot and steamy afternoon, to be greeted by a suspiciously empty looking airport, which I put down to it being a public holiday.

Although our arrival had been confirmed only two days before with our Thai agent, there was no sign of him nor any transport to convey us to the Oriental, the leading hotel in the city and to which my party was looking forward although, after some delay, was beginning to feel hot and sticky and not a little fractious. I somehow managed to find taxis to take us to the hotel, which was everything a hotel should be – a garden ablaze with exotic plants; huge leafed trees between which hammocks were invitingly slung; air-conditioned marble-walled reception rooms in which white coated staff were proffering iced drinks. Sensing trouble ahead, I urged my group to accept the drinks "on the house". The elegantly dressed receptionist, who introduced herself as Rita, greeted me with surprise that turned to consternation when I produced my booking form, which confirmed three doubles and ten singles – a tall order for any hotel.

"I not understand," she exclaimed. "Your agent rang this

morning to say you were delayed until tomorrow and Bangkok it is so busy I have disposed of all your rooms."

"You must get them back..." but even as I spoke I knew the futility of my words 'possession being nine points of the law'.

"How many share?" asked Rita hopefully. I knew the answer to this one too, without feeling the regard of nine pairs of hostile eyes trained on mine.

"Hilton next door with vacant rooms," continued Rita, "can manage six rooms here, you stay with me if want".

Doreen and Jean brushed past me. "We're at the hairdressers (luckily open) until our rooms are ready."

"What makes you think you are getting rooms," I muttered to their retreating backs. Two indeed did share. The rest of us moved to the Hilton for the night, returning to the Oriental for dinner and the next three nights.

My agent, Mr Seri, did eventually turn up that first evening and by the time he had metaphorically picked himself off the floor, promised us red carpet treatment for the rest of our stay in Bangkok. This indeed materialised, in the form of full compensation for our rooms, à la carte meals, free wine, air conditioned coach and limousine service for the non Hong-Kongers to the airport.

We dined in the candle-lit dining-room of the Oriental on that first night before the intervention of my agent, and watched the river outside alive with the movements of barges, skiffs and ferries that were plying a heterogeneous crowd of Bangkok's population from bank to bank.

Drained with emotion, I sat with Doreen and Jean and gratefully assented to a share of the hotel's most expensive wine. Over the next three days, with accommodation finally settled, we were able to relax and enjoy the stimulation and sheer pace of Bangkok. The vibrant colours of the river market, the glittering gold of Buddhist temples and the clamour of its population going about their business either on foot, by bicycle or in the jostling toc-tocs that buzzed like angry bluebottles all over the city. The mystery of the misunderstanding was never fully explained.

It was with a certain relief, tinged with trepidation, that I bade farewell to certain members of the group and flew onwards with the rest of the party to Hong Kong. At our Kowloon hotel I was greeted with the magical words "Good day, Madame, welcome to our hotel. Yes, we have all the rooms you require. Anything you want just ask for". The marathon was nearly at an end.

Nineteen

Mrs John de Witt Peltz or Mary Ellis Peltz arrived at Heathrow Airport in June 1970, wearing a stylish turbaned headdress that swathed most of her forehead. Apart from thinking it rather inappropriate for travel to the USSR in mid-June and remarking that her complexion was a bit mottled, I gave her no more immediate thought, pre-occupied as I was with gathering my flock together for their flight to Moscow. I had already learned that she was editor of 'Opera News' in New York and founder of the Metropolitan Opera Archives. It was not until we were actually waiting to board that I noticed one of Mrs Peltz's eyes was distinctly blacker than the other, and that there were by now other signs of facial wear and tear which disquietened me. She and her travelling companion, Mrs Emily Baker, were both from New York City and had flown in to London the previous day.

During our wait I managed to draw the latter aside and enquired whether her friend was feeling alright. After some hesitation she confided to me that she and Mrs Peltz had been to the opera the night before. On their way back to their hotel her friend had slipped on the escalator at Charing Cross underground and had plunged headlong on to the concrete floor below. A policeman had directed them to the nearest hospital. "Such a darling young man," murmured Mrs Baker reverently. "He gave each of us an arm to cross the road." In casualty, a young Indian doctor had examined his patient and pronounced no bones broken but multiple bruises and possible delayed concussion. He recommended complete rest for forty-eight hours and in no circumstances to travel by air. And here she was at that very moment being summoned to proceed to Gate 9 for the flight to Moscow, the forerunner of what promised to be a very strenuous twelve days of sightseeing. "But you mustn't let on I told you," implored a distraught Mrs Baker. "She said to me this morning, 'Now Emily swear you'll not tell a soul about my accident until we're aboard that plane.'"

Too late for recriminations now. These would have to wait. In the meantime, we had nearly four hours' flying time, which I had planned to spend reading and catching up on my homework. Instead I kept darting furtive glances across the aisle to where Mrs de Wit Peltz was sitting and drinking what could have been whisky (had I not read lately that stimulants were no longer recognised as being the correct remedy for shock?) and reading a history of St. Petersburg. After an hour or so, she removed her headgear – no doubt calculating that she could not be evicted from the aeroplane while flying several thousand feet above the earth, or merely because her head was beginning to ache. It was only then that one could appreciate the full extent of the damage meted out by the impact of her fall. A mass of ugly looking contusions merged with her hair giving her a grotesque and somewhat clownish appearance. I began to have serious doubts whether she would be let through the customs at Moscow Airport.

She smiled ruefully at me across the aisle having been told by Emily, no doubt, that I was in the know. "I'm alright dear," she declared. "I'm just fine." At my instigation the stewardess produced some ice in a plastic bag which I induced the victim to hold against her face in an attempt to reduce the swelling. This, however, had the effect of even worsening her appearance since the melting ice coursed down her cheeks, creating glacier-like fissures. A quick look at her passport, by then in my charge, revealed that she was nearing her eightieth birthday, which did little to relieve my anxiety. In due course we touched down at Sheremetyevo Airport in the midst of a full-bodied storm. It was teeming with rain and the sky was prune-coloured, I persuaded Mrs Peltz to re-wind her turban and to wear dark glasses, although the latter may well have caused her some pain.

As usual, the airport was seething with humanity and customs clearance seemed to take for ever. It was then that Olga, Intourist Guide, made her first appearance in my life and became from then on my mentor and friend and every-present help in trouble. I explained to her Mrs Peltz's predicament and she accompanied her through passport control, the bored soldier in charge stamping her passport with no more than a cursory look at its holder. Having located the rest of my group – thirty in all – and got them safely aboard our coach, we went on our way to the Rossya Hotel, that enormous, impersonal, excrescence towering over Red Square and the Kremlin – where it can take fifteen to twenty minutes to reach the restaurant from your bedroom. The hotel has four main entrances, all seemingly identical, and if a flustered traveller attempts to enter by the wrong door after showing his or her pass, the way is blocked by a formidable and weighty looking 'bouncer', threatening one with a volley of incomprehensible Russian.

During the drive, Olga gave an introductory talk on Moscow and the programme we were going to follow for the next twelve days. However, I could see that many members of the party were diverted by the curious appearance of Mrs Peltz, now looking rather glassily out of the window, but attempting at the same time to appear interested in Olga's dissertation. On arrival at the hotel I was all for depositing our patient in hospital there and then, or at least for calling the hotel doctor to examine her, but she would have none of it. "I know my own strength, dear," she kept assuring me. "A good night's sleep will see me right," but I felt anything but assured each time I looked at her face, which by this time resembled some surrealistic painting.

By the next morning she seemed improved and determined to take part in our every activity – although her rooming mate, Mrs Baker, confided in me that her compatriot had had a restless night and had complained of a headache. I again suggested that she should see a doctor, but the idea was brushed aside with an indulgent laugh.

For the next six days we explored the marvels of Moscow and its environs. We toured the precincts of the Kremlin, mesmerised by the quality of the treasures amassed by the Tsars, which were on show in the Armoury. We were ushered to the front of the local crowds queuing for admission to the great Cathedrals of the Assumption and of the Archangel Michael, scenes of the Tsars' coronations and burials, to stand transfixed in front of the jewelled iconostasis and frescoed walls. We stood, cameras poised (permission for photography having being granted) in front of Lenin's tomb, watching the chilling precision of the changing of the guard as, like automatons, the military figures goose-stepped across Red Square to take up their positions in front of the tomb, while the relieved pair performed an equally intimidating departure. We donned felt slippers and shuffled our way over the exquisitely restored inlaid floors which graced the former Sheremetyev family residences at Ostankino and Kuskovo and we paid homage to the unique and loveliest of monasteries at Zagorsk where the singing evoked the mysteries and sadness of the past. And on all these occasions Mrs Peltz photographed and admired, turning to her friend Mrs Baker from time to time with cries of "Oh my, Emily, all this gold and all this history," oblivious of the curious gazes from the serried ranks of Muscovites being herded round their heritage bequeathed to them by their deposed Tsars, destroyed by wartime bombs and now being lovingly restored by Soviet master craftsmen.

It was perhaps our flight to Leningrad by Aeroflot, notorious for its badly pressurised inter-city aeroplanes, that finally did for Mrs Peltz just a week after she had left London, or perhaps the *coup de grâce* was the deafening noise from the band that accompanied our dinner that first night in the Astoria Hotel.

During the meal I noticed that her skin had taken on a curiously greenish tinge, but put this down to the natural colour changes that bruises undergo. However her eyes seemed glazed and unfocused and at last she confessed she was not feeling "quite myself dear". I put her to bed and called the hotel doctor, who pronounced pneumonia and delayed concussion and prescribed immediate hospitalisation. The patient was mercifully past protesting further and I left her in the care of Mrs Baker while I went to alert Olga of the situation.

It was some time before the ambulance could be organised and when I was informed of its eventual arrival, the attendants had been inadvertently shown to the wrong room. Mrs Severne, my mentor and reason for being there at all, awoke from a sound sleep to find two white coated and masked figures standing over her. Convinced she was being taken off to a loony bin in Siberia, she gave a wild shriek and leaping from her bed came pounding on my door, to the consternation of the two male nurses who really did think they had a case of insanity on their hands. Hospitals in the Soviet Union are not very welcoming places, especially in the middle of the night, but the ward in which Mrs Peltz was finally put to bed was a small one and the night nurse sympathetic, although incomprehensible to both Mrs Peltz and myself. Olga was blessedly with me so was able to relay the information that patients depended on their families or friends to feed them, otherwise Mrs Peltz might have been left to starve to death.

The next morning I was informed that a head examination had been carried out and possibly an operation, although no permission given as far as I could gather. Having sent off the rest of my party on an introductory tour of Leningrad with Anna, a stand-in Intourist Guide and friend of Olga's, Olga and I repaired again to the hospital, aghast at the thought that we might well be confronted with a cabbage-like Mrs Peltz or gibbering idiot. But our American friend was made of sterner stuff and seemed remarkably unruffled by her first encounter with the Soviet medical service. She seized the oranges I had brought her with exclamations of appreciation and declared that she wanted nothing else except her French grammar books, which she needed as she was going on to Paris after our return to London and wished to master the irregular verbs. These were duly produced and on ensuing visits she appeared perfectly content construing French subjunctives, munching oranges and carrying on a sign language conversation with her two ward mates, elderly Russian women who seemed to regard Mrs Peltz as nothing out of the ordinary, offering her from time to time a piece of black bread and butter, herrings or a gherkin or two supplied by the dejected looking daughter of one of them.

Engrossed in her immediate surroundings, my client would wave rather absentmindedly at Olga and myself, who visited her each evening after the day's stint, a tedium that was, for me at least, mitigated by my ever-increasing knowledge of the Leningrad underground system, which had been a revelation on my first visit to the Soviet Union. I never ceased to marvel at the architectural beauty of the Metro: the chandeliers that adorned the vaulted ceilings, shining down on marble and inlaid walls that lined the platforms, themselves furnished with bronze reliefs depicting scenes from lives of the workers. The floors were spotless and I could not help contrasting the opulent cleanliness of these Metros with our own tube stations littered with rubbish, the only adornment being advertisements to out of date shows.

When I broached the question of his patient's future with her doctor, I was told "fourteen days in bed" and no question of flying to London in five days' time, which was our scheduled date of departure. When I broke this news to Mrs Peltz, her mouth set in stubborn lines.

"I am not" she repeated "not, staying here on my own" and gave a vicious jab at the orange which she was peeling.

"But Mrs Peltz," I protested, "you must do what your doctor advises. I cannot take the responsibility of allowing you to fly in the face of doctor's orders. I will contact your Consulate and they will look after you."

She continued mulishly to devour her orange but said no more. My advice obviously went unheeded, since two days later she announced she was flying back to London with the group and that she would take full responsibility for her actions.

"A corpse can hardly be expected to take responsibility for the consequences," I remarked sourly to Olga as we wended our weary way back to the hotel, to be met with the predictable meal of tomato and cucumber salad doused with sour cream, a hunk of unidentifiable meat – probably yak – and the ubiquitous saffron cake, for some reason called English trifle. Vodka and the excellent ice-cream were the only gastronomical consolations.

Mrs Baker disclosed to me the name and telephone number of a nephew who might be able to help, "in strict confidence of course". But telephoning from Leningrad in 1970 was not an easy matter and although I tried his number incessantly I never did succeed in contacting him. Instead I arranged for a wheelchair to take her to the aircraft at Leningrad airport and I rang our London office to arrange an ambulance to meet the flight at Heathrow and to book a room in a nursing home. Two days before our departure, Mrs Peltz discharged herself from hospital and when Olga and I arrived to collect her, all hell had broken loose, owing to her summer coat having disappeared. "My best blue summer coat," she wailed but no one admitted to having seen it, myself included, and we eventually had to leave without it, her doctor showing obvious relief at getting rid of his obstreperous patient. The coat was later discovered in the hotel cloakroom.

On the day before our departure I took my followers off to Novgorod for the day, leaving Mrs Peltz in bed at the hotel. For a time I was able to forget her, engrossed as I was in the beauty of this ancient city, Russia's former seat of government. An important trading centre until the 15th century when it lost its independence, the town stands on both sides of the River Volkhov and although badly damaged by the Germans in the Second World War, is renowned for its many churches and wooden buildings. It was not until our three-hour return journey to Leningrad later that June evening that my thoughts returned to Mrs Peltz. As the sun sank below the horizon of that relentlessly straight and uneventful road, punctuated at intervals by the occasional village of wooden houses and domed church, or a huddle of dachas, summer houses of the favoured few, I started worrying. I was tormented by the vision of our arrival in England with a prostrate American, seriously ill or even dying – my thoughts refused to go beyond that – and of being vilified by British European Airways for bringing an invalid aboard, or even worse refusing to take her. Steeped in apprehension and depression I arrived back at the hotel at about 10pm where I went to my patient's room. No sign of her. I finally tracked her down in what passed for a bar, where she was being the life and soul of the party, regaling to a spellbound group of Americans her account of life in a Soviet hospital. She hailed me with real pleasure, ignoring my frigid response. It transpired that she had spent the entire day at the Hermitage and was now celebrating her recovery.

Altogether, as she told me, "I've had a ball". Rigid with fury I told Mrs Peltz coldly and clearly that she was on her own now and that I could no longer be held responsible for her. I refused the vodka she offered me and returned to my room to pack and to spend the next frustrating hour or so trying to telephone my colleague at his home (luckily London was two and a half hours behind Leningrad time) and asked him to cancel both the ambulance and nursing home booking.

After an uneventful flight to London the next day, during which Mrs Peltz practised aloud her French verbs while consuming a hearty lunch and several drinks, we finally touched down at Heathrow. While waiting for our luggage to appear, she came up to me. Seizing both my hands in hers she exclaimed, "Dear Miss Wood, you've been the greatest and I know I've been a real trial to you. But I must tell you once again that I've had a ball and I guess you're mad at me but, dear, I do know my own strength".

Twenty

New Year celebrations in the USSR sounded promising and perhaps would find Intourist in rather a more relaxed frame of mind than hitherto. So here I was at Heathrow Airport, once again, on a chill late December morning, muffled to the ears in a fur-lined coat, Davy Crocket style hat and boots to match, checking in on a flight to Moscow alongside a young member of my party who confided to me that she had brought a new trouser suit for the festive occasions she had been promised, now safely packed away in her case. It was the last she was to see of case and trouser suit, which disappeared into limbo for evermore, but at least she and I were to have a tranquil outward journey before the loss was discovered.

On arriving in Moscow on that December afternoon, all sounds of traffic were muted, not that there was overmuch of that in 1973/74 apart from public transport and the sleek black limousines conveying party members about their business. The more modern buildings shed their forbidding aspect under a mantle of snow and the inhabitants, especially the women, looked more alluring in their fur hats rather than the ubiquitous headscarf worn by old and young alike. We were seeing in the New Year in the capital, since Christmas was not recognised under the Communist regime, and the population were bent on enjoying themselves, however little the shops had to offer or however long they had to queue for a handful of windfalls, the occasional bonus bar of chocolate or an extra bottle of vodka.

In contrast I and my group were to celebrate in typical capitalistic fashion, housed purportedly in a first class hotel. My guide on this occasion was a sad-looking individual called Vera. Dressed invariably, as we were to note, in a drab green suit topped by a leather jerkin and knitted hat, she looked as if the good things of life had passed her by, although now and again I thought I detected a faint glimmer of humour behind her tired eyes. She emanated a resigned dispiritedness that subsequently earned her the title of Dreary Vera amongst our group. Her mood of despondency I found infectious, especially when she told me we were staying at the Ukrainia Hotel, a pyramidic multi-tiered block, one of seven identical buildings that graced the city, one of them being the University. The foyer was graceless but the welcome was warm, the New Year spirit invading the staff generally. The lift lurched ominously as it creaked its laboured way to the twelfth floor where most of our rooms were situated, but which turned out to be spacious and well appointed, each with its aspidistra, table covered by a patterned rug, and a Bohemian style chandelier concealing, no doubt, a bugging device.

Apart from sightseeing, New Year's Eve was largely spent by me in trying to locate poor Miss Dennis's suitcase, without success. There was no record of it having turned up at any other airport in the Soviet Union, or even in Tokyo, as we had checked in next to those travelling to Japan. Admitting eventually to defeat I then tried to contact her father to ask him to send out a replacement suitcase of clothes, which necessitated several abortive calls before I finally traced him. Meanwhile various members of the group donated items of clothing and other essentials to the unfortunate girl who was being remarkably stoical in the circumstances.

Later that evening our party was ushered into the hotel's enormous dining room, decorated for the occasion with streamers and pictures of Saint Nicholas, proclaiming "Novi Gdom". For once the kitchens had surpassed themselves by producing mounds of caviar, smoked sturgeon, *bortsch* accompanied by newly baked *piroshki*, chicken Kiev and ice cream. Carafes of vodka stood on every table, flanked by bottles of sweet Russian champagne, beer and the robust Georgian wine, and the inevitable *sok* (insipid fruit juice). Since there was no incentive to finish the meal before the hour of midnight struck, we were subjected to a thirty-minute break between each course, which encouraged the replenishment of glasses and for the revellers to spill on to the dance floor – which appeared inadequate for the crowd of participants locked together in a frenetic aura of goodwill.

Most of Europe seemed to be represented, with the predominance going to Finland and the Eastern bloc. Oddly enough we appeared to be the only British party present and as the evening wore on, the majority of us threw off our British reserve and allowed ourselves to be swept on to the dance floor by farmers from the Ukraine government, officials from Czechoslovakia and the ubiquitous Japanese. Any small talk was extraneous, since an ear-splitting band made conversation impossible. On this occasion we had one man in the entire group, several years younger than most of his female companions, apart from Miss Dennis. I shall for ever remember Tony Holden with admiration and gratitude, as with commendable fortitude he led each member of the party in turn (including Vera) into the melée where his ballroom style gyrations did not stand much of a chance against the jostling couples around him.

On New Year's Day, after a leisurely morning and vigorous afternoon's sightseeing, we were to attend a ballet performance of The Nutcracker at the Bolshoi Theatre before driving to the station to catch the Red Arrow Midnight Express to Leningrad. Prior to leaving for the theatre I was engaged in the mundane task of checking the luggage, which was lined up neatly in the hall, and discovered that one of my own cases was missing.

On questioning the reception clerk I was informed that they were holding the case hostage until the telephone bill to Mr Dennis in London had been settled.

"But British Airways is settling this account," I protested, "they have already agreed to pay."

"I know nothing," came the well-worn refrain.

"Ring BA's office," I insisted.

"Closed for the New Year holiday," she retorted, not without a certain satisfaction.

"Ring the airport then," I cried, frantic by now with the thought of the imminent rising of the curtain at the Bolshoi, or even worse, of the Red Arrow steaming relentlessly out of Moscow station while I wrestled with Soviet bureaucracy.

By the grace of God, Reception somehow managed to contact Sheremetyevo Airport and the BA representative, who was *au fait* with the situation and managed to settle the matter. I sank into my plush seat at the Bolshoi in a thankful but drained condition. The ballet performance was magical and as snow fell on the stage in the closing scene, so the snow was falling as we emerged into Sverdlov Square.

We finally located our coach amidst the many lining the neighbouring streets and drove direct to the station. The very sight of the midnight express conjured up a vision of Anna Karenina, further enhanced by the hissing steam rising from the frozen tracks under the train and the tapping of the undercarriage by muffled-up railway workers which I had always imagined was theatrical license. Would that I had the necessary charisma to act out the role of the heroine but it was enough for me, with the help of Vera, to keep our group together and herd them into the right compartments.

All Moscow seemed to he on the move, with young and old clutching babies or bundles of bedding and wicker baskets bulging with provisions for the journey, being seen off by keening relatives, or entwined in a last-minute embrace. A band of merry, raucously singing porters helped to get us and our luggage aboard, their stubbled cheeks aglow with the cold and vodka. We were installed in 'soft class' with two to a compartment. Tony, our only man, was listed as sharing with a Mr A.N. Other, but having fought off several offers of company from Soviet citizens of both sexes, managed to retain a compartment to himself, much to the envy of the rest of the party. Fairly primitive toilets and an electric samovar were to be found at the end of each corridor, further banishing the more romantic notion of serfs bearing a steaming samovar with glasses from carriage to carriage. Vera and I shared a compartment but even during a seven-hour journey I was able to discover next to nothing about her background, except that she was forty-five and thought that I was younger than she was.

Leningrad station at 7am the next morning was comparatively deserted and as the train drew to a halt, blue-smocked porters were lined up at our carriage doors, ready to seize our luggage and load it on to the waiting coach. When things do run smoothly in Russia, it is such a delightfully unexpected surprise that one tends to forget the frustrations that test one's patience to the limit, until the next incident crops up as a reminder. We were staying at the Astoria, my favourite hotel in Leningrad, where by now mine was a familiar face and was greeted with smiles of recognition. Also awaiting our arrival was a small inconspicuous figure clad in a well-worn overcoat and astrakhan hat, his face framed by a goatee beard and kind eyes smiling shyly from behind gold-rimmed spectacles.

On one of my previous visits to Leningrad I was fortunate to be given an introduction to architect Professor Mikhael Kraminski, then in his late sixties, who had been much involved in the supervision of the restoration of the great palaces in the city's vicinity after the war, such as Tsarkoye Selo and Pavlosk, still undergoing repair. His brother Victor had emigrated to Britain, changing his name to Kennet and had married Audry Withers, one-time editress of Vogue. In 1970 he and his wife produced a book entitled "Palaces of Leningrad", which they dedicated to Mikhael. There was a problem getting the book to him in Leningrad and I undertook to take it with me on one of my tours although it was a moot point whether I would succeed in getting it through customs. In any event I popped it into my hand luggage (it was one of those coffee-table editions and weighed heavily) and hoped that the customs officials would be sufficiently dumb to believe that I was going to use it as a guide book. As luck would have it something more important distracted their attention and I was able to walk out of the airport with the precious book still safely in my possession. On arrival at our hotel I was able to hand over my burden, wrapped in one of Victor's cardigans, equally appreciated, to a grateful Mikhael. His gratitude was touching to see. Thanks to him we were able to see parts of buildings not normally open to the public and to watch the actual work of restoration in progress. As his English was nil and my Russian confined to phrases such as "more coat hangers please" or equally banal requests, our conversation was conducted in French.

On a previous occasion, he had invited me and two of the group, Lady Evershed and Mrs Norman, to have tea with him at his home where he had formerly lived with his mother and then his wife, now deceased. A large house in a once fashionable quarter of the city, it was now converted into ten apartments with a communal bathroom and kitchen. Mikhael told me that he had been given the chance to acquire one of the modern flats which had been built since the end of the war, each with its own facilities, but that he had preferred to stay with his memories. On the way there he took us to the former Yusupov Palace on the Moika River, scene of Rasputin's assassination and now a teacher's club where, on the threshold, he asked us somewhat apologetically not to speak too loudly in a foreign language. The Yusupovs had had their own private theatre within the palace, an exquisite piece of architectural design, restored to its original colours. From there we took a bus to his flat, which consisted of one largish room with a cheerful orange curtain dividing the living from the sleeping quarters. Rather at odds with the decor were treasures from the past: a crystal and lapis candelabra, rather a lovely icon and lots of family photographs. Of a gentle and modest disposition, he seemed to accept his lot philosophically. He talked much of his daughter as he spread a tempting array of food before us – salami and gherkins, smoked sturgeon, black bread and butter, wine and coffee. I only hope he enjoyed our company as much as we did his. On subsequent visits to Leningrad, he joined us on many excursions and to meals, as I always felt he did not have enough to eat. In more recent years I always heard from him at Christmas. Then one year there was no news and I heard sometime later that he had been run over and killed in a street accident.

One has only to read Suzanne Massie's 'Pavlovsk: Story of a Palace' to understand the research, sacrifice and dedication contributed by so many survivors of the Leningrad siege, which led to the almost unbelievable achievement of resurrecting, phoenix-like from the rubble, almost exact replicas of the palaces originally created for the Tsars and Tsarinas by architects and craftsmen such as Rastrelli, Quarenghi, Voronikhin and Cameron.

Tsarkoye Selo, or the Catherine Palace, named after Catherine I, wife of Peter the Great, must be one of the grandest of such palaces, richly embellished on the grand scale latterly by Rastrelli for the Empresse Elizabeth and Catherine II. The day of our visit was brilliantly sunny but freezing hard with snow lying deep on the ground. We had emerged from the sumptuously decorated interior and were making our way back to the coach across the great parterre, which stretches the length of the vast building. "Take great care," I shouted rather bossily to my party. "It is extremely slippery underfoot".

No sooner were the words out of my mouth when my feet shot from under me and I landed with some considerable force on my backside, my arms flailing in an effort to save myself. I thought at first it was my coccyx which had taken the brunt of my fall but in struggling with some humiliation to my feet, I noticed that my right wrist looked a bit odd and seemed to be back to front. We were on our way to a specially ordered lunch at the Sadko Restaurant in the Nevsky Prospect, since it was advisable sometimes to escape from the indifferent fare served at most of the hotels. After that, everyone was to be let loose in the Hermitage for the rest of the afternoon. Luckily for me I had in the group one of my partners, Diana Skene, who was travelling with a young Italian friend, Patrizia, to both of whom I confided my fears of a broken wrist. The lunch was enjoyed by all, especially by Mickhael Kraminski who, as yet, was unaware of my mishap, as were the rest of my companions. Fortified by an excellent meal and wine, I duly deposited my flock at the Winter Palace but retained the coach and my guide.

"Now then Vera," I demanded briskly, "where do we go to get this wrist seen to?"

Vera looked at me uncomprehendingly.

"Wrist?" she queried bemusedly.

"Yes, wrist Vera," I replied impatiently. "I think I've probably broken it. Do we go to a clinic or what?"

From Vera's expression I might have announced my intention to jump in the Neva. She obviously had not the slightest idea that I had damaged myself and was loth to believe me anyway. After a fevered consultation with the coach driver who proved a very present help in trouble, we drove off to a clinic where a young man in white overalls took a look at my wrist and clucked "Oi,oi,oi."

"Oi,oi,oi," I echoed. "What can you do for me?"

"Nothing here," he replied. "You must go to the Orthopaedic Hospital." This fortunately proved to be more centrally situated than the scene of Mrs Pelz's incarceration. The building could have stood in as a model for a poor-house in one of Dickens' novels. Its yellow brick façade was grimed by age and uncurtained windows revealed unshaded bulbs within, casting a harsh light onto the snow outside, for it was already nearly dusk.

The steps had been cleared of snow but sprouted moss and tufts of grass – a likely trap for the patients wending their unsteady way to the main entrance. Pushing our way through the door marked 'casualties', we were met by a blast of hot antiseptic air mingling with the smell of humanity. Vera explained the situation to a receptionist and we took our seats in the waiting room, next to a sorry looking individual with a heavily bandaged foot. Vera, whose face by this time had taken on a greenish tinge that matched her coat, looked as if it was she who was in need of treatment rather than me. Because of my tourist status, I was not kept waiting for long and was duly shown into the X-ray room where an efficient white-coated radiologist took a series of pictures of my, by now, quite painful wrist. Armed with these, I was then ushered into the presence of the surgeon who was to carry out the setting of the bone. She was a formidable looking lady of impressive height and girth.

"Alexandrovna," she introduced herself impassively, and taking the X-rays from me said to Vera in Russian in a tone of extreme boredom: "Another Collis fracture I presume".

Having lunched so well there was no question of my having anything but a local anaesthetic, so after motioning me to a chair, she gave a salvo of instructions to her assistant, a scared looking teenager who scuttled out of the room and returned staggering under a huge jug of water and a bowl of plaster of Paris. I learned later from Vera that trainee-nurses and even trained nurses, are regarded with contempt by the medical profession.

Alexandrovna then donned a mask – she was already clad in white overalls – above which a pair of grey eyes looked at me rather impatiently. She got down to work while Vera, who was acting as interpreter, grew greener and greener. I tried to fill my mind with thoughts of soldiers biting on bullets while their limbs were being amputated, or exchanging jolly quips with their surgeons during a stomach operation as I had once witnessed on some television programme. The only time, however, I tried to make some merry remark to Alexandrovna I was brusquely admonished and told to keep quiet. I did look down once towards the scene of action but as all I could see was what appeared to be a mammoth chisel sticking out of my wrist, I refrained from looking further. Instead I tried to concentrate on tomorrow's events. How was I going to pack? How was I going to check the luggage and get my chickens through customs? Alexandrovna gave a big sigh and paused for breath. I had not realised what hard work was involved in the setting of a wrist. Even with her strength and obvious experience, it took much effort before she could stretch the bones apart and reset them in the correct position. Vera by now had her eyes closed and a handkerchief to her mouth. What was she going on about? I asked myself irritably. She wasn't suffering. Not that I could confess to much pain. It was more the grinding and crunching noises that unnerved me. Finally with my right arm encased in plaster from wrist to shoulder, I was given a not-so-gentle pat on my left shoulder by my friend, accepted a packet of pain-killers, and was dispatched for more X-rays. All for free. I may say that on my return to London and my own doctor, most of the plaster was removed and replaced with something much less cumbersome, but the actual setting was pronounced first-class.

Diana that evening helped me to pack, and much more importantly, being several sizes larger than me, lent me a jersey that covered my plastered arm with ease. I gave the pain-killers to Vera, who I felt needed them more than I did. The next day I managed to dress myself and, with Diana's help, check the luggage and eventually we set off for the airport. As everyone knows who ever travelled to the USSR under Communist rule, a lot of paperwork was involved both when entering and leaving the country. Each member of a group had to sign a form on arrival giving exact details of all items of value and currency he or she may have been carrying, and the same procedure had to be followed before departure. It was strictly illegal to take any roubles out of the country and any unspent roubles had to be changed into hard currency. As sterling invariably seemed to be singularly in short demand, the British traveller had quite often to make do with dollars or even yen.

On this occasion all went according to rule except that it was abundantly clear that my signature, made with a functioning right hand when entering the Soviet Union, was not going to accord with the signature written with my left hand when leaving. It seemed unnecessary to have to explain why this should be, when the evidence in all its bandaged clarity was there in front of the cashier. Even Vera's expostulations produced no more than a stony-faced refusal to accept my surplus roubles which I had to have with me in case of emergency. In fact I was looked at with such suspicion and distrust that I took fright thinking that my arm might suddenly be seized and my plaster searched for illicit cash. In desperation Diana and I retired to a distant corner away from prying eyes, where she forged my signature and passed off my roubles as her own – two crimes which, if discovered, could probably have landed us both in the Lubyanka. This was Soviet bureaucracy at its most unyielding, but this time I defied officialdom even further and smuggled out three letters from Mikhael destined for England. Dreary Vera autographed my plastered arm and with a rare smile wished us all "Bon Voyage".

Twenty-one

Shahr-I-Sabz, originally known as Kesh or the Green City, lies some fifty miles south of Samarkand. It was the birthplace of Tamerlane (Timur) who had subsequently build his palace there – the Akserai or White Palace – which, so I had been told, was fast deteriorating into a ruinous state. I had heard also that although the building still retained vestiges of its original tiling and mosaic decoration, there was talk of dismantling the site and dispersing anything of value to local museums.

The reason why I was interested in this particular place was that in 1976 I had been asked to arrange a visit to Leningrad and Central Soviet Asia for a group of academics, which included Sir Denis Wright, ex-ambassador to Persia, and his wife. I remember with gratitude them both receiving me and my party at the British Embassy in Tehran, even though it was on the eve of his departure from Persia. Also in the present group was Mrs Searight, a well-known entomologist specialising in the study of fleas, and her husband (who was the owner of an important collection of oriental water colours, which I later understood he donated to the Victoria and Albert Museum), and several other distinguished and learned members of society. I had been specifically asked to include in the programme an excursion to Shahr-I-Sabz and, although I had by then learned not to commit myself to any promises connected with Intourist, I had undertaken to do my best.

I first approached Intourist in London, who referred me to Intourist in Moscow. My former liaison there, La Tigressa, was now making life difficult for Canadian travel agents, but on writing ahead to her replacement I received a reply telling me to wait until I reached Moscow and to plead my case there and in person. As we were spending barely twenty-four hours in

Moscow, this was a tall order, but I could but hope. On finally arriving in the city, I despatched my group on a tour of the city and was finally able to confront Moscow Intourist.

It was here that I was allotted the guide who was to accompany us on the rest of our tour. Galena was a plump blonde with a nice sense of humour and no moods. From the start, she entered with enthusiasm into my quest for permission to visit Shahr-I-Sabz, although to her it was but a vague name in her country's history. She led me to some higher authority at Intourist who introduced me to Dmitri, a bland-voiced official, who informed me politely enough that only the Samarkand authorities could grant me permission for such a visit and that I must approach them on my arrival. With that I had to be content.

We flew that night to Samarkand – a journey of great discomfort and little sleep – and checked in early the next morning at our hotel, an uninspiring building but with adequately furnished rooms and ablutionary requirements. It was also centrally situated.

Although Galena was to accompany us throughout the tour, it was Intourist's policy in those days to allot a local guide to take charge of us at each destination. In this instance we were appointed Irina, a tough cookie from outward appearances, and very much the one to dictate terms to Galena, who became a mere cipher.

Over breakfast of rock-hard boiled eggs, good black bread and butter and the inevitable *sok*, I engaged Irina in conversation.

"Irina, we want to go to Shahr-I-Sabz. Can you manage that for us?"

"You cannot go to Shahr-I-Sabz."

"Oh! Why is that?"

"It is not included in the programme."

"Oh indeed it is – and we have left space tomorrow for such an excursion."

"There is no coach available."

"But we requested a coach and the cost of it is included in the tour price. I have a receipt for it."

"I know nothing," said Irina woodenly, reverting to the well-known refrain I had met so many times in the past.

"Well take me to someone who does," I retorted briskly.

After lunch Irina told me to follow her and led me to a drably furnished room on the fifth floor of the hotel, where a harassed looking man stood behind a baize-covered table, on which stood a samovar but with no glasses near it or sign of reviving tea. His greeting was dispirited.

"Here is Comrade Direktor of the hotel," announced Irina in a tone which conveyed "and the best of British luck to you".

"Good afternoon Comrade Direktor. Please, my group would like to go to Shahr-I-Sabz."

"You cannot go to Shahr-I-Sabz."

"Oh, why not?"

"The road is blocked. There is no other route."

I was not accepting this. "Please make an appointment for me to see the Direktor of Intourist Samarkand," I demanded coldly.

My request was eventually complied with and this time I was ushered into the presence of a rather jolly looking female dressed in a modish battledress type dress in air force blue. Her hennaed hair was piled high on the crown of her head. She looked at me appraisingly.

"What can I do for you Madam," she enquired, stifling a yawn behind a well-manicured hand.

"Good afternoon Madam Direktor. My group would like to visit Shahr-I-Sabz. I understood from Intourist London that you could arrange this for us."

"You cannot go to Shahr-I-Sabz."

Why can't we go to Shahr-I-Sabz?" The monotony of these conversations became mesmeric.

"No-one goes to Shahr-I-Sabz," she smiled at me indulgently.

I sat up abruptly. I brightened visibly. This was much more the answer I wanted to hear. It meant that there was no valid reason for our not going to Shahr-I-Sabz – no blocked road, transport available to take us there, free time on our agenda; just the usual bloody-mindedness of our host country.

"But surely," I argued, "you should want to show overseas visitors a place as important as Tamerlane's birthplace. It could become one of your regular excursions and we would be able to extol the co-operation of Intourist," I ended obsequiously.

The comrade lady shrugged her shoulders and waved her hands deprecatingly.

"I'm sorry. Perhaps next year."

I had to admit defeat to my expectant group who had been encouraging me from the sidelines. During dinner that night Irina approached our tables.

"We start for Shahr-I-Sabz tomorrow at 8.30am" she announced impassively. "With picnic lunch," she added repressively as a wave of applause and laughter erupted round the room.

"Thank you Irina," I acknowledged gravely, trying not to respond too blatantly to Galina's grin of triumph from the far end of the table.

In the event we were accompanied by Galina, Irina and two officials from Intourist, none of whom it was clear had been to Shahr-I-Sabz before. The coach was on time, the road to our destination was devoid of obstruction and once above the town the mists cleared and the sun came out. The birthplace of Tamerlane lies some fifty miles south of Samarkand, the road flanked by cotton fields, vineyards and fruit orchards. On arrival in the town, we drove to the site of the ruler's great palace, little of which then remained, except for fragments of the impressive portal. These vestiges none the less conveyed a tantalising idea of what the palace must have looked like in its heyday. The piers were covered in tiles decorated in exquisitely worked designs, ranging from circular medallions in black, gold, blue and white to delicately traced white lilies, the surrounds inscribed with Arabic writing. Some flooring remained, also covered in tiles or turquoise and white interspersed with others of a lovely yellow, outlined with gold filigree lines. Small boys bounded excitedly in and out of the ruins intent on hacking off pieces of statuary, which they proffered to us and were visibly puzzled at our protests against what they considered to be signs of friendship and appreciation of our visit.

By the time we had visited the Kak Gumbaz or Blue Dome Mausoleum, burial place of Sah Shamsedin, Tamerlane's spiritual adviser; the Jalan Gir Mausoleum containing tombs of two of the Emperor's sons; and the site of his own intended sepulchre nearby – only unearthed in 1964 under the house of a local inhabitant – we had gathered round us a horde of friendly Uzbeks, mostly women in baggy trousers carrying tightly swaddled toddlers on their backs. Clearly unused to tourists, they chatted eagerly amongst themselves, pressing upon us grapes and almonds, which we purchased for a few kopeks or handful of cigarettes. We finally drove out of the town through avenues of cannas and stopped beside a cotton plantation, where the flowers were just beginning to burst from their pods into a sea of pale pinky-yellow blooms, faintly rose-like in appearance. Here we ate our picnic of goat cheese, hardboiled eggs, grapes and the local bread. During our return journey to Samarkand, I was asked by one of the Intourist officials to write down my impressions of Shahr-I-Sabz. On subsequent visits to Uzbekistan I understand that some years later, a glossy new hotel was erected in the town, but that even less of the palace remained intact.

Twenty-two

My final brush with Soviet cussedness came about as a result of the shooting down by a Soviet plane of the Korean airliner in 1983. I was on the point of departing for an eight day tour in Leningrad with a group of twenty-eight members of the British Museum Society when the news came that our Prime Minister was threatening to ban all flights that flew over Soviet occupied territory as from 15th September. We were due to leave for Leningrad on 11th September but our return flight was scheduled for 18th September. Both Intourist and the Russian Embassy in London guaranteed us a safe flight home on that day, but we were duty bound to give our clients the option of cancelling with a full refund. In the event twelve opted out, leaving fifteen and myself to face any music that came our way.

Heathrow Airport was bedlam on the day of our departure, with everyone trying to seek assurance from their relevant airlines that they would eventually get home. A rival group was in close proximity to us in the aeroplane and I got into conversation with the young courier, who had never been to Russia before. On hearing that I had had twelve cancellations she retorted smugly, "We only had two, but I expect the rest knew they were in good hands".

Such complacency made me vow that come what may, I had to get my group back to England on the scheduled day. After a three hour delay, we finally touched down in Leningrad at 10.30pm local time, with no Intourist Guide in sight – the first time ever – but was told she would be at the hotel. Customs took even longer than usual with almost every piece of luggage searched – mine for some reason was an exception – and endless perusal of all reading matter including magazines. We finally reached the hotel Europeyskeya at 1.10am. Still no guide, no mineral water, no sustenance and Intourist had never passed on the message that we were now sixteen instead of twenty-eight. Better that way round at least. I managed to prevail upon the 'house mothers' on each of our floors to brew up hot drinks, at the cost of several pairs of nylons.

Our guide, Zoja Belikova, turned up at breakfast. I knew from the moment I saw her that there would be a clash of personalities. She was older than the average guide, with much experience, and remarked rather ominously that she had heard of me from other guides! She was obviously a party member as she had been five times to the UK and had a husband in high places, which entailed a fine apartment in Leningrad and two dachas in the country. She was obviously riled at being landed with a group of a mere sixteen people instead of twenty-eight and irked by our slowness that first morning – after all we had had a very short night and some of us were not in our first youth. Unfortunately, one of our party was a chronic asker of futile questions, while one of the male members insisted on stopping to photograph a scene or monument from five different angles. I spent my time in rounding up the laggards, but towards the end of the morning, after a particularly idiotic and provoking remark about the regime, Zoja threw a tantrum and got all choked up. We got through the day by playing her along and jollying her up and she eventually got our measure and we hers, but of all the Intourist guides I have ever had she was the least co-operative, probably due to the aftermath of Western censure following the Korean affair.

Luckily, after years of experience I was beginning to know the ropes, but I could not help wondering how my smug little friend from our rival group was faring, until I remembered that she had with her as lecturer Prince George Galitzine, and felt discouraged once more.

During the following days Zoja and I managed to conduct a reasonably harmonious relationship, but at no time did she mention, or seem to concern herself with, our departure, which occupied most of my waking hours. Direct flights from Leningrad to London had now been cancelled, as had most flights from the

Soviet Union to Western European cities. I had every confidence, however, in John Winser, our totally reliable managing director, and knew that he would be beavering away on our behalf from the home front. From time to time a rumour would reach me that we were to go home via Dublin or Finland, but it was not until two days before our departure that I was informed by Intourist that we were booked on an Aeroflot flight to Prague and from thence to Manchester, airline unstated. Sure enough a telegram was delivered to me the next morning – a feat in itself – from John which read, "Booked you 1245 Aeroflot Leningrad/Prague/Manchester STOP Sodding coach will take you London via Harpenden Four Bells STOP Good Luck John" I felt rather as Bletchley must have felt when confronted with Enigma. I soon deciphered 'Sodding' into Soden's, a coach company we often used – although for a brief moment I wondered if John had lost his cool – but the last few words totally defeated me. Why Harpenden and why the Four Bells? Did he think we would be so in need of a drink by the time we landed in Manchester that we had to be revived en route? But why Harpenden? All was revealed when I sat next to two of my flock that night at dinner.

"What are you doing when you reach Manchester," I asked Colonel Bell, as I knew he lived in Skye and might not wish to go to London. "Oh, we're spending a couple of nights with friends in Harpenden," he replied. The penny finally dropped. For "Four Bells" read "for Bells".

We passed our final day happily enough, everyone having become resigned to the change of plans. After all, they had been warned that there might be complications in getting home. After an engrossing and totally satisfactory afternoon spent in the Hermitage, including the viewing of the Scythian treasure, we repaired to the hotel, prior to dining out at the Pritakitskaya Hotel, one of Leningrad's newest and glossiest of hotels overlooking the Gulf of Finland. A specially arranged dinner ensured better food than usual with a generous supply of vodka, champagne and Georgian wine.

On arrival at the hotel I was called to the Service Bureau where a lethargic looking blonde lady was powdering her nose. "There is a little problem over your flight home tomorrow," she announced morosely.

"What problem?" I enquired uneasily.

"No flight Prague to Manchester."

"Why not?"

"I know nothing."

"What is the alternative?"

The blonde lady shrugged. "You stay in Leningrad extra day and night then fly Prague Monday for night. Czech airlines flight home Tuesday."

"Who pays?"

"You must pay."

"Absolutely not," I shouted, "and what about our visas? They expire tomorrow."

More shrugs. The blonde yawned and raised her eyebrows at two colleagues who were lounging in the background. "Do not argue with us" she intoned flatly. "Go argue with Madame Thatchair". I would willingly have argued with Madame Thatchair just then if I had had the opportunity, or more likely have wrung her neck. What right had she to land us in this dilemma? I took a deep breath and spoke as calmly as I was able.

"Surely there must be other means of getting to England?" I asked. My persecutor regarded me with hostile eyes, behind which I tried to detect the faintest hint of sympathy.

"Go speak with Aeroflot," she suggested, obviously only too ready to get rid of me. "There might be a flight to East Berlin and after that ...," her lips twitched briefly in a travesty of a smile.

"But where are my tickets?"

"They come soon from other office. I call you."

Zoja, who had gone to change, duly returned and I briefed her and the members of the party as to the latest developments. At least I knew they were going to eat well and consume a large amount of liquor. I thought I glimpsed a glint of satisfaction in Zoja's cold eyes at the thought of how I was to spend my evening, but she offered no advice or assistance apart from offering to drop me off at Aeroflot's offices, where I spent the next two hours wheedling, pleading, coercing, haranguing and threatening. Finally I got hold of a delightful girl who did everything in her power – which was not too much – to help. She spoke no English but mercifully French and having first told me that all planes tomorrow were full to every port of call in Eastern Europe, she proceeded to put through numerous telephone calls on my behalf. The mere fact that she was really trying made me feel better. In any event by this time I was almost beyond caring and ready to let fate take a hand in any way it liked. There were frantic figures of all nationalities jostling each other in an effort to get near the counter, all in the same predicament as myself, but at last my saviour arrived with the news that she had managed to get me sixteen seats on the midday flight to East Berlin at Aeroflot's expense. I would then have to get myself and my group back to England as best we might. She swore that we needed no visas beforehand to cross into East Berlin and that we could buy visas for West Berlin at the frontier with US dollars, a currency I always carried with me when visiting the USSR. She also added that she had requested seats from West Berlin on a flight leaving for London at 5.40pm but had no guarantee of their availability. I pledged to her my undying gratitude and presented her with a fountain pen with a picture of the Queen and returned to the hotel to lay on breakfast and a coach to take us to the airport the next morning. The buffets were all closed so I could not even buy a bun or banana and had to fall back on my emergency ration of vodka and two barley sugar sweets.

I managed to contact Zoja at the Pritakitskaya and tell her of tomorrow's plans and to ensure that I saw everyone on their return to the hotel. They eventually arrived back in a very jolly frame of mind, bearing with them two bottles of champagne for my consumption – ungratefully I would have welcomed food in their place – and received with somewhat euphoric equanimity news of the latest developments. Having taken down messages for, and telephone numbers of, relatives or friends meeting individuals, I tried for the next three hours to contact John Winser at his home, to no avail. I heard later that he had been to a party and only got home at 2am on the Sunday morning, to be woken by my renewed telephone call at 5am. I explained our movements as at present and the possibility of a flight from West Berlin. He in turn said he would keep in touch with British Airways throughout the day and his nice imperturbable voice interspersed with his familiar schoolboy wit helped to restore my equilibrium.

After a breakfast of the not unusual fare of hardboiled eggs and yoghurt with an interminable wait for coffee or tea, we clambered into the bus. I warned my fellow travellers that our worries were not yet over and ascertained who amongst them were German speakers, since this was not one of my languages. Zoja turned up five minutes before our departure from the hotel when all the luggage was aboard and once at the airport abandoned all pretence at helping me to check in – an unheard of dereliction of duty where Intourist guides are concerned.

The airport was thronged with visitors desperately trying to leave the country before their visas expired and I had to use my elbows to battle my way to the check-in counter, where I handed over my tickets. The Aeroflot woman counter clerk gave them a cursory glance and handed them back to me.

"Not on list," she snapped and continued to talk to her colleague.

"They are so," I snapped back, pushing the tickets at her.

"I said names not on passenger list," she shouted, this time throwing the offending tickets at me. Desperate at the thought of being incarcerated with all my flock with out-of-date visas in this God-benighted country I seized the tickets and thrust them under my tormentor's nose.

"They bloody are," I yelled "Look!" This was sheer bluff on my part as I had no way of telling if our names were on the list or not but at least my invective had the result of stunning two of them into looking properly at the list. By God's good grace our names were there and both officials sullenly acquiesced, issuing boarding cards without comment. We weighed in our luggage, changed our money and passed through customs and passport control suspiciously easily. I suppose the authorities were only too glad to see us go. We then had a half-hour wait in a departure lounge jam-packed with humanity – mostly Finns going home, but our flight, when we finally scrambled aboard, was full of Germans flying to East Berlin, with a six-hour coach drive afterwards to Hamburg.

We were served not a bad meal in flight and eventually touched down at East Berlin at 1pm, local time. The visas into West Germany, as predicted by my Aeroflot friend, presented no difficulty thanks to my dollars, which were handed over in exchange for a piece of paper resembling a cloakroom ticket. No porters or trolleys being available we staggered our way out of the airport with our luggage and across the road to the appropriate bus stop for West Berlin. Being a Sunday, departures were few and far between. One bus was on the point of leaving but refused to wait for the few stragglers, less quick on their feet than the rest of us. I was not unduly worried, until I was told that the next departure was at 3.15pm and that it sometimes took an age to cross the frontier. However, by this time a kind of devil-may-care attitude had been adopted by most of us, although there were one or two who had important meetings the following day and were perturbed at the thought of missing them.

I discovered that there were singularly few members in my group who spoke German and my volunteer-interpreter, the retired army officer of Four Bells fame, had not been to Germany for some years. Even with the English language, he had to give great thought before any utterance, which must have driven his wife into a frenzy of frustration at times.

"Colonel, could you please ask how long the bus journey will take to the airport?"

"Well, the last time I visited Berlin must have been before the Second World War – do you remember Joyce? Was it 1938 or 1939? We had just got married, so it must have been 1939. We went by car of course from England so it wasn't quite from this direction."

"Please, Colonel, could you ask how long the journey will take?"

I accompanied him to the ticket bureau, where even I could understand the official to say it would take between one and a half and two hours.

My heart sank. Even allowing for no delays, it left us exactly 25 minutes from the time of our arrival at the airport to the estimated flight departure time, provided John had finally managed to get us on a flight.

"Trouble is," mumbled the Colonel, "they speak a different lingo here, difficult to understand."

Clearly the army was not going to alleviate my burden in any marked manner. The bus duly rumbled up and we all clambered aboard with our luggage, along with a handful of other stranded passengers – mostly American. The driver proved sympathetic but adamant.

"We are only allowed to go to the telefunken" he announced through his loud-speaker.

"Ask him where that is," I hissed at the Colonel.

"He says about two miles from the airport."

"How do we get to the airport from the telefunken?"

"By taxi if there are any about on a Sunday," translated my interpreter lugubriously.

"But tell him we are sixteen passengers with lots of luggage." On hearing this, the driver looked unhappy but remained obdurate. I sat myself down behind him so that he could see me clearly in his mirror and began ostentatiously counting out dollar bills in front of his wary eyes. "Offer him cigarettes," suggested one of my party. I had given most of mine away to my Russian friends and helpers – none to Zoja naturally – and only had one or two packets left for emergencies.

Soon, however, I had collected a pile of packets from members of my group. as well as from the Americans who were as anxious to reach the airport as we were. I smiled encouragingly from time to time at our Herr Chauffeur through the mirror, who was by this time looking distinctly uneasy and was nervously licking his lips. It was not so much the distance which took the time; it was the interminable stops at the checkpoints at the Eastern and Western

German borders. Although our 'wall' was only a suburban wall in the East German sector it was crawling with guards and police dogs and the driver had to navigate the zig-zag hazards designed to prevent vehicles from making a quick dash to safety. We all had to leave the bus while it was searched for contraband. I had whisked dollars and cigarettes into a shopping bag, which I clutched to me during the individual frisking and declared that I was carrying duty free and money for my group. Once we were over the frontier into West Berlin, I gambled the lot and poured them out in front of the driver accompanied by a rather long drawn out and no doubt slightly incoherent plea from the Colonel. Hans, as his name not surprisingly turned out to be, after turning off his loud-speaker and scanning the horizon, nodded briefly and muttered quickly, "I take you to airport". There was a loud cheer which he drowned with a blast of music from his radio which he had hastily turned on again, and I blew him a kiss through the mirror which so unnerved him that we nearly left the road.

We made the airport by 4.30pm. Imploring the Colonel to come with me, I made a dash for the British Airways desk, entreating the rest of the party to follow me as quickly as possible. Once there I made contact with a delightfully co-operative English speaking British Airways representative. "Yes", she confirmed, she had been in touch with BA in London. "No," we were not on the flight originally scheduled but thirteen of the party were booked on a flight leaving then and there for Düsseldorf (fully paid up) and thence to Heathrow.

"We are holding the flight for you," she told me. "Where is your party?"

"Right here," I replied confidently turning round to a vista of nearly five hundred yards, devoid of any sign of humanity, much less fourteen passengers hurrying towards me, their luggage and passports at the ready. "Where are they?" I shouted distractedly at the Colonel, who was stumbling down the corridor breathing heavily – I had outdistanced him early on in the race to the check-in counter.

"Don't know," he gasped. "They seem to have disappeared". My

British Airways friend looked anxious.

"Where is your party?" Where indeed? At that moment one of the younger members of the group appeared on the horizon strolling leisurely towards us. On seeing my frantic signallings, he broke into a run.

"Where is everyone?" I called shrilly as he approached.

"In the Duty Free Shop," he answered laconically.

"Well tell them to get the hell out of there or they'll miss the flight home."

By this time I was definitely becoming slightly hysterical with worry and frustration. Throwing me a startled glance he trotted off towards the Duty Free, obviously fearing for my sanity, the Colonel panting in his wake calling "Joyce, Joyce". Unrepentant, my flock at last appeared, burdened with bottles. I had the reluctant task of detailing two of my travellers, the young sheepdog and Mr Eric Porter, an older retired academic, to stay behind with me, with no guarantee of a flight out that day. There was no time to ask for volunteers nor to have inevitable ensuing arguments. What I hadn't yet been told by BA in the turmoil of the last half-hour was that the three of us would in fact probably manage to get on a Global Charter plane to Gatwick, provided a party of forty who had got lost in East Berlin failed to turn up. I was also to detain Mrs Crowther for this flight as John Winser had instructed her husband to meet that flight at Gatwick, it being nearer to their home. None of this was relayed to me until after the flight to Düsseldorf had left, so while Pam Crowther was winging her way to Heathrow, her husband was to be dementedly looking for her at Gatwick. I later heard that they were finally reunited at about 2am.

My two press-ganged companions and I revived ourselves with orangeade, liberally laced with vodka, while British Airways continued their struggle on our behalf through the good offices of a most helpful and engaging man called, I believe, Taylor – to whom I shall always be eternally grateful. As time progressed, our thoughts turned to the possibility of spending the night in West Berlin, but eventually, and to our immense relief, we were confirmed on the Global Charter flight, which left West Berlin at 7.25pm. I sometimes wonder what happened to the missing forty and whether they are for ever encircling the city's limits.

I think the three of us gained on our fellow travellers in the long run, since we travelled on a brand new 727, were served a delicious meal, or so it seemed after a diet of Russian fare, and were much cosseted, being treated rather like heroes who had survived an arduous ordeal, a role I was more than ready to accept. We touched down at Gatwick at 8.30pm, the three of us being first off the aircraft, and found our luggage whirling round the turntable. Not long after my arrival home a telephone call confirmed the safe arrival of the remainder of my party, all of whom had been reunited with their families, except for the unfortunate Mrs Crowther – but luckily for my peace of mind I was not to be aware of this drama until the following day. Later on I heard that the rival group had travelled by train to Helsinki, where they had spent a night before catching a flight home, arriving a day behind schedule. Honour was satisfied.

Twenty-three

Over the years, it did happen on occasion that we were told on arrival at a hotel (usually in Eastern countries) that we had been transferred to another hotel, since some Head of State had annexed all accommodation (Mrs Ghandi on a visit to Tehran; the Shah of Persia at the Shah Abbas Hotel in Isfahan for a private family party). Despite the fact that the rooms had been booked and confirmed months before, censure not unnaturally fell on the tour leader, who had to submit to cries of "shameful, disgraceful treatment, unacceptable", although invariably alternative accommodation had been found in advance.

Far worse was to arrive at a destination where, if things went wrong, there was literally no alternative comparable accommodation – as once happened to me in Cochin, where we were to stay at the Hotel Malabar, ravishingly positioned on the lagoon. We had confirmed our booking from Bombay the night before and touched down in Cochin in high spirits, looking forward to lunch and a leisurely sail on the lagoon. We were met by our agent, Mr Tamphi, an overweight individual and unusually unsmiling for an Indian, but who, when asked if all was in order, replied with the invariable "no problem". On arrival at the hotel, Mr Tamphi went ahead. I followed in time to hear an altercation in progress. My heart lurched. Not enough single rooms. Far worse. No rooms at all. A Club Mediterranée group had arrived earlier that morning, apparently booked in by the same agent, and were now happily installed in our rooms. I argued for half an hour while my group was tucking into rather good fish and chips. The conversation went rather like this.

"So sorry I have no rooms for you."

"What do you mean no rooms? We reconfirmed yesterday."

"Your group arrived. All rooms taken."

"But *we* are that group. You must get rid of the other one."

"You here already. Can do no more. Tomorrow OK. Tomorrow No problem. Today problem."

A commiserating laugh, a shrug of the shoulders and I knew I was defeated. I knew it was useless trying to persuade the other party to quit, especially as they were French. Having to break such news to my group is like an officer having to tell his troops that leave is cancelled and that they have to go into battle forthwith. They were remarkably supportive.

I sat them down with limes and sodas and for the next hour I and Mr Tamphi, who had suddenly come to life with a catastrophe brewing and face to be lost, searched by telephone for alternative accommodation. Having drawn blanks at eight hotels in descending scales of comfort and grades, we finally struck, if not gold, at least some vacant rooms at an establishment called the Sea King, which offered us eleven of the sixteen rooms required. I told them to hold them until our arrival, boarded my party on to our coach, which was still piled high with our luggage, and set off through the New Town of Cochin – every street of which appeared to be under repair, resulting in devious detours. It also seemed to be Cochin's rush hour and what with deviations, impediments from a throbbing mass of humanity on foot, in trucks and on bicycles, we took nearly an hour to go four miles. We stopped at a dreadful looking dump on the main street which, for one dire moment I thought to be our destination, but Mr Tamphi had so bestirred himself to think of ringing ahead to the Sea King to see if they had uncovered any more rooms. He was triumphantly told two. Only three to go! We finally drew up outside a respectable enough looking building, well clear of the main thoroughfare. I braced myself and told my slightly uneasy looking party in as masterful tones as I could muster, that if I was satisfied the hotel was clean, this was where we were spending the night.

I heard later that during my absence, one of my party, a retired army colonel, Philip Erskine, had exhorted his fellow-travellers to rally round their leader and was warmly applauded. With this encouragement, I set to sorting out the accommodation. Basic as this was compared to the Malabar, the rooms were clean and adequate, despite the sanitary arrangements being admittedly fairly primitive. The 'en suite' bathrooms consisted of a curtained-off partition with at least a WC flushed by the bucket method, and a shower that emitted gusts of boiling water or none at all. The twin beds besported one sheet between them and the ratio of towels was one to each room. However most of us had bathing towels with us, and I managed to buy a pile of sheets and towels at the local bazaar nearby for a handful of rupees. The staff could not have been more welcoming and our luggage was delivered to our rooms by a diminutive boy of about ten who was barely bigger than the cases he carried with smiling enjoyment.

I despatched the group to a performance of Kathakali dancers with Mr Tamphi who, in the face of adversity, was becoming more and more humanised and helpful. Meanwhile members of the hotel owner's family were entering into the spirit of this unexpected invasion, and they, together with Isobel Clarke, who happened to be on the tour, and myself, helped to make up the beds. The dancing brigade duly returned, having enjoyed the performance, and were further relaxed by several drinks on the house and an excellent dinner in the hotel's Chinese style restaurant, consisting of several mammoth sized local fish, smothered with herbs and almonds and served with a delicious lemon sauce. Sated with this feast, most of us were ready for our beds, however spartan these might turn out to be.

One couple became faintly hysterical when they found a beetle in their room, so Isobel and I elected to change with them having found no livestock in our room, apart from the odd mosquito. Needless to say, they immediately found a beetle in our room.

"Probably brought their own," muttered Isobel mutinously "and anyway why come to the East if you can't put up with a beetle or two."

"Well they weren't included in the tour price," I responded and we both laughed uproariously with light-headedness and fatigue at our own silliness.

Breakfast was rather a travesty of the word, consisting of bread and *gee* and a nameless jam and very strong tea. Luckily I always carry large jars of Nescafé when visiting the East, so this saved the day for the coffee drinkers. My own aim was to keep members of my group from visiting the kitchen adjoining the breakfast room, as this was crammed with family retainers lounging about smoking cigarettes or pipes, hawking and coughing while our diminutive porter brewed tea out of a muslin stocking-like object, turned russet-coloured through age and tannin, which hung from a nail from the ceiling.

Oddly enough we all survived the night's ordeal without anyone becoming the worse for wear. Ramjan, a gentle student guide, took the party off on a sightseeing tour of the old town of Cochin, a former Portuguese trading centre, and Fort Cochin, famous for its singular Chinese cantilevered fishing nets, while I departed to the Union Bank to cash some money with which to pay off the Sea King. The entire bill for twenty-two of us – including dinner (with beer), bed and breakfast, came to £42.00.

The cashier looked at my passport, looked at me, looked again at my passport unbelievingly and exclaimed, "Mees Wood? Mees Wood? Still not married? Have a cup of tea".

It was the first time I had really laughed in the last twenty-four hours, except for the beetle episode. I also sent a telegram to John Winser at Specialtours, asking him to make sure there was a substantial refund awaiting each member on their return home. Later we were waved off by cheering staff at the Sea King, whose kindness I will long remember, and thereafter the rest of our stay in Cochin was magic.

Having installed ourselves back at the Malabar Hotel, which is situated on the tip of Willingdon Island and has superb views over the harbour, we embarked on a privately hired brig which was tied up at the hotel's landing stage at the foot of the garden. We sat on deck, fanned by a cool breeze, and set off across the lagoon. The water was limpid clear and we passed a number of yawls whose crews were getting ready for the evening catch. Sailing near the shoreline, fringed with palm trees and dense vegetation, we could see the fishermen and their womenfolk mending nets. Now and again we came to a clearing surrounding a village of thatched houses, the inhabitants of which would run down to the water's edge offering us pineapples and coconuts. At one such village, school was coming out and the children, scantily clothed in gaily coloured frocks or shorts, flitted like dragonflies along the shore, singing and yelling with laughter as we sailed by.

We landed at the island of Allepey to visit a coir-making factory, several amongst us buying door mats attractively decorated with lozenged patterns. I pondered briefly on the fun the buyers would have in getting them home.

Our crew-master took on board some bottles of Todi, the local drink, for us to try. Most of us found it totally disgusting, based as it was on fermented coconut milk. Our final call was to Bolghatty Island, where we walked in the garden of the former Governor's house, now a hotel (with a mere eight rooms alas!), the evening air heavy with the scent of cassias, frangipani and cannas over which bee-eaters were swooping. On the way back to the hotel we sighted two black and white kingfishers, more bee-eaters and a flock of green parrots that sped over our heads with raucous cries. We tied up at the quayside, just as the lights from the shore were coming on, while out on the water the winking lanterns from the fishing boats traced their route across the ocean. As I stepped ashore, looking forward to the luxury of a hot shower, I felt the catharsis of all the tensions that had gone before and with my worries behind me for the time being, was able to enjoy a dinner of the curried prawns for which Cochin is renowned.

Twenty-four

A reconnoitring visit to any country in advance of the "opening day" was of course invaluable. Moreover it was usually hugely enjoyable without the encumbrance of individuals with widely differing views on all subjects. These ranged from the desirability of including in the programme a trek up an Iranian rock-cliff to view the incomprehensible inscription (to all but the most learned) celebrating Darius' triumph over Gaumatas, while the less mobile members of the party had to wait below in the coach; the choice of a second-class hotel in delectable surroundings, as opposed to a deluxe establishment in the city centre, to the merits or demerits of including the cost of all meals in the tour price, thus inhibiting the more adventurous members from finding hidden gastronomic delights or disappointments on their own.

In the early 1970s, Afghanistan was beginning to appear on group tour programmes. I was eager to get in on the act before it became too commonplace a destination. (In fact, we were just in time to carry out three visits in successive years before the Russians moved in.) So, with the help of Ariana Afghan Airlines, it was duly arranged for me to visit Afghanistan in November 1973 with a view to promoting tours there with a cultural slant.

My flight was due to take off at 4pm, but six hours later I was still sitting at Heathrow Airport in the company of the Afghan Airlines manager, from whom I had gleaned much useful information about his country in the intervening hours. From time to time one of his compatriots would join us and by the time my flight was called, a formidable array of empty glasses was spread before us and my expectations of their host country were very rosy indeed.

We touched down only once en route for Kabul. Any airport in the middle of the night is fairly dispiriting and Istanbul was no exception. Every kiosk was closed, lights glimmered low and the lounges yawned heavy with emptiness apart from a number of white-robed figures stretched out on the few available benches. Back in the comparative cosiness of the aeroplane I managed to snatch some sleep, awakening in time to eat a reasonable breakfast while gazing down on the snow-capped summit of Demavend, prince of the Elburz range of mountains, with not a cloud above it.

On disembarking at Kabul Airport in mid-morning, I survived the tedium of passport and customs control and finally emerged, luggage intact, into the arrivals hall, where I was speedily identified and scooped up by René, an Afghan Tours representative, smelling strongly of goat. He led me to the company car, emblazoned with "Afghan Tours" where lounged Kharami, who was to be the guide throughout my visit. A good looking young Afghan with adequate English and a languid manner, it was clear from the outset that he regarded the forthcoming days with misgiving. To begin with I was a female, old enough to be his mother and a foreigner at that. The task of conducting such a person round Afghanistan was no doubt in his eyes a degrading one and resentment quickly showed.

It soon transpired that his knowledge of the places I wanted to visit was fundamental. However, armed with Nancy Duprée's excellent guide book and Kharami's knowledge of the language and customs, I felt reasonably confident that I would achieve my goal. Having deposited me at the Hotel Intercontinental, where I was to be the guest of Afghan Tours for the night, no one seemed to know what to do with me next.

After a short nap, I called on Mr Jalawan, the manager of Afghan Tours and outlined to him the itinerary I had in mind for our forthcoming tour the following year. There was a distinctly defeatist air about Mr Jalawan, which blended with the drabness of his office: beige walls, dusty desks and tattered posters that did not inspire me with optimism.

I had hoped for a dynamic personality who, fired with enthusiasm at the thought of incoming tours from England, would suggest places hitherto unvisited by the tourist, or at least applaud my own suggestions. However, Mr Jalawan seemed more inclined to discuss the relationship between our two countries, his theme being eternal friendship between the nations of the world and more specifically between Afghanistan and Great Britain. Considering the past history of his country and its geographical position I felt that he was either a born optimist or merely trying to divert me from the facts and figures which I was in need of. Friendship could develop later – indeed I hoped it had already arrived – but what I had to have right then was his co-operation and a price in order to be able to advertise the forthcoming tour – which was, after all, less than a year ahead.

Mr Jalawan sighed heavily, spread his hands deprecatingly and called for tea.

"Hotels not give tariffs yet," he intoned gloomily. "New ones not printed. Not like many single rooms."

I did sympathise with him there.

"Why British not like share rooms, share bed?" he asked. "Is frigid race?"

I did not want to embark on the sexual habits of my compatriots but attempted an explanation. "We have too many widow women nowadays and many women want to travel instead of staying at home."

"Young widow women?" he enquired hopefully.

"No," I admitted ruefully, "mostly elderly."

Mr Jalawan looked gloomier still. After rather more haggling and further cups of tea I was promised a negotiable price by the time I returned from my reconnaissance. A car and driver and the unenthusiastic Kharami would be at my hotel the following morning and at my disposal for the next five days to drive me to all the sites mentioned in my itinerary. Meanwhile I was free to visit Kabul on my own.

Spectacularly situated, the city is dominated by two high mountain ranges, the Shar-i-Darwaza to the south and the Koh-i-Asmai, with the Kabul river cutting a swathe between them. At 5,900 feet on a November afternoon the air was crisp and invigorating but fairly thin, as shown by my somewhat laboured breathing as I headed up the slope to my hotel, with the sun setting on the distant ranges. I reckoned that with fairly primitive accommodation in the remoter parts of the country, my visitors would appreciate a little luxury at the beginning and end of their tour, so had decided on the Intercontinental, Kabul's then leading hotel.

A Penn Overland Bus Tour had just arrived and was disgorging its weary looking travellers – a medley of Europeans and Asiatics – who were in the midst of a marathon ten-week journey embracing London, Europe and Asia. I managed to cash in on their buffet-style supper, where I was introduced to *arsk*, a delicious cold soup well flavoured with lemon and coriander and particularly refreshing on a hot day, as I was later to discover. This was followed by a pancake stuffed with spinach and served with sour cream. A palatable, very light local red wine accompanied the meal, served in a pretty turquoise earthenware carafe. After this satisfying repast, I slept soundly and set off the next morning with my reluctant guide, Kharami, and Abdul the driver, a soft-spoken man with a gentle manner, much older than his compatriot but with no English.

Ghazni, to the south of Kabul, was our first destination, approached by a good but rather monotonous road. We passed several derelict caravanserais, a few camels, a handful of sheep but no goats. Perhaps they had all been commandeered for the national game of *buzkashi*, played mainly in the north in winter. Played at full tilt on sturdy mounts, with no boundaries and with a decapitated goat in lieu of bat, it resembles a particularly lethal game of polo.

During the drive, Kharami unbent enough to divulge that he was married with one wife, although he was on the look-out for another – four was the permitted maximum – and six children. He looked little more than a sixth-former himself. He had been to one of Afghanistan's three universities and spoke Farsi, Pushtu and a passable amount of English.

In November, the countryside through which we passed was grey and barren, but as I was to see on future visits, with the coming of spring a startling metamorphosis took place – all too briefly. Then the whole land changed into a vivid kaleidoscope of green, shot through with a rich variety of wild flowers of all colours.

Two toll gates announced our arrival in Ghazni, once a Buddhist centre and later the thriving capital of an Empire that stretched well into Central Asia. After successive invasions it was finally razed to the ground by Genghis Khan. Dominated by the citadel, the town is strikingly ringed by hills and contains what was purported to be a first-class museum, which I was determined to visit. It was obvious that Kharami's heart was not really in sightseeing. He would much rather have been haggling over a bag of rice at the nearby market, to which his eyes swivelled furtively. With a fair amount of prodding, we managed to enter the museum before it closed. Remarkably, all the exhibits were labelled not only in the local dialect but in French and English, which made Kharami's lack of knowledge easier to bear. Afterwards we bumped our way down dust roads to the two great minarets of Ghazni, then drastically crumbling, and continued to the Palace of Sultan Mas'ud III, presently being excavated by an Italian archaeological team under the supervision of Professore Tucci, who had also been responsible for the excavations at Persepolis. Being winter, most of the dig was under tarpaulins, but we were able to see a section of the dado to the marble screen, splendidly decorated and carrying the date of the palace's completion in 1112.

We lunched in a run-down joint called Ferroki, renowned for its kebabs. However, being one of the three meatless days in the week, imposed by the neo-President, we had to make do with the other speciality of the house – much to my relief – a tasty mess of eggs, tomatoes and onions cooked in oil called Karoyi Kabab. This was eaten with one's fingers, with the help of slabs of nan, the local unleavened bread. Outside every eating house or humblest *chaikhana* was a tap for washing of hands, a rigorous performance both before and after a meal and especially necessary after a dish such as we had just eaten. At the more far-flung restaurants we visited, I was invariably the only woman present but my presence rarely caused comment or the raising of eyebrows, apart from occasionally being offered a spoon in lieu of fingers.

We returned to Kabul for the night and woke the next day to a brilliantly sunny dawn with just a tinge of mist lying above the town, which nevertheless cleared very soon. Kharami, taciturn as ever, called for me at nine and we sped round the sites of the city, me taking copious notes while my companion smoked throat choking cigarettes and chatted up the passing population. We visited Babur's garden, legacy of the Moghul Emperor, with its delightful summer pavilion, the veranda fringed by slender pillars, the interior decorated with painted ceilings. Fine plane trees lined the path leading to the lovely marble mosque built by the Emperor Shah Jahan to celebrate his capture of Balkh. Babur's tomb was modest enough, but spoilt by the erection over it, despite the Emperor's plea that his grave should remain uncovered. I galloped round the Kabul Museum full of interesting treasures and again well labelled in three languages. We emerged just in time for me to be electrified by the boom of the Noon Gun which fired daily at midday. My discomfiture was the first time I heard Kharami laugh.

Having exhausted the cultural sights of Kabul at breakneck speed (to be researched at leisure and for which I would allow at least two or three days' exploration time on future visits), the three of us left the capital and set off for the north. Abdul proved an excellent driver and was as helpful and enthusiastic as Kharami was moody and lacklustre. I wondered if the latter had lost face amongst his cronies for undertaking such an excursion. Scenic-wise the day was stupendous. We passed many mulberry groves and vineyards and a number of grape-drying towers with vented windows, through which the air could pass and thus dry the grapes stored therein, converting them to raisins.

The road, a good one, ran along the Hajar valley, its river looking promising for the angler. Beyond the busy town of Charikar we turned off the main road leading to the Salang Tunnel and Pass, and continued towards Pul-i-Mattak, where

Kharami insisted in stopping to go in search of the snuff for which the town is renowned. I did not desist as I hoped (in vain) that it might take the place of cigarettes. Here, tarmac gave way to dust. However, the Peugeot's springs were good and we bounced along not uncomfortably, winding our way between hills punctuated with the ruins of Buddhist monasteries and crumbling walls of caravanserais signalling the former prosperity and importance of this trade route.

At Chahr eh Ghorband we stopped to eat the contents of our respective lunch boxes in a vine-ceilinged *chaikhana* where a samovar was boiling away over a fire of scented wood – willow or poplar? Abdul produced an inviting looking cold omelette and Kharami some vile looking meat, which he pronounced delicious. My own rations were what one might expect from an international hotel – cold chicken, a hard boiled egg (possibly bantam by its size) some nan and an apple. Green tea accompanied this and I, to whom tea in any guise has always been anathema, found myself becoming a temporary addict.

After we had finished eating, I left the two men smoking and walked on ahead. Inevitably after a few minutes I was joined by a half-a-dozen schoolboys on their way back to afternoon classes. They were a cheerful bunch, Mongolian in appearance with high cheekbones and narrowed eyes, and glad of any distraction from their normal routine. They plied me with questions in rudimentary English embellished with graphic gestures. Where did I come from? Why was I alone? How many children had I and who was looking after them? What did my husband do? The usual stock questions demanded of any stranger abroad of whatever age – although one ten-year old with a livelier curiosity than the others enquired cheekily if my husband beat me, seizing a large branch from the roadside the better to mime the husband, much to the hilarity of his colleagues. I normally carry with me in far-off lands a trove of cheap pens and chewing gum and these I doled out amidst much acclaim. The Peugeot then caught up with me with Abdul at the wheel and Kharami lolling by his side enjoying his siesta. I waved goodbye to my young friends and we proceeded on our way.

At first we drove through fertile land where hand-driven oxen were ploughing, but soon we were climbing steeply towards the summit of the Shibar Pass and to the watershed of the Oxus and Indus rivers. The higher we climbed, the more rugged and mountainous the landscape, as we came eventually in sight of the awesome range of the Hindu Kush. It was like driving through a lunar world with forbidding looking boulders perched precariously on jagged rocks, the sombre greyness of them shot through with mineral streaks of gold, silver and greenish or turquoise blue. The isolation and remoteness were accentuated by the dearth of habitation. No sign of life from either man, animal or bird. On reaching the summit we found ourselves on the high plateau of the Shibar Pass, nearly 11,000 feet high as our breathing – or lack of it – told us, the minute we got out of the car.

The air was like iced liquid, cutting short the little breath we could muster and very soon we were glad to return to the comparative comfort of the car and to make our cautious descent towards Bamiyan. Heralding the minuscule village of Boloah were the arresting remains of a once impregnable fortress or *quala*, its turrets and encircling walls fitfully reflecting the rays of the afternoon sun that penetrated with difficulty this rocky ravine. We reached Bamiyan in mid-afternoon. All around us towered the mountains of the Hindu Kush, capped with the first snows of winter. The town itself, though sited on a high plateau at an altitude of 8,000 feet, seemed like an oasis cocooned within its valley, overlooked with a brooding intensity by the two great Colossi of Bamiyan, the Great and Lesser Buddhas, now alas destroyed by the Taliban.

Those immense statues were proof that Buddhism had finally reached the Bamiyan valley in the third to fifth centuries AD. In the second century, the Kushan ruler, Kanishka, had recognised the potential of his country's position at the very centre of the Silk Route with trade to India opening up to the south, with China to the east and with Rome, then approaching the zenith of its powers, to the west. By this time Hinduism was ousting

Buddhism in India and it was no easy matter to infiltrate his own faith along the trade routes. However by powers of persuasion and the astute use of his immense wealth, Kanishka was able to encourage missionaries of the Buddhist faith to visit the valley and set up a chain of *stupas* and monasteries en route.

The culmination of his dream, which he did not live to see, was the erection of the two giant Buddhas, the smaller one dating from the early fourth century, the larger one possibly a century later. Both statues were carved from the cliff itself, which acted as their backcloth and were covered in a mixture of mud and straw – in the case of the larger figure with a drapery of ropes prior to the mud treatment, before being finally painted, blue in the case of the smaller statue and red to the larger. Both had gilded faces and hands. The cliffside surrounding the two figures was pockmarked with myriad caves which led to deeper caves and grottoes, many of them retaining vestiges of painted statuary and sculptured ceilings.

Kharami and I walked down the main street, lined with hippies and boutiques, the latter selling sheepskins and jackets reeking rancidly of uncured leather. It was still the era of the flower people and its disciples for the most part appeared to be living off the local population, poor enough themselves, often for nothing or in exchange for a pair of threadbare jeans or well-worn shoes. My aim was to find a guide to take me to visit the large Buddha before the sun set and it was with evident relief that Kharami handed me over to a local schoolmaster-cum-guide and departed with Abdul to arrange our accommodation for the night. Our ascent was a slow one, my breathing not yet being accustomed to the rarified air, and as we drew nearer to our goal I could feel the all-seeing eyes of the Buddha viewing us puny mortals with disdain.

Once there, we were able to clamber on to the head of the statue, then partially missing both face and hands, and from this vantage point I could examine in detail the remains of the wall paintings that decorated the cliff-face and were even then sadly dilapidated. My perch on the Buddha's head was like being on top of the world. From there I had an uninterrupted view of Bamiyan and the surrounding range of the Hindu Kush. The latter, a marvel of colour, is also miraculous in formation. Folds and curves give way to layered seams and pleats; boulders of rock are streaked with eau-de-nil; a glint of amethyst darkens to purple, merging with strata of apricot and sepia, gradually fading to a universal grey with the going down of the sun. Stupefied with so much beauty and mystery, I stumbled my way down the cliffside and was directed to the hotel where we were to spend the night and at which, I hoped, I and my future groups would stay.

The Yurt Village and Bamiyan Hotel stood high on the plateau overlooking the Buddhas and consisted of a main reception block containing two dining rooms and a small number of bedrooms. The latter were adequately equipped with a pipe stove and in a few cases a bathroom adjoining, the functions of which appeared somewhat primitive. Nearby was a so-called 'motel' with a bar and additional dining space and six quite well appointed bedrooms with a bathroom to every two rooms. Scattered round the plateau within easy distance of the reception block were several clusters of yurts – felt-lined tents exuding cosiness – the majority of which had extensions containing a shower and WC. Luxury indeed. For those without such amenities it meant a hundred yard dash (at 8,000 feet) to the ablution block.

Amongst a group of 15-20 individuals, most of them retired and many with decisive characters and well-heeled backgrounds, it is very difficult to please all tastes and to decide what will be the most acceptable to the majority in the way of sightseeing, accommodation and menus. I have found over the years that although those who travel under my wing consider themselves to be travellers rather than tourists, they are not averse to their creature comforts, however remote and adventurous the journey. A further problem is that due to the preponderance of lone travellers (many of them widows), very few of whom are prepared to share, the ratio of single rooms to doubles required is of necessity a high one, much to the dissatisfaction of hotel managers. Rather than lose business they will promise you the desired number of single rooms, only to find on arrival that due to some "oversight" there are fewer than those promised, leading to much argument with the management, and recriminations from those unfortunates who might have to double up for a night or two.

Once or twice there are genuine misunderstandings, as once in Hamadan. Sir Ronald Mylne was travelling on his own but the hotel protested vehemently that his name was not on the rooming list. Seizing the list, I found him registered under Mr Sir, a mistake similar to one made when a certain peeress (Lady Normanby) once travelled round the Soviet Union with her visa stamped in the Cyrillic form of Marchioness, which meant feverish last-minute changes to luggage labels and rooming lists to conform with her new designation. At Bamiyan, after discussion with the hotel manager, I opted for the yurts – figuring that at least they would be a novel experience to most, if not exactly grand confort, but added the proviso that they must all have 'facility extensions', as the bathrooms were delicately described. Having made my decision I thought I had better try one myself that very night, a decision I was to regret. Because the hotel was surprisingly full with members of an Indian film unit, and because I was trying to keep costs down as much as possible, I was appointed a yurt with no 'facility extension'. Before retiring to my room, I ate in one of the dining rooms in company with many of the film company. I was informed by my solicitous waiter that the star was due to arrive that night but knew neither his name or in what picture he was to appear. The food, though spicy and appetising, was tepid – high altitude I told myself placatingly – and it was even possible to have a fair-sized glass of drinkable red wine at 150 afghani (about £1).

After dinner I groped my way to my yurt to write up my notes, which was a mistake. The light was dim and fitful, given to eccentric flickerings and culminating in a sudden burst of light, before reverting to dimness, which proved a strain on the eyes. The air was icy, despite a stove which I kept on all night, ignoring the suspicion that I might be found dead in the morning overcome by carbon monoxide fumes. Judging by the gusts of freezing air which seemed to penetrate every crack in the yurt's felt-lined construction, there seemed little chance of that. How I envied Kubla Khan with his ermine and sable-lined tent. When the time came to visit the ablution block, it took me minutes to summon enough courage to make the two-minute dash across a windswept expanse of grass. It was only an urgent bladder and the fact that I had been in close proximity all day with Kharami and Abdul, both inveterate smokers and eaters of garlic, cooped up in a fairly ancient Peugeot redolent of petrol fumes and oil, which prevented me from chickening out and going unwashed for the night.

My arrival at the ablution block – a stark concrete building reminiscent of a prison house, coincided with that of a group of Japanese ladies, come to wash out their billycans after an evening meal in their yurts. The ablutions were open plan, that is the washbasins were in one long row adjacent to each other. The shower I had tried but the water like the soup was tepid. My teeth chattering with cold, I bowed to the billican ladies and indicated that I was going to brush my teeth. They bowed back with much hissing and showing of gold-filled teeth and continued with their washing up, accompanied by high-pitched chatter. Teeth done, I washed my face and gingerly removed my mackintosh, my one aim being not to expose more than one part of my anatomy at a time, not because of prudery but because of the elements. Before giving my Guerlain soap an airing and attacking my upper limbs, I bowed again to my companions which induced more hissing Japanese chat. Doggedly I descended to my nether regions which produced a gale of giggles which were delicately stifled by hands placed before mouths. With a last hissing and clashing of billycans, the ladies mercifully departed into the night. "Bring bath plugs", I remember saying to myself as I tried to wash out my smalls in running water – my second mistake that evening as they were still drenched the next morning, hung even as near the stove as I dared.

I shivered my way back to my yurt under a brilliant canopy of stars and dived into my bed where I found solace in my first piece of forethought, a hot water bottle which I had cajoled the cook into filling after complimenting him on his dinner. My second godsend was a pair of woollen bedsocks knitted by Katie, our former cook, and which had lain neglected while living a sybaritic existence in a centrally heated flat.

Calling blessings on Katie's greying head, I pulled them over my frozen toes, donned a couple of pullovers and was toying with the idea of continuing my notes when the lights, such as they were, went out. I later learnt that all lights were extinguished at 10pm in order to save the meagre amount of electricity supplied by a generator. Then the music started up with drum accompaniment – no doubt the Indian film unit at work or play, and no doubt too with Kharami as an ardent spectator or even hopeful would-be participant as local colour. He had played cassettes of Afghan and Indian music non-stop in the car until I asked him to stop – it was unfortunately before the time of earphones – after which he sulked like a reprimanded child.

Despite a restless night I awoke feeling surprisingly fit and after a breakfast of omelette and Nescafé (the latter supplied by me) we set off for the small Buddha. The air still cut like a knife and I only hoped it would be considerably warmer in May for the sake of my less resilient companions. This ascent was even more arduous than that of the evening before, since it involved climbing a series of very deep uneven and steep steps with no hand rails, which makes it even worse coming down than going up. We crossed behind Buddha Minor's head, also minus its face and hands. The paintings in his niche were in an even worse condition than those behind Buddha Major. Nearby there were still more caves dug into the hillside, some with ceilings carved to simulate wooden beams and resting on stone pilasters; others with designs of birds, scrolls and vases, and one with a remarkable lantern roof.

A ten minute drive from the Buddhas took us to Shahr-i-Gholghola (The Silent City), once a thriving community with a proud citadel at its centre, now but a rubble of stones, but still commanding a breathtaking view of the valley below. Further on at Saidabad were the ruins of the walled Qala-i-Dokhtar (the Daughter's Castle), so called after the daughter of Jalal-al-Din, ruler of Bamiyan in the early 13th century. It was she who, according to legend, on hearing that her father was to marry a Princess from Ghazni, betrayed him and his kingdom to Ghengis Khan, who razed the city to the ground in 1221, leaving nothing living in the ruins including, I was pleased to hear, the princess.

Abdul, who looked as if he had been joining in the previous night's revels, admitted to having missed his breakfast, so we stopped at a kebab stall before setting off for Pul-i-Khumri. Having finished the film in my camera, I found to my chagrin that the winder had jammed and, being the most amateurish of photographers, a trait obviously shared by my two companions, and with little chance of finding a dark room in the immediate vicinity, I was faced with the abandonment of photographs for the time being. Half an hour's drive led us past the jumbled remains of Shahr-i-Zohak (the Red City), once one of the most important fortresses which guarded the Bamiyan region under the rule of the Shansabani kings in the 12th and 13th centuries.

Here, on a later expedition, I was to experience one of the most enjoyable picnics ever, described on page 319. The road led on through a ravine bordered on either side by sheer rock rising steeply upwards and enclosing us, as it were, in a narrow corridor that seemed to brook no escape, as mile followed mile without change. We were following the course of the Darishokori

River and just as I was thinking I couldn't stand much more of this claustrophobic atmosphere, the valley broadened out with the rock cliff giving way to shale covered slopes.

I found this landscape in turn wholly mesmeric but was brutally brought out of my trance by a sudden and almighty crash, followed by a hoarse cry from Abdul, as the car swerved violently sideways to be brought to an abrupt halt by coming to rest against the hillside, now covered in scrub.

Bewildered but seemingly unhurt, the three of us looked about us. Kharami was muttering Afghan curses, or it may have been prayers, but Abdul was galvanised into action and was already out of the car. Spread out on the bonnet like an outsize feather duster lay an enormous eagle, quite dead. Its amber eyes were open and glaring, its beak and talons cruelly curved, as if even in death the bird was about to seize and devour its prey. The sun shone down on its dark brown plumage, its tawny tail feathers marbled with grey and brown.

We had been on the point of emerging from the ravine into the beginning of a plain. The road stretched straight ahead and in the distance a speck appeared travelling fast. Quick as a flash Abdul, with the help of Kharami, who could also move fast if he thought there was anything in it for him, removed with considerable effort the corpse from the bonnet and bundled it into the boot. The wing span was awesome – four to five feet at least.

Meanwhile, the speck materialised as one of the gaily decorated trucks which abounded in the region, its driver and numerous passengers eyeing us curiously as they drew alongside. They were obviously intrigued by our unorthodox position and offered to help but Abdul, afraid no doubt of a telltale feather lying around, assured them we were OK. I hoped he was right and indeed the car seemed miraculously undamaged apart from some scratched paint. I learned later that owing to a drought the preceding summer and dearth of water in the preceding spring, food had become scarce on the ground in the form of rodents and other small animals and several eagles had been sighted recently flying at a much lower height than normal in their search for nourishment. My two companions were cock-a-hoop.

"What will you do with the bird?" I asked curiously.

"Sell it in the market. Will bring much money."

"How much money?" Kharami translated.

Abdul shrugged and muttered a figure.

"He says 3-5,000 afghanis, maybe more", Kharami laughed exultantly.

I fervently hoped that we would not have to wait until our return to Kabul in three days' time before disposing of their booty. I was not filled with delight at the thought of a rotting carcass jolting about behind me, however valuable the prize, and it was obvious anyway that I was not to be offered any share in the profits.

With combined effort we finally extricated the Peugeot from its resting place. Not even the windscreen had sustained a crack and once Abdul assured himself that the steering was undamaged, and had been complimented on averting what could have been a serious accident, we were on our way. By now we were travelling through a fertile valley, which looked promising picnic country – although rather devoid of shade, I noted mentally for future reference. The landscape grew ever gentler in contour, although being late in the year the earth was brown, varying from shades of biscuit, light buff, through café au lait to occasionally a rich chocolate. We passed various signs of life: a donkey turning a wheel being used as a rice thresher; several oxen ploughing, their creamy flanks blending with the earth. Occasionally we would come across nomadic tribes on the move, the women dressed colourfully in richly embroidered dresses hung about with gold and silver jewellery. Most were mounted on small sturdy horses with gaily bedecked bridles and saddle bags, festooned with cooking pots, swaddled babies and a hen or two.

The road at times was very twisty and I for one was not sorry to reach Doshi, where we stopped to lunch at rather a bleak *chaikhana*, which offered the usual menu of pilau, nan and green tea. Afterwards I walked on ahead for my daily constitutional, which turned out to be quite a long one since my colleagues appeared in no hurry to catch me up. Perhaps they were even then haggling over the price of their bounty. By now we were back on tarmac which made walking easier. The air was deliciously invigorating, with a light breeze to temper the sun. I was offered several lifts from passing traffic, although had I accepted such an invitation it was anyone's guess as to where I would have sat. Most trucks were packed with drums of kerosene, goats and a sea of humanity. I provided much merriment amongst the local population as I strode by, untrammelled by possessions, and provoked much giggling, waving and whispered chatter as I returned their greetings.

Eventually I was retrieved by Abdul and continued on our way to Pul-i-Khumri (Bridge of Doves) where we were to spend the night. We reached there shortly after 3pm and I decided to carry on for another twenty minutes to Surkh Kotal (the Red Pass), which housed one of the most famous sites in Afghanistan, the important religious temple founded in about 130 AD by King Kanishka, he who had introduced Bhuddhism to the Bamiyan valley. I had read that excavations had been carried out since 1952 under the supervision of Daniel Schlumberger and was keen to include a visit in my programme for my forthcoming tour. But I was unsure whether a bus (our intended means of transport) could reach within moderately easy walking distance of the site. The alternative was a long steep and very dusty walk by a stony track, which I doubted would be possible for some of the less mobile members of my party. The only way to find out was to see for myself.

Kharami, who had now become Crummy in my own vocabulary

and estimation, had grown increasingly uncooperative as the day progressed, replying in monosyllabics to any questions and generally behaving like a sulky schoolboy. Earlier I had had a surreptitious look in the boot on some pretext and saw to my relief that the bird had metaphorically flown. Whether his part in the transaction had not worked out to his liking, or whether his matrimonial plans for wife No. 2 were hanging fire, I could not know. He may have had a stomach ache due to over-indulgence with the film set the previous night, or again he was just being his usual perverse bloody self.

Whatever the cause, when I announced my intention to inspect the excavations at Surkh Kotal, he exploded into incoherent anger.

"No time for this," he spluttered. "Enough for one day".

It was then barely 3.15pm and it was thanks to Abdul, as I pointed out, that we had started late. True, the latter had driven hard and well but he was not being asked to do anything but wait in the car for the next hour or so, and Kharami had spent most of the day sleeping, whingeing or listening to his damned cassettes. I thought it time to turn tough.

"Now look here, Kharami. Mr Jalawan (his boss; my agent) has had a copy of the places I intend to visit, including Surkh Kotal, and has approved them. I am paying for this expedition and if you'd rather leave us now and make your own way home, that is all right by me and I will explain the circumstances to Mr Jalawan when I get back to Kabul."

I had little doubt that Mr Jalawan thought as did Kharami, that I would be content with gazing at sites from afar but his subordinate was not to know that. I knew I was calling my guide's bluff as it was very unlikely that Abdul and I, left to our own devices without a common language, would make much headway. "Anyway" I concluded, "yours is a marvellous country and I intend to enjoy it. Why can't you?"

He looked at me in real astonishment. This was a point of view he clearly had not considered before and he was properly startled at any suggestion of enjoying himself. My words must have had some effect, for apart from a scowl and ungracious shrug of the shoulders, he complied with my request. Although we were never to become soul-mates, there was never any open rebellion after that.

Having given instructions to Abdul to see about accommodation for the night, Kharami and I set off along an unpaved road that climbed upwards for about three kilometres – but we were now down to an altitude of about 2,000 feet, so the going was comparatively easy. The hardest part was trying to keep our footing on the loose pebbles that kept skidding from under our feet, causing much slithering and cursing (on Kharami's part). We finally made it to the foot of the monumental staircase, five flights high, each with a terrace between. To reach the temple excavations we had to negotiate an even more slippery and steeper path. Luckily my companion had no breath left for reproach and I could not have retaliated in any case. Achieving our goal, I collapsed on to a boulder and surveyed the scene before me.

Being November, digging was at a halt and for one bleak moment I thought all had been covered over, with nothing to reward our labours. But sufficient excavations were on view and with the help of a plan of the work in hand affixed to a wall, I was able to have an idea of what the site signified. Obviously one would have to request one of the members of the archaeological team to act as our guide. A temple had already been excavated, surrounded by a paved colonnaded courtyard as well as a number of rooms, unidentifiable to me as yet. I had already been informed that several inscriptions had been discovered and that these, together with a huge headless statue purported to be that of Kanishka, were now on view in the Kabul museum. Across the hills one could see the cemeteries of Pul-i-Khumri, and by the side of the road as we descended lay relics of King Kanishka's fort. On our way down we stumbled on an alternative path, rather longer but less severe, which could be offered to the less mobile or lazier members of the party who could dally there and search for wild flowers.

Honour and investigations satisfied, I returned to the patiently waiting Abdul, who had already reconnoitred our accommodation for the night. Pul-i-Khumri is a fairly large and prosperous town standing at the crossroads of the main routes to Kabul, Kunduz and Mazar-i-Sharif. To reach our hotel, we passed the Ghori hydro-electric station, one of the most important power-producing plants in Afghanistan. The hotel itself was entirely adequate for the three of us, but posed a problem for me, as it appeared only to have six bedrooms in all. The manager assured me that many more were being built in the annexe and would be ready by the spring, but I could see no sign of builders or construction work in progress and had grave misgivings. I was shown to my room – almost a grand suite and luxurious by preceding standards – and somehow out of place. I felt I had once more entered civilisation and was not sure that I welcomed it.

However, any such doubts vanished when I discovered a bath crouching behind a plastic curtain decorated with seagulls. Deterred only momentarily by a bewildering array of levers attached to a geyser, I pulled the most likely looking one, spurred on by the thought of washing away all that dust from my skin, hair and belongings. With a ferocious hissing, a cloud of steam erupted in my face causing me to start back in fright, only to get entangled in the curtain bringing it down together with the rail, seagulls and me. After much ostentatious farting, all the rusted taps could produce was a trickle of water, scalding it is true, but a rich peat brown in colour. Thoughts of washing my hair or person having evaporated, I extricated myself from my plastic shroud and went in search of the brandy, which I always carry with me for 'medicinal purposes'.

This was a further solace to be denied me, since I discovered that the plastic container had split (I suspect the impact of a mighty predator thrown on top of my hold-all had proved too much for it) and that its precious contents were now well and truly absorbed into my one change of clothing. I had been subconsciously aware of an alcoholic odour pursuing me on the way to the room and had noted the inquisitive sideways glance of my escort, but with my bathing problems to contend with, such thoughts had vanished from my mind.

While eating my dinner – an unappetising stew of goat piled high with vegetables – I explained my predicament to a sympathetic waiter who spoke good English.

"I bring you water," he exclaimed – which he eventually did and hung around until I managed to extract some cigarettes, smelling faintly of brandy, from my luggage with which he departed delightedly. I doused myself in the water, then my clothes which I draped around the hot-water pipes.

After an uneasy night I awoke feeling distinctly queasy but with the help of hot green tea and a couple of Alka-Seltzers (my ever present help in trouble) I managed to endure the 51-mile run to Samangan without mishap. After a dull run through a flat uninteresting plain, we arrived at the site of Takht-i-Rustam (Rustam's Throne) – in my opinion one of the most exciting places I had so far visited in Afghanistan. In the 1960s, excavations under a Japanese mission brought to light evidence of a once flourishing Buddhist community dating from the 5th and 6th centuries. Some of the caves had carved or vaulted ceilings, similar to those at Bamiyan, and contained niches for statues. Others served as bath houses or latrines.

Crowning the summit of the hill in front of the monastery stands the *stupa* cave itself, carved out of solid limestone with an ambulatory surrounding it to allow pilgrims to pay their respects, and topped with the limestone *harmika* which originally held the umbrella or *chatri* pole. In Ferdowsi's poem, the Shåhnameh, the hero Rustam marries the lovely daughter of the King of Samangan and, to celebrate the occasion, drinks from the basin at the head of the *stupa*.

The sense of serenity was all-pervading and I withdrew reluctantly from this magical spot to join the others for the drive to Mazar-i-Sharif. An unremarkable landscape accompanied us until we reached the spectacular Tashgurghan Gorge, which heralds the approach to Khulm, a centre for the fruit trade. Here we stopped briefly to explore the enticing covered market selling figs, pomegranates, dried mulberries and apricots as well as a tempting display of spices and nuts, gaudily painted lacquer ware and embroidered caps. It was amazing to watch how Kharami came to life amidst such surroundings.

After a mild verbal skirmish with the latter, I persuaded him to accompany me to the Bagh-i-Jahanama, the former gardens to the palace of the Amir Abdul Rahman. These we entered by an elaborately carved wood gateway and, although the grounds were overgrown with a tangle of grasses and unpruned rose bushes, and the pretty terraces sadly neglected, the whole setting was delightful and well worth a few moments' dalliance. There was talk of converting the palace into a hotel. If that was so, I only hope the treatment is in keeping with its setting.

We reached Mazar by midday and I saw our guide eyeing the seedy looking Balkh Nights Hotel with obvious favour. As it was cheaper than most and seemed clean enough inside we dropped our bags there. We then heard there was to be a game of *buzkashi* in Mazar that afternoon – some said at 2pm, others seemed to think 3pm more likely. As none of us felt like eating we decided to visit Balkh first, before returning to Mazar for a late lunch and the *buzkashi* game. I had just been reading Cassell's 'Les Chevaliers', a gripping tale centring round the life of a great horseman and *buzkashi* player, and although I was not keen on the thought of a decapitated goat being used as the target, I was reassured by the reception clerk who told me that blown up bladders were used nowadays.

Balkh lies eleven miles west of Mazar, with the extensive ruins of the ancient city lying north of the modern town. Successive teams of archaeologists have yet to establish the exact date of the earliest foundations but it is thought that they go back to the Jushan period or even before that to Zoroastrian times, although the massive walls surrounding the city – now badly deteriorating – were rebuilt during the Timurid period. The city was razed to the ground by Genghis Khan and his followers in 1220.

Small boys and persistent youths were thick on the ground, pestering us to buy shards of pottery and bronze figures, all of which were naturally "anteek". We passed the shrine of Khwaja Abu Nasr Parsa, full of praying Moslems. The building, though dilapidated, was embellished with lovely coloured corkscrew pillars. I was also shown on demand, and with bad grace on the part of Kharami, the Mosque of the Nine Domes (c. 1000 AD), again in a ruinous state but still retaining some splendid ornamentation on its decaying arches and pillars. We had to circumnavigate a dreadful mud and dust road in order to get there and my heart went out to Abdul, who had taken the trouble to wash the car that morning, thinking we were finished with dust roads. There seemed to be more and more people converging on Balkh and we soon discovered the reason. The *buzkashi* game was to be staged there and not in Mazar as we had been informed. I was partly relieved, although I would have liked to have studied the technicalities of the game.

As we still had the sights of Mazar to visit, we returned there for lunch in a typical Afghan *chaikhana*. By this time I was feeling very much better but thought it prudent to stick to green tea and a mouthful of bread. I was the only woman present but was assured by the owner that I was very welcome. During the meal I was intrigued to see an enormous tray being prepared with heaped plates of rice and kebabs and the ubiquitous tins of Coca-Cola. This was then carried out to a large limousine in which reclined several heavily veiled ladies and some children. I could only feel thankful I was not travelling in their car that afternoon.

After lunch we went to look at the Caravanserai, a very modern and delightfully situated hotel some way outside the town, all the rooms with bath or shower, which would do admirably for my pampered groups. Here I ran across a party of German tourists, housed in one of those enormous coach/homes fitted out like a railway carriage with sleeping cubicles for forty passengers, furnished with upper and lower berths, the corridor used for hanging space and an ablution space at one end. The rear of the vehicle let down to reveal a mobile kitchen from which soup and stew were being doled out. The group had come from Frankfurt and were to be on the road for thirty-eight days. My mind reeled at the very thought of such a marathon. I was, however, able to invoke the help of one passenger who, like most Germans, was an ardent photographer and was only too happy to show off his prowess by unjamming my camera and inserting a new film.

I wandered round the town on my own looking at the Shrine of Hazrat Ali and the Mosque. I could not enter the latter, it being a Friday and likewise the museum was closed. Instead, I found a number of carpet vendors who invited me into their shops, where I passed a happy time sitting on a pile of carpets drinking tea, as rug after rug was unrolled before me. I finally came away with a very pretty Turkoman prayer rug tucked under my arm for which I paid the princely sum of £15 in Afghan money. I had soup (tepid as usual) and more tea for supper, which I drank while sitting on my rusting balcony watching and listening to the Mazar crowds below and to the ceaseless honking of car horns. Early the next morning a camel caravan passed under my window, the beasts grunting and disdainful, urged on by the raucous cries of their keepers. Two doves flew by like messengers of fate, outlined against an aquamarine sky, aiming for a nearby minaret. The call to prayer was summoning the faithful and from my balcony I witnessed many Moslems prostrating themselves in the direction of Mecca. Dust arose from the street and it was time to leave. A pot of tea and we were away before eight.

Thanks to starvation, I was mercifully myself again but it was Kharami's turn to feel sorry for himself with a sore throat, a nasty hacking cough and much hawking and spitting. We sat interminably behind a queue of lorries at the one and only petrol station on the outskirts of the town. No use to ask Abdul why he couldn't have filled up prior to departure. It was the East and what did time matter? It was tarmac today with many sights to divert us along the way. Herds of sheep and goats being propelled by a ragged urchin and mangy looking collie-like dog; a string of camels led by a donkey and in the rear a baby camel. Most villages we passed through possessed a *chaikhana* or two frequented by cross-legged worthies drinking tea and smoking. We passed turbaned figures and others swathed in material as a protection against the dust that swirled about their heads; barefooted children begging by the roadside or offering nuts or fruit;

and heavily-veiled women bearing baskets or babies on their backs. A raven flew into our windscreen. Not such a dramatic occurrence as before, but the victim was despatched with equal haste into the boot. The wings were of an inky black glossiness, and the eyes like amber stones. We were retracing our steps towards Khulm and Pul-i-Khumri before returning to Kabul via Doshi and the Salang Pass. Some way beyond Khulm I pointed out a tiny shrine perched on the top of a hill and could palpably feel Kharami's relief as we drove past it. Later on we came across a falcon sitting on a fence, motionless in the sun.

Once I left the car to look at some pistachio trees. They are small with a broad flat leaf and are in great profusion between Samangan and Pul-i-Khumri. Cotton and sugar beet were also much in evidence. Shortly before entering Doshi we nearly ran down a holy man carrying begging bowl and prayer mat tucked under his arm. We did not tarry at Doshi but continued through the pretty, fertile valleys of the Anderab and Khinjan Rivers, both rich in trout, so I was informed. Mulberry trees were abundant but grown for the fruit rather than for silkworms – dried mulberries are one of the specialities of the region. I tasted some and found them to be tasty and crisp. The locals mix them with walnuts, or brew them into a hot invigorating drink.

We stopped for lunch at a delightful *chaikhana* situated at the foot of the climb to the Salang Tunnel, sitting on a terrace high above the river. Thankfully (for me) it was another meatless day, so we were served with a bowl of arsh – a robust soup of beans, vermicelli and root vegetables accompanied by sour cream and a plate of well cooked plain boiled rice. A purée of dried apricots and the inevitable pot of green tea completed this satisfying meal.

We set off for the Salang Tunnel, then the highest in the world at 11,100 feet and over a mile long, punctuated by a series of galleries. Once through the tunnel the road drops away rapidly and runs parallel to the Salang River, overlooked by a number of villages perched precariously on the rocky hillside. Emerging from the mountains at Jebal Seraj, we stopped there for Kharami to buy a hen for his aunt. His choice was a nice looking reddish brown bird with a bright eye who showed its resentment at being popped into a plastic bag by much clucking and squawking. It then lay under Kharami's seat with tied feet and its head sticking out, looking like an outraged old woman. We also stocked up on bags of pistachio nuts, small but crisp, almonds and walnuts and in Kharami's case a sack of dried mulberries.

On leaving Jebal Seraj we crossed the Ghorband River by a grandiose newish looking bridge. At Chahrikar, a town teeming with activity, we had to stop again, so that Abdul could haggle for a cooking pot. By this time there was a sort of end-of-term party spirit amongst the three of us. I had accomplished, after a certain amount of battling, largely what I had set out to do; Abdul must have been feeling a sense of achievement at having covered so many miles in difficult terrain without mishap – so far - and even the surly Kharami had come to life and was quite chirpy at the thought of shortly getting rid of me.

After leaving Charikhar I was on the look-out for a Buddhist *stupa* known as Tope Darra (Valley of the Stupa). It was Abdul who first spotted it, standing as it was high above us – but one really needed binoculars more powerful than my own to distinguish more than its outlines. Just before entering the outskirts of Kabul we ran out of petrol. I had espied a pump in Charikhar but did not think it worth the argument which would have ensued had I mentioned it. In any case we did carry a spare can, the contents of which would get us to our destinations. Afghan petrol smells quite different and much worse than ours at home. I thought it was rotting fruit at first or perhaps our friend the raven who, I had remarked, was still with us, its sheen somewhat diminished, and was thankful we were nearing our journey's end.

We deposited Kharami with his mulberries and hen near his home on the outskirts of Kabul – our parting was civil on both sides – and Abdul then drove me to the Intercontinental Hotel, where I banished all thoughts of being a traveller rather than a tourist and wallowed in the luxury of a hot, scented bath while attempting to wash the dust out of my hair. My coat disappeared into the hands of a willing house-boy and was returned soon afterwards, miraculously de-dusted and pressed. Feeling more civilised, I went to call on Mr Jalawan, only to discover to my slight relief that he had been called out of town. His deputy reiterated the promise of a firm quote before the end of the year. I duly returned to the hotel, where I had an interview with an efficient assistant manager ready to carry out my every whim in regard to next year's visit. It was only at the last minute that he disclosed he was being posted to Pakistan in three months' time and could not therefore guarantee that his successor would adhere to his wishes.

My journey home by Ariana Afghan Airlines was only marred by a blaring blast of music played incessantly throughout the flight to Istanbul. First we flew over the Hindu Kush – looking superb in the clear morning light – and later caught tantalising glimpses of Demavend and the Caspian Sea through an obscuring haze. Istanbul's airport I found as unappealing by day as it was by night, but at least I was able to stretch my legs and buy peeled pistachios.

I managed to arrange three tours to Afghanistan before the Russians invaded the country in 1979. The first covered very much the ground I had reconnoitred; the second included Iran, with entry to Afghanistan through Herat; and the third and final entailed flying to Karachi and making our way to Jalalabad via the Khyber Pass, perhaps the most thrilling of all three variations.

Reflections

Twenty-five

I have often been asked if I ever had to cope with a death while on tour and can thankfully say that I was the only one amongst my colleagues who escaped this trauma. Kay Turnbull, in fact, earned the title of Killer Kay, so regularly did she have a death to contend with. I did however have some near misses which, in their way, could be equally problematical.

On one occasion an American lady visiting England under my wing had a severe heart attack in the early hours of the morning at our hotel in St Ives in Cornwall. She was rushed into intensive care at Penzance Hospital where she lay between life and death for the next forty-eight hours. I was to lead my party (all Americans) back to London by various stages, so rang the American Consulate to ascertain the correct procedure should the worst occur. I explained the situation to the duty officer. A laconic voice answered me:

"Lady," it said. "If she lives she's all yours; if she dies she's all ours".

She did indeed survive and complained bitterly at being moved into a public ward, until it was pointed out somewhat tartly by the sister-in-charge that it was the British taxpayer who was paying for every penny of her illness and she should be duly grateful.

"Especially," continued the ward sister, "since, if the boot was on the other foot and I was ill in America there would be no such reciprocal arrangement."

There were other dramas to contend with: civil disturbances in countries to be visited, air strikes, bombing attacks on London by the IRA, which deterred our American clientele in large part from visiting Britain; earthquakes or floods which precluded travel, sometimes to the extent of having to cancel a tour altogether. This happened once in the case of a tour to China, fully booked with twenty-five participants and fully paid up. Barely a week before departure date a major earthquake badly damaged the area included in our programme. The Foreign Office advised us against going but cautioned us to wait until we heard from the Chinese authorities since, if we cancelled the tour, we would brook no compensation. Good counselling indeed, as shortly afterwards our Chinese agents refused to take the responsibility of our arrival and cancelled the tour themselves. We had perforce to refund all 25 participants in full – a considerable sum of money – and await repayment from China. This took several weeks to arrive and in the meantime the exchange rate had so changed in our favour that we finally made a very handsome profit for a tour that never took place. It so easily could have gone the opposite way.

Another question that cropped up at intervals was, how did we cope with muggings or robberies? The answer, I suppose, is that when taking a party of well-heeled travellers to less affluent parts of the world, one must be prepared to accept the fact that thefts with violence could occur and to be constantly aware of this. All one can do as a tour leader is to warn one's fellow travellers to be alert and to try and impress on them the folly of carrying with them on excursions anything of value, including passports. Even so, such warning could fall on deaf ears.

Sicily, although one of my favourite countries on account of its architectural legacies from the Greeks, Romans, Normans and Classicists, was also one in which especial vigilance was needed against attacks of violence, thanks to the Mafia. It was in March 1977 that Specialtours arranged two tours to Sicily for members of the National Art Collections Fund. The first group was under the guidance of Diana Skene, who by now lived in Italy and would therefore prepare and smooth out any hiccoughs before my arrival. She had with her as lecturer a volatile Italian lady called Claudine Gnoli, while mine was an amiable English academic, Sir David Scott-Fox, whose knowledge of Sicilian history was proficient but who rather lacked the wherewithal to put it across to his audience.

Two days before I set out for Sicily with my group, Diana telephoned me in London. She sounded somewhat distracted.

"You'll never believe this," she exclaimed with a rueful laugh, "but I've had my handbag stolen".

Why should I not believe her when for the last three days she had rung me to warn of the likelihood of such an event?

I conjured up sympathy. "What happened?"

"I was counting everyone into the coach when a youth zoomed up on a Vespa, snatched my bag off my shoulder and, pouff, away."

She sounded increasingly outraged.

"What did he take?"

"All my money and cheque book to pay for dinner, but worst of all the key to the hotel safe deposit box in which I had recommended everyone to put their valuables. And now," she continued "the safe has to be blown open which I understand is very expensive, so I'm afraid you will have to go to the bank and bring out enough lire to finance its replacement."

Figures and references followed, ringing off with the usual exhortation, "Be absolutely sure to warn everyone of the dangers and to take nothing of value on their persons".

Despite a certain humiliation on Diana's part at being hoisted with her own petard, we could not but see the funny side of the situation.

So here was I some two days later with my group on an Alitalia flight coming into land at Palermo Airport, notorious for its high ratio of accidents in recent years. I was seated behind a very vociferous family of Sicilians within good view of the cockpit, which remained open to view through the entire journey. At take-off my confidence in the pilot was not heightened when they all crossed themselves fervently and pressed kisses on photographs of the Virgin Mary, which they produced from their pockets. The journey from Rome was mercifully a short one, since waves of garlic and unwashed humanity emanated from the seats in front. A certain tension, accompanied by more crossings and kissings, at the order to fasten our seatbelts announced our imminent landing. I derived little comfort from the rear view of the pilot, who appeared to be smoking a cigarette and looking out of the window, but our landing was accomplished smoothly and competently followed by a spontaneous and enthusiastic round of applause and cries of *"bravissimo"* from my Sicilian friends, in which I joined wholeheartedly. Our captain responded with a jolly wave of his hand and I wondered if he was a relative.

Having cleared our luggage and boarded the coach under the guidance of our driver, Augustino, a small and rather elderly man who I hoped would have both the stamina and fortitude to stand up to any vicissitudes which might beset us, I gave my usual pep talk and added an account of Diana's misfortune for good measure. We were staying at the Jolly Hotel in the centre of Palermo, a fairly modern establishment with spacious rooms and lofty-ceilinged dining room, reminiscent of Edwardian days. In hindsight the hotel was probably one of the Mafia strongholds in the city in the spring of 1977, judging by the nefarious happenings that occurred within and around its precincts, but we were only to learn that by experience.

The first morning's sightseeing was pure pleasure, with visits on foot to some of the city's many treasures. We were on our way back to the hotel for lunch from the Palazzo dei Normanni when two of my party decided to stop and take photographs. I was entrusted with their handbags while they rehearsed how they should walk close together with their camera cases in between. A hundred yards from the hotel a sneak-thief crept up on them from behind, barged between them, all but knocking them off their feet, and made away with his plunder – two cameras and accessories. One of the victims, Miss Day, showed commendable spirit by chasing after the robber for a distance with well-bred cries of "Stop thief, stop thief". This only incited the thief to increase his speed and invited no more than shuttered, indifferent looks from a few onlookers who were all too familiar with such incidents and whose one aim was not to be involved in such. The two robbed were rueful but philosophical and unharmed. All three of us made our way to the nearest police station, suspiciously handily situated at the end of the street. Here we spent lunchtime filling up forms in septuplicate. Who, I wondered, were the seven recipients? Not surprisingly, the carabinieri treated the whole affair as a normal daily occurrence, too trivial to merit more than a shrugging of uniformed shoulders and a sympathetic pat on the back. *"Che misfortunato signora."* The three of us having missed our lunch, we repaired to the hotel bar for an espresso and *tosti*.

We were going that evening for drinks at the Palazzo Gangi in a fairly insalubrious quarter of the town and in the afternoon I went off there to tie up arrangements, leaving Sir David to take the group on a further sightseeing tour of the town. My walk took me through a maze of back-streets, many of them festooned with the day's washing, hung out to dry on crumbling balconies decorated with a potted plant or two or a subdued looking canary or mina bird. Dressed as I was in a well-worn raincoat and carrying a clipboard, I was afforded only the occasional disinterested glance. These decaying streets with their peeling paint suddenly erupted into a piazza dominated by the 18th century Palazzo Gangi with fine Baroque window frames and wrought iron balconies. A double staircase leads from the courtyard to the piano nobile and to the great ballroom, featured in the film 'The Leopard', with its magnificent tiled floor and unique ceiling. It was here that our reception was to take place that same evening although thankfully, as it turned out, the owners were not to be present, leaving the steward to do the honours. The sun was low in the sky as I retraced my steps towards the hotel. Nearing my destination I became aware of a commotion in the street ahead. Even from a distance there was a certain familiarity about some of the figures in the tableau and it was with a sinking sense that I identified them as mine. A very diminutive lady, Miss Rainbow, was bleeding copiously from a headwound, and Mrs Ehrenberg, a voluble member of the party, was bewailing for all to hear, the theft of her handbag.

"What happened?" I asked Sir David, who was standing by rather helplessly.

He looked stricken but defensive. "It was such a marvellous afternoon. Everyone wanted to walk the last lap and Augustino persuaded me it would be quite safe." His tone implied that the latter had let him down by this assurance. "These two youths – boys really – seemed to appear from nowhere and attacked these two ladies and disappeared before any of us were aware what had happened".

Both victims had been knocked to the ground and both bags seized. The *carabinieri* were quickly on the scene and for the first and hopefully last time in my life, I had the dubious thrill of travelling in a police car with sirens blaring and blue lights flashing. We went first to the hospital where Miss Rainbow's wounds were attended to in a highly efficient and sympathetic manner. Luckily the cut to her head, though bleeding profusely, was superficial and turned out to be less serious than at first suspected. It transpired, however, that despite all my exhortations she had been carrying her passport in her bag. "Why", I asked myself "do I waste my breath?" She was none the less being so stoic throughout her ordeal that I had not the heart to upbraid her too harshly. When I rang the British Consulate later that evening to report the loss, he replied wearily "that is the thirty-ninth today". At the police station where we were finally deposited I was hailed as an old friend.

"*Buona sera signora. Ancora lei. Come sta?*"

More forms in septuplicate and a long drawn-out argument between Mrs Ehrenberg, and an official as to what items she was carrying in her bag. "How should I know," she protested belligerently. "I don't make a list each day of what I take out with me". I was thankful I was not in her position, as being ready for any emergency, my own bag was apt to contain a number of items supplementary to normal accessories such as money, credit cards and cosmetics. These might include a waiter's friend (penknife complete with corkscrew and bottle opener), folding scissors pinched from my father's fishing bag, a pocket calculator as a safeguard against unscrupulous traders, a bottle of McKenzie's smelling salts (for travel sickness) and a rudimentary first-aid kit, including a miniature bottle of brandy given free on the plane. The last would have stood me in good stead in this particular instance in lieu of my clipboard.

Somehow the tour got under way and my four victims seemed to have put their troubles behind them and were determined to enjoy the rest of their visit. For the remaining visits in Palermo itself, we did in fact have a police escort in the guise of two rather sheepish looking gentlemen who were obviously rather humiliated at the role allotted them. One afternoon we were invited to the country home in the Conca d'Oro belonging to members of the Visconti family. Here we were given *biscotti* and the local wine and left to wander in the surrounding orchards where we picked and ate cumquats, oranges and lemons off the trees and were the objects of much interest to the assortment of ducks, guinea fowl and bantams which were roaming free, not to mention a variety of dogs.

We left Palermo the next day and somehow, with the sloughing off of the city's precincts, our spirits lifted. The weather was perfect and only Philistines could fail to be other than seduced by Sicily in the spring. Cloud-free skies, undulating valleys punctuated with fields of artichokes or fennel, greenhouses of carnations, the pink feathered branches of tamarisk trees and the heady scent of mimosa wafting through the open windows of the coach; wild marguerites and oxalis scattered amongst meadow grasses and the gold of broom everywhere – surely these sights must be balm to any bruised spirit or body and even Sir David was to become more expansive, although his after-dinner talks tended to send his audience nodding. And vying with nature were the architectural marvels created by ancient civilisations, destroyed by their enemies and painstakingly recreated by later generations of Corinthians, Greeks, Carthaginians, Romans and Normans all playing a part in construction and destruction and, as if to prove the futility of their strivings, the force of nature would intervene and wipe out with the eruption of a volcano or the upheaval of an earthquake, the life's work of successive cultures.

Our drive that day included a stop at Segesta where mules took the weaker members of the party to the temple. Brooding in its majestic solitude, its pillars open to the broom-scented air, it was not difficult to imagine those honeyed stones being witness to some sacrificial rite. On to Selinunte which takes its name from Selinon, the Greek word for the wild celery which grows in profusion around the fallen pillars. The magic of the site lies in its position high above the shores of the Mediterranean and in its deserted stillness, silent except for the keening of seabirds. Once a teeming acropolis with commercial port and military garrison, complete with underground escape routes, only vestiges remain of the former Byzantine village and necropolis. Our next port of call was at Agrigento, where we were to stay at the Villa Athena surrounded by an almond grove, alas! its trees no longer in bloom.

I knew the hotel from the sixties when, scarcely completed, it presented a few problems such as defective ball cocks and stray tools outside causing a sprained ankle. But in 1977 we were greeted warmly by the manager, Signor Casterini, who had shared my problems of those early days. Everything worked in well-equipped rooms and the food was delicious. After dinner we walked in the garden, now free of hidden obstacles. The night was cool but drenched in the heady scents of mimosa and wild thyme. The larger of the temples that dominated the area were floodlit, and beyond the reach of the lamplight lay pools of shadow in which could be seen the faint outlines of some pillared portico, transformed now from the honey-coloured stones of daylight to a sombre black in the fainter light of a half-moon. I shivered suddenly, not with cold but with the feeling that the spirits of the Gods and Goddesses of those Greek legends were perhaps still haunting these stones, or entombed in some catacomb unable to break free.

During our travels I had kept in touch with Diana, who was three days ahead of me with her group and also not without vicissitudes of her own. Whilst in Taormina, where they were now installed, a small party had opted for an expedition up the side of Mount Etna with a local guide. Sheila Folkard, the NACF representative, had slipped on the shale and had been carted off to hospital with a suspected broken leg. I mentally deleted any optional visit to Mt. Etna from my itinerary.

The marvels of Agrigento and Syracuse and the outstanding Roman mosaics at the Villa Imperiale at Piazza Armerina I leave to the guide books. I skipped on to Taormina for two days' relaxation before catching the train to Rome and onward flight home. We were staying at the delightful Hotel San Domenico – a converted monastery, its former austerity having given way to comfort and luxury. My mind went back to an earlier visit in the 1960s, when I had with me an unworldly young girl from the Midlands who had lost her heart to our then driver, Sebastiano, a lusty lothario.

We were to travel overnight by train from Taormina to Rome in comfortable two-berth wagons-lits and thence by air to London. Augustino drove me down to the station that last afternoon to confirm arrangements and to ensure that porters would be available. The train was not due to leave until 9.45pm so we had plenty of time to enjoy a good and fairly hilarious dinner with liberal quantities of wine at a boat-shaped restaurant called La Cambusa. We arrived at the station; efficient and willing porters were at the ready to deal with our luggage and the train came in on time. I was looking vainly for the wagons-lits section when a distraught official announced that owing to a lightning strike (as common as daylight throughout Italy), all wagons-lits had been shunted off.

The alternative was second-class compartments with rigid seats, most of which appeared to be filled already with unsavoury looking humanity. I was told by the station master that nothing could be done until we reached Messina in an hour's time, where there was a ten-minute halt. There I should go directly to the *capo della stazione* and explain my predicament. I was aghast. Nine hours sitting upright in cramped accommodation was not going to please my flock, especially the ones with chronic indigestion, unsteady stomachs or hip replacements. Lady B. (as she liked to be called), a very elderly member of the party, already boasted two such false limbs. Outwardly I remained calm and explained rather tersely what had occurred and that I hoped to improve the situation in Messina. Everyone seemed surprisingly philosophical thanks, no doubt, to Bacchus.

With the help of Augustino, whom we were leaving behind, and the porters – vociferous but sympathetic – we managed somehow to find seats for everyone within shouting distance of each other. I squeezed myself into a confined space in the guard's van, already stacked with crates of poultry and cardboard boxes, around which I wedged my eighteen pieces of luggage. Every time the train started, slowed down or stopped, a pile of cases would veer towards me and just as I was about to be swamped, would lurch in the opposite direction as the train changed speed. This luggage barrier did at least serve as a buffer against the amorous inclinations of the very drunken guard who insisted on sharing my vigil with me, while I felt he should be attending to more important matters.

"Bellissima", he hiccoughed owlishly, leering at me across a piece of Samsonite luggage then, caught off his balance as the train increased speed he keeled backwards pulling several cases on top of him. This game continued for the next half hour with me trying to dodge teetering suitcases on one hand and evade my maudlin companion on the other. Rescue came in the form of Miss Knight, who had managed to extricate herself from an overcrowded compartment in order to keep me company and with her arrival, we managed to persuade the guard to move.

The train drew in to Messina Station, which appeared enormous and alive with activity. Passengers were to and fro-ing; trolleys piled high with postal bags and boxes labelled 'Alive! Handle with care' weaved a precarious way between the crowds; and a mechanised buffet car was plying its wares with offers of 'sandwich, salami, potato crisps' and the ubiquitous Coca-Cola.

Leaving Miss Knight in charge of the luggage and exhorting as many of my group as I could locate to stay put in the train but to be ready to move at a moment's notice, I set off in search of the *capo della stazione*. I was pointed in a general direction over a bridge and across several platforms and finally reached my goal, a cramped untidy shed-like building, the interior reeking of tobacco smoke. *Il capo* was a villainous looking individual hunched over an enormous bottle of *vino rosso*. He looked at me with a bleary stare in which interest played no part. My spirits sank to zero. Here there was no possible help. The next few minutes taught me never to judge people by their appearances.

"*Buona sera, signore*", I began breathlessly having run from the train at top speed. "*Ho una problema*". The word "problem" obviously made no impact on the listener, being so banal and commonplace a noun that it merited but fleeting attention. His face remained impassive. I struggled on, painting as graphic a picture as I could in my somewhat limited Italian of our predicament, the halt and lame under my care and what a pity it was that a perfect holiday in glorious Sicily should end in this disastrous way. I was quite carried away by the eloquence of this speech but not seemingly so *il capo*. But suddenly as if a squib had been lit under him, he came to life. Leaping to his feet with remarkable agility considering his bulk, he strode from his office bellowing instructions to minions who appeared as if from holes in the ground.

"*Presto, presto*", he shouted urgently to me as I followed hard on his heels. "*Il treno per Roma parte in cinque minuti*".

Reaching our train I hounded my party out of their carriages and at my mentor's command herded them into others which miraculously appeared across the platform. The minions seized the luggage which was still intact under Miss Knight's guard and threw it in after us while *il capo* seized Lady B. and carried her bodily across the divide – both of them enjoying themselves immensely – and I bundled the odd remaining holdalls into whatever carriage presented itself, while members of an Italian football team cheered us on our way. Whistles blew, doors slammed and my saviour, still bellowing, waved aside the wad of notes I was trying to press into his hand and strode off, no doubt to a well-earned glass of *vino rosso*. While containing no wagons-lits, our replacement train was at least a *rapido* offering a choice of six-berth couchettes or first-class seats backed with lace antimacassars. A cheerful steward came round with soft drinks and sheets for the couchette users. A party seemed to be taking place in Sir David's compartment, which he appeared to be sharing with five ladies. Mentally I wished him luck, sat back with my head on the antimacassar and fell asleep.

Over the years the chances of being attacked in Italy did not decrease, and in the mid-eighties a much more serious mugging took place, again in Sicily, which made the headlines in both the British and Italian press, one of the captions being "OAP tourists have a go", which mortified the participants rather more than the attack affected them. Diana was leading the group on this occasion, which once more consisted of members of the National Art Collections Fund, amongst whom were a dowager Duchess, a retired bishop, the former director of the National Gallery of Ireland and many other distinguished figures in the art world.

The group had been attending an evening performance at the puppet theatre in Palermo and was on its way back to the hotel by coach, which was ambushed by three youths on motor bicycles, two of them brandishing pistols. The driver was forced, at gunpoint, to back into a dark alleyway and, with further threats, to open the passenger door. His eleven-year old daughter was among the passengers, having been invited by Diana to attend the show, so naturally he did as he was told. While one of the thugs acted as look-out, the two armed bandits boarded the bus.

> **LATE NEWS**
> O.A.P. TOURISTS HAVE A GO!

One held Diana and the driver at gun-point while the other went systematically through the coach, robbing passengers of their valuables including rings and watches. Two men travelling together attempted to hide their signet rings and watches in their shoes but were in such a state of nerves that they dropped the lot and watched their property roll relentlessly to the feet of their plunderer who immediately pocketed the articles.

An elderly farmer from the West Country, sitting next to his wife, was so incensed at the indignity of the situation that he produced from a pocket a pruning knife – history does not relate why he was carrying such an article on holiday – and proceeded to defend himself. He was immediately fired at, the bullet grazing his wrist before ricocheting out of the window, skimming through Diana's hair en passant. His friend sitting behind him leapt to his defence, only to be hit over the head with the butt of a pistol. The ensuing blood and the sound of the pistol shot so unnerved the attackers that they leapt out of the coach and on to their motorbikes and made off with their spoils, leaving a somewhat shocked but undefeated party behind them. The retired bishop was asked afterwards by the media, "Did you think of praying, Bishop?"

"Good heavens no", replied the Very Reverend, "I was busy trying to hide my ring somewhere safe."

The wounded were duly taken to hospital and the Mayor of Palermo appeared at the hotel shortly afterwards. He told Diana that he was mortified that such an incident should occur to guests in his town (although his must surely have been a daily mortification) and that the local mafia would be much displeased that these riff-raff thieves could behave in such a manner when foreign tourists were so important to the town's economy. Financial aid swiftly followed to compensate for money that had been stolen; free wine henceforth was served at every meal throughout the tour and flowers appeared in every room. A police escort accompanied the coach on all its expeditions and free flights home were offered to the two injured men and their wives. They, however, declined the offer and after a stitch or two at the municipal hospital, the heroes of the moment were on parade for sightseeing the following morning, which impressed the mayor and hotel staff more than anything else.

The first we knew about it at home was when the Daily Mail telephoned the office, the first of all the daily press to do so and incidentally the only paper to get the story right. The Dowager Duchess and her travelling companion, being tired, had not attended the puppet performance. They admitted to feeling cheated!

When terrorism in the air was at its height in the mid-eighties, yet another group came under attack, this time in Rome. Our party was on its way home and Diana was on her way back to Florence where she lived, having checked everyone in at Leonardo da Vinci airport. Passengers were waiting in the departure lounge to board their plane when assassins burst upon them and began spraying the area with machine gun bullets. A wretched Alitalia official was then seized as hostage and marched off to the runway where he was shot dead and an aircraft set on fire. Members of our group, thanks to the advice of one of the men in the party, lay flat on the ground while bullets pinged around their heads, and got somewhat shakily to their feet after the all-clear had been relayed by loud-speaker to all travellers. Travelling with the party was a Miss Mallet, an elderly lady of somewhat severe appearance with a keen sense of etiquette, combined with a dry sense of humour. She travelled with us regularly and invariably wore a Queen Mary style toque. When the gunmen had been disposed of she was approached by a young Alitalia air stewardess.

"*Tutto va bene, signora?*" she enquired solicitously.

"Quite all right dear", replied Miss Mallet "but just tell me if my hat is on straight, because I expect the Press will want to interview me." She was right. They did. The news was relayed to us at home and when I telephoned Diana I found her to be blissfully unaware of the entire episode, as it had not yet appeared on Italian television.

Twenty-six

Since childhood I have had an addiction to picnics, so it is likely that those who have travelled under my wing have had at least one alfresco meal thrust upon them.

To reach the Caspian Sea from Tehran, we had first to cross the Elburz Mountains, a spectacular drive which plunges you into a lunar landscape only to emerge minutes later into a brilliantly green world of pastureland, interspersed with villages – their houses often erected on stilts – tea plantations and orange groves. Once over the crest, the descent at breakneck speed is precipitous, culminating in flatter, duller country until the Caspian in all its disappointing ordinariness breaks into view – reminiscent of the coast at Worthing.

However there was the hilarity of choosing our picnic lunch in the town's market place and with the help of our fat guide, Malek, we bought yards of the delicious biscuit-textured bread which served as a plate for the rest of the food; sheep's cheese wrapped in vine leaves, smoked sturgeon hanging in festoons from sticks carried over the shoulders of the vendor, knobbly green pickled cucumbers piled high beside pyramids of yellow oval-shaped tomatoes; oranges and raisins. To finish off the meal a box of 'gaz' was handed round – a sticky, nougat-like substance, ruinous to the teeth. Liquid refreshment came in the form of 'durgh', a mixture of yoghurt and soda-water very refreshing in hot weather, the ubiquitous Coca-Cola, green tea and for those with stronger tastes, a glass of vodka or the good light local beer.

This banquet was consumed sitting on a couple of upturned boats, abandoned on the shore, our feet dabbling in the warm greyish sand or in the sluggish tepid waters of the Caspian lapping lazily beyond. Inevitably we collected an audience – a small band of schoolboys who sang to us Persian songs, recited the few English words they knew and laughed with delight at their own cleverness. No problem as to what to do with any surplus food. It disappeared like magic into those eager small hands, and like magic their smiling owners faded into the Persian distance.

High up in the foothills of the Hindu Kush there lie the remains of the once noble city of Shahr-i-Zohak (the Red City), formerly the principal fortress protecting the entrance to the city of Bamiyan in the 12th and 13th centuries. Now, sacked and devastated by invading hordes, its ruins bask brooding in desolate loneliness atop a high hill. On a cloudless still morning in May, with the air crisp and invigorating, some fifteen of us in assorted shapes and physique, set out to climb the considerable ascent to these ruins. The first stage was easy going, the second rather more onerous and the final leg a distinct challenge – at least to some of us. With the help of a local shepherd, however, who leapt from pinnacle to pinnacle like one of the mountain goats that viewed our progress with some astonishment, a fair handful of us made the summit. Before us lay the debris of a once teeming acropolis. All that remained were vestiges of crumbling sandstone walls, glinting red in the sunshine and pierced at intervals by elaborately decorated turrets, former watch-towers that guarded the town from marauders below.

Our descent was even more hazardous than our ascent, with loose pebbles impeding our progress, but on reaching the valley floor we found gaily patterned rugs spread out in the shade of a pistachio grove beside a clear-running stream. There, reclining at our ease, we devoured the local pipe-shaped bread scattered with poppy-seed, goat's cheese, hard-boiled eggs and fruit.

Then along the riverbank came a procession of diminutive boys, the leader bearing a samovar almost as big as himself, followed by another with an armload of wood and the rearguard proudly holding aloft a tray of delicately painted china teapots and glasses. The samovar was filled with water from the stream, the fire stoked by many willing small hands accompanied by a volley of instructions from their bearded and turbaned seniors, and in a very short time a glass and steaming teapot of fragrant green tea was placed at each elbow. Nectar of the Gods indeed it seemed, consumed in that idyllic setting.

A third memorable picnic took place in India and was a breakfast affair combined with a tiger hunt. We were staying in fairly primitive quarters in Corbett National Park, which lies at the foot of the Himalayas where dawns are ice-cold and noons hot and dazzling. Called as the first streak of light was breaking, we dashed freezing water over our faces, flung on jeans and several layers of sweaters and clambered inelegantly aboard our steeds. These were a number of elephants, patiently awaiting us and scarcely darker than the air around them, each beast in the charge of a turbaned driver. Our goal was to watch a tiger make a kill from a look-out tower up which we groped to stand vigil for the next half-hour. The lure was a wretched little bleating kid, tethered to a stake, and I for one was vastly relieved when, after three 'beats' of the surrounding grasses which stood in places six feet high, there was no sign of any tiger. By this time we were numb with cold, but around us the day was coming alive in a series of ever-brightening swathes of colour from pale amethyst to deeper tones until suddenly the sun exploded into the sky blinding us with its almost painful light.

We abandoned the kid to its fate, mounted our cumbersome transport, and moved with astonishing rapidity and even more astonishing sure-footedness across the plain, over dried-out riverbeds and up into the jungle. We were now on the look-out for wild elephant and soon the sight of trampled earth, fallen trees and the sound of distant trumpeting, heralded the arrival of a herd of about twelve fully grown beasts with their young. The two smallest were enjoying a trunk-to-tail game of follow my leader.

By this time we had shed our sweaters and were feeling a bit dehydrated as well as hungry. We made a somewhat uncertain descent from our mounts, who took advantage of the halt to fill their trunks with water from the river and give themselves a well-earned bath.

We would-be hunters meanwhile attacked a sustaining breakfast fare of curry puffs, hard-boiled eggs and chappatis with melon and ginger jam, accompanied by deliciously refreshing iced tea. By now the sun was high and after some time spent in photography and exploration of the area, we climbed aboard our patient beasts and headed for camp. The swaying movement of the elephant, and the position in which one has to sit, proved too much for me and some two miles from home I had to cry for mercy and finish the journey on foot.

Twenty-seven

One would think on reading the foregoing that all our tours were fraught with drama or crisis, but those of course are the ones that make the most impact and remain embedded in the memory. Fortunately, over the years, trouble-free and totally enjoyable travels were predominant and as time went by so did our tours and destinations expand. On 1st October 1974, our embryonic beginnings with Twickenham Travel, to whom we owe so much and to Bruce Lyons in particular, finally crystallised with the establishment of Specialtours, based in Chester Row, London SW1, which I am happy to say is still in being today.

Here John Winser and I were joined by Kay Turnbull and Jean Neilson in what were still fairly cramped quarters. The seventies and eighties were exceptionally busy with more and more people joining up for group travel and wanting to break new ground as far as countries were concerned. Arrangements for a tour had to be made at least a year in advance so timetables were imperative. This was where John's graphs came to the fore, showing when payments were due to hotels and airlines; when itineraries and tickets had to be dispatched; notes to be written for current tours and the brochure to be published for the following year. John and his graphs were the hub of office life, especially when the rest of us were away on tour or on recces to new destinations such as Ethiopia and Uganda, China, India and Afghanistan.

Meanwhile incoming groups increased rapidly, both from Italy and more especially from America. We had difficulty in persuading our American travellers that it was not a good idea or, even feasible, to visit Britain in one fell swoop, rather than exploring a particular region with its multiple treasures at a more leisurely pace. Tours had a variety of interests. There were horticultural forays to Persia during the Shah's reign, under the guidance of Mary Burkett, former curator of Kendal Art Gallery, who spoke Farsi and was a leading expert in felts. With our government's blessing, we were allowed to bring back rare specimens in our spongebags, but only if they were not endangered species. To this day I am called Twickers by Mary as it was in the very early days we began to do tours together, she as lecturer and myself as tour leader. Then there was a visit to Scotland by members of the Association Française d'Orchidophile and the Association Franco-Ecossaise under the leadership of the redoubtable Mademoiselle Drouilly before which I spent hours scouring the Scottish countryside searching for the likely domain of wild orchids and persuading kind owners to receive the party and show them their precious hothouse collections.

Museums, too, liked us to organise a visit based on a current exhibition, or to an exhibition in one of the world's capitals, while Diana Skene on several occasions had to include the Palio in Siena in one of her many Italian tours. As the years advanced, so too did technology in the guise of the telex and answering machines and so, inevitably, did competition increase with more and more tour-operating companies specialising in similar cultural tours and later on some of our original sponsors decided it would be more profitable to run their own tours. Politics and the state of the world also played a part in the fluctuation of our fortunes. The IRA bombings in London deterred many an American from visiting Britain, as did riots or strikes in the Middle East or Europe disrupt our arrangements for visits in these countries.

In 1986 we had an ill-starred marriage of short duration with another company called Grand Tours, with similar ideas as ours. The merger failed, however, after nine months due mainly to the incompatibility of personnel. As Diana and I both grew older – after all we were not in our first youth when we set up our own company, we had to look to the future. New blood was introduced in the form of Lucy Knox, who blew in like a breath of fresh air bringing new ideas and an exotic wardrobe into our rather more staid surroundings. Sadly for us, but happily for her, she met and married David Abel Smith and eventually produced Eliza Violet. Naturally her time for touring was somewhat curtailed but she became increasingly interested in the then Czechoslovakia, to which I had already taken many a party.

It was during my first visit to Prague that Daniella Retakova entered my life. Although a qualified psychologist, owing to the severe unemployment in the country at that time, she was forced to take a secondary job as a tour guide under the auspices of my agent in Prague, Mr Jelinek, a slightly dispirited character but who could usually be enlivened with a bottle of Scotch. Young and attractive with good English, mine was the first group for whom Daniella worked and on many subsequent visits both with me and with Lucy. She always maintained that she learned the rudiments of guiding from me who, like Angus before, brooked no short cuts. In those early days, when Czechoslovakia was under communist rule, it was very difficult for a Czechoslovak resident to obtain a visa to come to England, unless one had a sponsor who took full responsibility for her conduct. On the first occasion in which she succeeded in entering Britain Daniella stayed with me at my London flat where the telephone rang incessantly – seldom for me – with a stream of admirers wanting to date her, or calling with bunches of red roses and invitations to some nightclub. I had to play the heavy-handed chaperone on some of these occasions. After all I was totally responsible for her whilst she was over here and I knew next to nothing about her would-be suitors – and the quest for a British or European passport was the all-time mecca for many young girls from a communist state.

She eventually married a Czech doctor and continued to work for Specialtours with Lucy and later worked for a time as interpreter and assistant to Vaclav Havel on one or two visits he made to London, when she was sometimes accompanied by her son, Pavlik, aged then about five or six.

Sadly her first marriage ended in divorce. However, some years later she married an American, Harold Linden and lived at Boca Raton, in the state of Florida. After some months he encouraged her to take Pavlik with her on a visit to a friend in Switzerland

and on her return, she found a flat devoid of everything but a broken vacuum cleaner. After the defection of her second husband, she brought up her son on her own – and with such success that Pavlik, or Paul as he prefers to be called today, was offered a place at four of America's leading universities, viz. Princeton, Yale, Exeter and Harvard. He is now studying philosophy and politics at Harvard, plays the cello more than moderately well, is a very good tennis player and has beautiful manners. A moving testimony to his mother's upbringing. Lucy, meanwhile continued to research Czechoslovakia, resulting in a guide-book on Prague and other publications. She now takes tours as lecturer and guide to the more far-flung regions of Albania and Romania, where she recently acquired a house.

Kay was the first of our early team to retire, a sad loss to her many faithful followers who had travelled the world with her. I recall a hilarious recce I made with Kay to France one year when I drove and she navigated expertly. To keep costs to a minimum we stayed at the cheapest of hotels – on one occasion most likely a brothel in Lyons where she was assailed with an apple core by a drunken tramp. Her place at Specialtours was taken by Edith Ferguson, red-haired and Irish, with a zest for living and much experience in the travel world, particularly where skiing was concerned.

Diana retired about the same time as I did, in 1987, leaving the Italian side of Specialtours in the more than capable hands of Susie Orso, by then an experienced and much loved leader of tours and now a director of Specialtours, together with Frances Roxburgh. The latter is talented, unflappable, elegant, imaginative and relentlessly hard-working. I can think of no two individuals whom I would rather have as inheritors to our beginnings. Before that, Lucy was Chairman for some years and the firm was joined by Karen Saville-Sneath, with whom I enjoyed a number of enjoyable tours, strictly as a passenger, before she left to organise tours of her own.

I was to have handed over to Lady Jane Howard (Ginny), a dynamic character with much experience in both guiding and the ways of the world. She seemed, outwardly at any rate, to have much self-assurance and had a considerable flair for bringing to life every aspect of the tour in which she was engaged. Americans loved her. She was to have worked alongside me, both in the office and in the field, but fate decreed it otherwise.

Lunching with Alys Acworth, daughter of my late employer, who lived in a mews house in Ennismore Gardens Mews, I inadvertently slipped, on descending the spiral staircase to her basement entry, landing with considerable force on the concrete ground. It was raining hard and some considerable time before the ambulance arrived and carted me off to hospital, where I lay for five weeks with various broken bones and other complications, and a further two weeks in a convalescent home named Unstead Park, near Guildford, inevitably called by its patients "Unsteady Park". Thus the wretched Ginny was left to pick up the ropes as best she could – which may have been better in the long run, rather than with me breathing down her neck all the time.

Diana retired to Scotland where she immersed herself in her family, the life of the locality and an increasing involvement with the process of healing. I saw much of her after our retirement, both in London and in France, where I had acquired a house in Provence, until her untimely death from cancer in 1996.

More recent members of Specialtours are Nicola Howard and Antonia Lloyd-Owen, a daughter-in-law of Ursula Barclay, my old friend from Caserta days. I have travelled with them both, strictly incognito, although by the end of the tour I have usually been rumbled when a fellow-traveller has come up to me and congratulated me on being the co-founder of such a splendid travel organisation and to thank me for such an inspiration. I can surely hear Diana saying "Darling, we made it!".

So many real and lasting friends I have made over the years, both in Georgian days and later, alas! now so many since gone. I hesitate to mention any specifically since so many more deserve an equal tribute. But a few stand out in their continuous fidelity. Elizabeth MacNiece, who clocked up fifty tours in two decades and whom I always contrived to place next to our host or hostess on the occasions of a private visit, on account of her chic and wonderful manners.

Nancy Fisher, niece of the former Archbishop, and headmistress of, first a school in Africa, and later of Wycombe Abbey. History has it that owing to a bicycle accident she was awarded a lot of money in damages which she spent on travel. Not quite in the same league as Elizabeth MacNeice, she did succeed in taking part in nine tours one year, some admittedly rather brief ones. Strikingly tall with a dominating personality and an erudition, especially in all things ecclesiastical, she had a disconcerting habit of eschewing a meal in order to visit a church on her own and would be discovered much later flat on her back in the middle of an aisle, when I, with beating heart and thinking "My God, a heart attack", would be met with a calm gaze and the comment "so much better, dear, to view that wonderful vaulting from this position".

Nancy Saunders, a passionate gardener but totally deaf, would be half-way up a Persian mountain in quest of the elusive fritallaria, oblivious to the increasingly desperate shouts from the rest of the group that the coach was about to leave. Elizabeth Hickok, an indefatigable photographer from Pennsylvania, who always swore she would follow me to the edge of the world, once saved face for me by buying a carpet in Kashmir at vast expense after several dozen had been laid before our increasingly embarrassed eyes, whilst sipping the ubiquitous cups of green tea.

John Codrington, late of the Coldstream Guards, landscape designer, voluntary fire-fighter and member of the Bach Choir, was another regular. Where others photographed, John set himself down on his campstool which he carried everywhere and did a series of pencilled sketches which he transferred into oils or watercolours at a later date, one of which adorns my walls today. On his death I was told that he had left me some pieces of Persian pottery, which were at first found to be just that, but later some genuine pots were discovered, which gave me much pleasure. Michael Cartwright-Sharp, a fund of knowledge on every conceivable subject would, while imparting some obscure historical fact, invariably open his dissertation with the words, "As I am sure you already know," which made us feel almost intellectual equals.

So many Georgians, some of them cantankerous, some maddeningly slow, some *trop bons viveurs* but all humbling in their loyalty. Only a handful sadly now remain, apart from those previously mentioned in earlier chapters: Cloë Carr, always impeccably dressed and coiffed; Elizabeth Winn, with her wicked mimicry; Mary Cosh, writer of many books on Scottish architecture and other subjects; Reresby and Penelope Sitwell who, on a visit to Russia, always insisted in sitting at the rear of the coach and heralded late morning and early evening with cries of "nipski time", accompanied by the clinking of glasses and joyous laughter. One much lamented friend was Tom Hutton (General Sir Thomas Hutton, retd), a Georgian member in those early days who travelled frequently with both Diana and myself. When asked by a mutual friend with whom he preferred to travel, he was purported to have replied diplomatically, "I love them both, but Hazel might put a hot water bottle in my bed if I was feeling poorly".

I cannot omit mention of all my American clients – many of whom became life-long friends. Most of them required much cosseting – much more so than their British equivalent. It was no use giving them a day off to do their own thing. They had to be led by the hand. All those enthusiastic Guides of Winterthur Museum who had to be deterred from turning furniture upside down in privately owned houses in an effort to discover the maker's name; Smith Alumnae led by Virginia Eley, whom I bequeathed to Susie Orso to become firm friends; Mary and Jack Hopkins; Morris Arboretum, led by Elizabeth McLean, historian and lecturer.

So many more and if I have omitted to mention any, or at times get a fact or two confused, it is because of advancing years myself. I have also mixed some events into a single tour, with the result that some participants may be inclined to question my memory. Indeed, my memory is not as it should be, so put it down to poetic license. Meanwhile, mention a name from the past and I shall surely recall the face with a smile of recognition – or in one or two cases – a certain wariness?